# THE WORLD'S GREATEST
# ROYAL SCANDALS

# ACKNOWLEDGEMENTS

AKG, London 47, 57, 83, 95, 113, 120, 147, 181
Corbis UK Ltd 9, 11
Hulton Getty Picture Collection 30, 46, 62, 67, 72, 84, 101, 111, 125, 126, 133, 142

# THE WORLD'S GREATEST
# ROYAL SCANDALS

**Nigel Cawthorne**

CHANCELLOR
PRESS

This 1999 edition published by Chancellor Press an imprint of
Bounty Books, a division of Octopus Publishing Group Limited,
2-4 Heron Quays, London E14 4JP.

© Octopus Publishing Group Limited

Reprinted in 2002 (twice), 2005, 2006

All rights reserved

ISBN 0 75370 091 3
ISBN 13 9 780753 700914

Printed and bound in Great Britain by Mackays of Chatham

# Contents

Introduction 7

1 • A Fairy-tale Too Far 8

2 • Familias Horribilis 25

3 • Edward and Mrs Simpson 44

4 • Bertie, Prince of Wales 54

5 • Mrs Brown 65

6 • The Delicate Investigation 71

7 • William IV and Mrs Jordan 78

8 • The Badness of King George 83

9 • The Lesbian Queens 93

10 • Restoration Comedy 97

11 • Gay Times 110

12 • Virgin Sovereign 118

13 • The Six Wives of Henry VIII 124

14 • Camelot, It's Not 137

15 • The Raving Romanovs 140

16 • Scandinavian Scandals 146

17 • Here Comes the Sun 152

18 • The Lubricious Ludwigs 158

19 • Serbian Shenanigans 162

20 • Mystery at Mayerling 169

21 • Farouk, King of Playboys 170

22 • The Bribery of Prince Bernhard 176

23 • Fall from Grace 178

# Introduction

The royal scandals of recent years have filled newspapers and TV screens world-wide. Largely, though, modern royals have only been doing what the rest of us do in our private lives, only very publicly. However, when those set above us reveal their feet of clay, we find every detail of their scandalous misbehaviour compelling. Here are our own human frailties writ large.

But in former times, royal scandals extended far beyond the scope of ordinary mortals. Kings and queens misbehaved in ways that ordinary people could only dream of. The fascination of historical scandals is the nagging question – given unlimited wealth, power and leisure time, wouldn't we behave just as badly? Kings have frequently used their rank to help themselves to the wives and money of their subjects and Catherine the Great of Russia remains one of history's most celebrated nymphomaniacs.

Closer to home, Henry VIII was one of the most bloodthirsty tyrants in British history. But the fact that he had six wives – divorcing two and executing another two in scandalous circumstances – has made him one of the most beloved figures in British history. A good royal scandal is something we can all enjoy.

Even in our own century, we thrill to hear of the scandalous excesses of the gluttony, gambling and womanizing of King Farouk. And who can fail to show interest in the scandalous allegations that Princess Grace of Monaco, the virginal Grace Kelly of the silver screen, was an insatiable nymphomaniac who became embroiled in a kinky suicide cult? How the mighty are fallen.

# 1 ❖ A Fairy-tale Too Far

It was a fairy-tale wedding of the 20th century. Over 750 million people around the world watched as the heir to the British throne and his shy virgin bride descended the steps of St Paul's Cathedral on 29 July 1981 to the cheers of the crowds. Just 11 years later, with the publication of Andrew Morton's *Diana: Her True Story*, the fairy-tale turned into a farce and the greatest royal scandal for more than half a century began to unfurl.

In many ways, one of the functions of a royal family seems to have been to amuse its subjects with periodic royal scandals. It keeps the public's minds off important things like war, pestilence, famine, crime, death and taxes. It forges a nation into one people who share common emotions as they witness the outrageous antics of the royals. And it gives them something to talk about. When Charles II frolicked with the orange-seller and actress, Nell Gwynne, people were shocked and scandalized. Yet they were also grateful that the newly restored king was not one of those dull old Puritans who had, a decade before, banned Christmas. Oranges were on sale openly on the street. The theatres were open again, so the public could see actresses – and, most particularly, actresses' legs – once more. And there were plenty more buxom young ladies like Nell who would give a gentleman a whole lot of fun for sixpence.

However, the scandal of Charles and Di's sham marriage and its shocking exposé was taking things a bit too far. For more than six years, it rocked the monarchy to its foundation. It led to the Queen complaining of at least one *annus horribilis*. And she was forced to scale down the civil list and pay taxes.

It is not difficult to see how the scandal came about. Prince Charles had been brought up steeped in history. In royal families, it is generally accepted that married people fool around, but stay together for the sake of propriety. In the British Royal Family, particularly, it was the men who fooled around and their long-suffering wives were supposed to put up with it. The first king in the current dynasty, George I, arrived in England from Hanover in 1690 with two mistresses – dubbed the 'maypole' and the 'elephant', one being tall and thin, the other short and fat. He left his wife behind, imprisoned in a castle because she had had the temerity to take a lover.

**Prince Charles with Diana Spencer at the announcement of their engagement**

Charles's great-great-grandfather, Edward VII – the notorious Prince of Wales known to actresses and prostitutes across the world simply as Bertie – scandalized the nation with his salacious goings on while his dutiful wife, Queen Alexandra, not only put up with his infidelities, she was kind to his mistresses. She even allowed one of them to visit him on his deathbed.

Although, as a rake, Charles was nowhere near Bertie's league, he had sown a few wild oats. Several of his early entanglements made the newspapers. According to the Fleet Street scandal sheets, Charles lost his virginity to Lucia Santa Cruz, daughter of the Chilean ambassador, when he was a student at Cambridge in his early 20s. She was a post-graduate student, three years his senior. Later, it is said, the plucky Prince scaled the walls of the all-woman Newham College to share the bed of Sybilla Dorman, daughter of the Governor General of Malta. Soon after, he was photographed escorting Audrey Buxton to the May Ball at Trinity College.

He managed to keep most of his aristocratic escorts out of the newspapers. There was Lady Jane Wellesley, daughter of the Duke of Wellington; the daughters of the Duke of Northumberland, Lady Caroline and Lady Victoria Percy; the Duke of Westminster's daughter, Leonora, and her sister Jane, who became the Duchess of Roxburghe; the Duke of Rutland's daughter, Lady Charlotte Manners, and her cousin Elizabeth; the Marquis of Lothian's daughter, Lady Cecil Kerr; the Duke of Grafton's daughter, Lady Henrietta Fitzroy; Lord Astor's daughter, Angela; Lord Rupert Nevill's daughter, Angela; Sir John Russell's daughter, Georgiana and so on through *Burke's Peerage*. He kept these amours quiet by entertaining the young ladies concerned at Broadlands, the country estate of his Uncle Dickie – Lord Mountbatten.

However, some slipped under the wire. There was a good deal of fevered press speculation about Prince Charles's relationship with Lady 'Kanga' Tryon and some snobbish tut-tutting about his sipping at the lips of Sabrina Guinness, daughter of the famous brewing family.

When he took up with the rich and stylish Davina Sheffield, her jilted lover James Beard spilt the beans of their cosy cohabitation in the Sunday papers. And when Prince Charles started seeing Lord Manton's daughter, Fiona Watson, the papers had a field day. The curvaceous Fiona had once stripped off for the soft-porn magazine *Penthouse*, so here was a royal scandal complete with juicy pictures.

Then in 1972, Charles met the love of his life, Camilla Shand. He was introduced to her at the upmarket Mayfair disco, Annabel's, by Andrew Parker-Bowles, the guards officer whom he would later cuckold as her husband.

Camilla made no secret of her scandalous intent. She introduced herself to the Prince as the great-granddaughter of Alice Keppel – the last mistress of Edward VII. Alice had once famously remarked that her job was to 'curtsy first and then hop into bed'.

Camilla and the Prince got on famously. They shared a love of riding, the countryside, gardening and architecture. They also both had the same juvenile sense of humour. However, duty intervened. As heir to the throne, Charles had to do his bit in the armed forces. Reluctantly, in 1973, he left Camilla on the dockside and shoved off in his ship *HMS Minerva*. It had already been made clear to Camilla that she was not the material queens were made of. Four weeks after she had kissed her sailor prince goodbye, she accepted the proposal of Andrew Parker-Bowles. Within months they were married, and the very next year Prince Charles became godfather to the couple's first child.

Prince Charles consoled himself with other women. After dining at his flat in Buckingham Palace, many women would stay the night. The prince's valet would often find items of ladies underwear concealed around the house. These would be laundered and returned in an Asprey's box, if the owner was known. Otherwise they would be given to members of the Palace staff, many of whom were gay.

The Palace managed to keep the details of these affairs out of the press.

At the time, Prince Andrew told a girlfriend that Charles was trying to compete with Warren Beatty who, it is said, had laid every starlet in Hollywood. The *Daily Mail* even reported that Charles had a slush fund to buy the silence of women who objected to being used once and then cast aside.

During this period, Charles was seeing Sarah Spencer, Diana's older sister, who was deemed unsuitable as a wife because she was a heavy smoker. Meanwhile, his younger brother, Prince Andrew, was having a brief dalliance with Di herself.

Charles was now 30 and the pressure was on for him to do what heirs to the throne are supposed to do – produce more heirs. The race was on to find him a suitable wife. Foreign princesses, including Marie-Astrid of Luxembourg, were vetted. But all those of a suitable age and disposition were Catholics. Under the Act of Settlement (1701), it is deemed unlawful for the heir to the throne to marry a Catholic.

So the Royal Family looked closer to home and their eyes soon alighted on Diana. She was everything they could have wished for – English, upper class, naïve and, by her own admission, none too bright. More importantly, she was a virgin. At least this was the firm assertion of her uncle, Lord Fermoy, though no one asked how he was in a position to know.

Her virginity was also important under English constitutional law. Catherine Howard had been executed for treason, not just because she had fooled around after her marriage to Henry VIII but also because she had lost her maidenhead before it.

Randy Andy, apparently, had got nowhere with Diana. Neither had author and socialite, George Plumptree, with whom she had been going

**The wedding of Charles and Diana**

out for more than a year. Or, at least, they were not saying. The public swallowed this, not least because she looked the part. With her blushing good looks and her innocently averted gaze, she could have been tailor-made for the role. She was everyone's idea of the fresh, unsullied maiden who gets to marry Prince Charming.

But Charles was not Prince Charming. In fact, his coolness towards his delightful young bride was palpable. In the couple's first face-to-face interview with the press, he was asked whether he was in love with her. He replied, awkwardly: 'Yes, whatever that may mean.'

'I think an awful lot of people have got the wrong idea about love,' he had said in an interview four years earlier. 'It is rather more than just falling madly in love. It's basically a very strong friendship. I think you are very lucky if you find the right person attractive in both the physical sense and the mental sense. If I am deciding who I want to live with for 50 years, that's the last decision on which I would want my head to be ruled by my heart.'

He could have been talking about Camilla.

The problem was not just that Diana was not Camilla. She was not of royal blood, nurtured in regal seclusion. She had not been brought up to play aristocratic games, to turn a blind eye to her husband's misdemeanours and conduct her own affairs, if she felt the need to have any, discreetly. She was a modern young woman who expected more. She wanted to be loved and she was not going to put up with her fiancé fooling around.

And fooling around he was. While they were courting, Charles was seeing Davina Sheffield and Anne Wallace, who in turn was seeing other men. He was also maintaining an interest in Camilla Parker-Bowles. Just weeks before the royal wedding, Diana found a bracelet in Charles's desk drawer. At first, she thought this expensive gift was for her. But on closer examination, she spotted the initials 'F' and 'G' engraved on it. In intimate conversation, Charles and Camilla had adopted the Goon Show nomenclature, 'Fred' and 'Gladys'.

Diana was heartbroken; Charles nonplussed. He could not see what Diana had to complain about. It seemed perfectly normal to him to carry on an active love life with other women, even though he was getting married. After all, his father, the Duke of Edinburgh, had been doing that very thing for all the long years of his marriage to the Queen. That is what royals did. Besides, the wedding plans were almost complete. Heads of state from around the world were on their way. The TV networks had cleared their schedules. The world was waiting. It was too late to back out now. The fairy-tale wedding had to go ahead.

The nightmare situation she had innocently walked into must have been apparent to Diana from the very first night, which the young couple spent at Broadlands. Instead of extending that first night of bliss long into the following day, Charles slept off the exertions of their long and tiring wedding day, then leapt from his marriage bed bright and early the next morning to go fishing.

Their honeymoon on the Royal Yacht *Britannia* was more successful. Apparently, they went to bed early and rose late. Rumours spread that they had taken candid pictures of each other. Some said that these pictures fell into the hands of the press but, so far, no newspaper has dared to publish them.

However, instead of having intimate dinners *à deux*, evening meals were formal affairs, surrounded by staff. Even when they were alone, Charles would propound his great thoughts on such weighty topics as world affairs and mysticism. He was old beyond his years and she was just a normal 20-year-old airhead, whose interests did not extend beyond clothes, make-up, pop music and babies. Not only was she bored by him, she was hurt, too. During the cruise, pictures of Camilla fell out of his diary. She also realized the significance of the entwined 'CC's on the cufflinks he wore. Fortunately, as a balm for his boorish behaviour, there were plenty of handsome young sailors to flirt with.

Back on dry land, Diana flirted openly with the President of Portugal, the dashing Mario Soares. And there were others. But the story circulated in the press that this was just the high spirits of a sexy young woman and the marriage was solid. This was far from the case.

Within a year of their marriage, Charles made it clear to Diana that he had no intention of giving up his friendship with Mrs Parker-Bowles. As heir to the throne, having a *maîtresse en titre* was not only right and fitting, it was practically his duty. Diana did her duty, too, and produced Prince William in 1982.

Soon after giving birth, Diana overheard Charles on the phone saying: 'Whatever happens I will go on loving you.'

These are the words every young mum would love to hear from her husband, but not when he is saying them to his mistress.

With the birth of a second son, Prince Harry, securing the succession, Diana's duty was now done. Publicly, she was seen as a loving mum and she loyally turned up at Charles's side at state occasions. Otherwise her life was her own. Soon the press got wind of the fact that, like his mother and father, they slept in separate bedrooms.

Once, while Charles was away, Diana went to an all-night party.

Afterwards, she spent the weekend with Philip Dunne. Then she was seen at a David Bowie concert with Major David Waterhouse.

The gossip columns were soon reporting that Diana had an unusual number of close male 'friends'. Names were bandied around. There were Mervyn Chapling, Roy Scott, a friend of hers from the days before she was married, and Nicholas Haslam, hi-fi dealer to the aristocracy. Once the affair with Haslam was over, it was reported later, she became a phone pest.

The name that provoked the most heated rumours was Captain James Hewitt. He had taught Prince William to ride and eased Diana back into the saddle. Hewitt's long-term girlfriend stormed out of the relationship, claiming that he was besotted with the Princess. During the Gulf War, Hewitt was posted to the Middle East and he and Diana exchanged torrid love letters.

Next, there was the upper-class car dealer and scion of the gin family, James Gilbey. They had been friends in her single days and, trying to put the best possible construction on the Princess's increasingly reckless social life, it was generally assumed that she was using him merely as a shoulder to cry on.

But Diana was now being tailed by journalists. At 8 p.m. one evening in 1989, they saw Diana's bodyguard, Sergeant David Sharp, drop her off at Gilbey's flat. They waited. No one left or entered the flat for the next five hours.

At 1 a.m. she emerged, slightly dishevelled. Sergeant Sharp drove up. Furtively, Diana got in the car and they sped away. When journalists asked what the two of them had been doing for five long hours, Gilbey gallantly said that they had been playing bridge. But you need four people to play bridge.

By now the press was feverishly speculating that there was something wrong with the royal marriage. Buckingham Palace managed to keep the lid on it. Then Andrew Morton's sensational book, *Diana: Her True Story*, blew the whole thing out of the water.

Although everybody – including Morton – stoutly denied it at the time, it was plain that the book had been produced with Diana's active co-operation. After her death, it became clear that she had actively colluded with Morton on the book. It was her mouthpiece. The book exposed the marriage as a sham from the very beginning. The Royal Family had employed her simply as a baby machine. In fact they had isolated and excluded her to the point that she fell prey to the eating disorder, bulimia nervosa. And Charles's cold and unfeeling behaviour had driven her to attempt suicide.

Andrew Morton's book was quickly followed by *Fall of the House of Windsor* by Nigel Blundell and Susan Blackhall. It maintained that it was Diana's petulant tantrums that had alienated the Royal Family. Charles, it said, had been driven into the arms of another woman by his young wife's unreasonable behaviour. It also mentioned the existence of the notorious 'Squidgygate tapes'.

On New Year's Eve 1989 and 4 January 1990, secretarial agency manager Jane Norgrove and retired bank manager Cyril Reenan had recorded mobile phone conversations between two people who were obviously physically intimate with each other. One purported to be James Gilbey; the other the Princess of Wales.

They had been touted around Fleet Street for two years. In 1992, they surfaced in the USA. It was only then that the British press ran them. At first derided as fakes, they pretty soon proved to be the real McCoy. In them, Diana cursed 'the f***ing family'. Now the Royal Family had a full-scale scandal on their hands.

The tapes were known as the Squidgygate tapes because throughout Gilbey refers to Diana as 'Squidgy'. They went like this:

GILBEY: You know, all I want to do is to get in my car and drive around the country talking to you.
DIANA: Thanks (laughs).
GILBEY: That's all I want to do, darling. I just want to see you and be with you. That's what's going to be such bliss, being back in London.
DIANA: I know.
GILBEY: Kiss me, darling. (Blows kisses down the phone.)
DIANA: (Blows kisses back and laughs.)
GILBEY: Squidgy, laugh some more. I love it when I hear you laughing. It makes me really happy when you laugh. Do you know I am happy when you are happy?
DIANA: I know you are.
GILBEY: And I cry when you cry.
DIANA: I know. So sweet. The rate we are going, we won't need any dinner on Tuesday.
GILBEY: No. I won't need any dinner actually. Just seeing you will be all I need...
 (Pause.)
DIANA: Did you get my hint about Tuesday night? I think you missed it. Think what I said.
GILBEY: No.

DIANA: I think you have missed it.
GILBEY: No, you said: 'At this rate, we won't want anything to eat.'
DIANA: Yes.
GILBEY: Yes, I know. I got there, Tuesday night. Don't worry, I got there. I can tell you the feeling's entirely mutual.

Next they talked about making babies.

DIANA: You didn't say anything about babies, did you?
GILBEY: No.
DIANA: No.
GILBEY: Why darling?
DIANA: (laughs) I thought you did.
GILBEY: Did you?
DIANA: Yes.
GILBEY: Did you, darling? You have got them on the brain.
DIANA: Well yeah, maybe I...
   (Pause.)
DIANA: I don't want to get pregnant.
GILBEY: Darling, it's not going to happen.
DIANA: (Sighs.)
GILBEY: All right?
DIANA: Yeah.
GILBEY: Don't worry about that. It's not going to happen, darling. You won't get pregnant.

The tapes continued in the same vein.

GILBEY: Oh Squidgy, I love you, love you, love you.
DIANA: You are the nicest person in the whole wide world.
GILBEY: Pardon?
DIANA: You're just the nicest person in the whole wide world.
GILBEY: Well, darling, you are to me too.
DIANA: You don't mind it, darling, when I want to talk to you so much?
DIANA: No. I love it. Never had it before.
GILBEY: Darling, it's so nice being able to help you.
DIANA: You do. You'll never know how much.
GILBEY: Oh, I will, darling. I just feel so close to you, so wrapped up in you. I'm wrapping you up, protecting.
DIANA: Yes please. Yes please.

GILBEY: Oh, Squidgy.
DIANA: Mmm.
GILBEY: Kiss me please. (Blows more kisses.) Do you know what I'm going to be imagining I am doing tonight at about 12 o'clock. Just holding you so close to me. It'll have to be delayed action for 48 hours.
DIANA: (Titters.)
GILBEY: Fast forward.
DIANA: Fast forward.

These were plainly two people deeply in love who could not wait to get their hands on each other. But they had to be careful.

DIANA: I shall tell people I'm going for acupuncture and my back being done.
GILBEY: (Giggles) Squidge, cover them footsteps.
DIANA: I jolly well do.

If all that was not damning enough, there was a portion of the transcript that was so hot that the newspapers did not dare publish it. Of course, journalists and other insiders knew what was said and this helped fuel the scandal. The omitted section was about masturbation.

GILBEY: Squidgy, kiss me. (Sounds of kisses being exchanged.)
GILBEY: Oh God, it's wonderful, isn't it? This sort of feeling. Don't you like it?
DIANA: I love it.
GILBEY: Umm.
DIANA: I love it.
GILBEY: Isn't it absolutely wonderful? I haven't had it for years. I feel about 21 again.
DIANA: Well, you're not. You're 33.
GILBEY: Darling, mmmm. Tell me some more. It's just like sort of mmmmm.
DIANA: Playing with yourself.
GILBEY: What?
DIANA: Nothing.
GILBEY: No, I'm not actually.
DIANA: I said it's just like, just like...
GILBEY: Playing with yourself.
DIANA: Yes.
GILBEY: Not quite as nice. Not quite as nice. No, I haven't played with

myself, actually. Not for a full 48 hours. (They both laugh.) Not for a full 48 hours.

ALTHOUGH no one could doubt their authenticity, there was still a mystery that surrounded the tapes. From the tapes it is plain that James Gilbey was talking on the mobile phone in his car. As he drove, the phone would automatically be passed from station to station in the cellular network. So an amateur radio enthusiast tuning into the call would catch only part of the conversation before it jumped frequency between stations. It was quickly concluded that the recording had been made using a bug in the land line at Diana's end, then rebroadcast on a fixed frequency in the hope that someone would pick it up.

Who could have done such a thing? Suspicion fell on the security forces – MI5, Special Branch, the Royal Security Squad or the government listening station in Cheltenham, GCHQ. Plainly, orders to tape the phone of the future Queen of England would have to come from the highest authority. Diana's supporters suspected Charles. They said that he used the security forces to gather evidence he could use in a divorce, but had leaked the information to get his own back for Diana's collusion in *Diana: Her True Story*.

With the press on his tail, James Gilbey went into hiding. But Diana pressed home her advantage. She demanded an immediate divorce, a sizeable financial settlement, unfettered access to her sons, the retention of her royal titles and a court of her own.

The Palace fought back. It leaked stories that Charles and Diana had had a romantic reconciliation at the annual Ghillies' Ball at Balmoral. ITN aired an hour-long documentary, assuring the world that divorce was off the agenda.

But Charles's faction could not sit still. They said that the Prince loathed Diana, and that he considered her co-operation in *Diana: Her True Story* an act of betrayal. They said that he called her 'Diana the Martyr' and that the Squidgygate tapes had given her a dose of her own medicine.

The Palace insisted that the couple made once last attempt to bluff it out. Together they made a state visit to South Korea. It was a glittering occasion with plenty of photo opportunities for the world's press. But it was plain from their body language that the royal couple detested each other.

With the two parties still clearly at each other's throats, something had to be done. It fell to the luckless Prime Minister John Major to make a statement to the House of Commons.

'It is announced from Buckingham Palace that, with regret, the Prince and Princess of Wales have decided to separate,' he told the packed chamber. 'Their Royal Highnesses have no plans to divorce and their constitutional positions are unaffected. Their decision has been reached amicably, and they will both continue to participate fully in the upbringing of their children. Their Royal Highnesses will continue to carry out full and separate programmes of public engagements and will, from time to time, attend family occasions and national events together. The Queen and the Duke of Edinburgh, though saddened, understand and sympathise with the difficulties that have led to this decision. Her Majesty and His Royal Highness particularly hope that the intrusion into the privacy of the Prince and Princess may now cease. They believe that a degree of privacy and understanding is essential if their Royal Highnesses are to provide a happy and secure upbringing for their children, while continuing to give wholehearted commitment to their public duties.'

Fat chance.

Mr Major added that the succession was unaffected and that when he became King, Charles would still become head of the Church of England. Some doubted that. Even senior churchmen shook their heads at Charles running around with a married woman and made it clear that if he attempted to marry Camilla they would press for the church to be disestablished.

*The Sun* proclaimed that John Major's announcement was a 'Victory for Di'. But she felt that she had been outmanoeuvred by the Palace, which was seeking to sideline her. The game was far from over though.

That there should be one tape could be considered a misfortune, but that there were two smacked of carelessness. But two there were.

The second came to light in Australia. It purported to be a telephone conversation between Prince Charles and Camilla recorded on the night of 18 December 1989 – two weeks before the notorious Squidgygate tapes. Its authenticity has never been questioned because its content was so sensational.

A man claiming to be a radio ham sold the tape to at least one national newspaper, but it was thought too tawdry to use. However, in January 1993 an Australian magazine called *New Ideas* got hold of a copy of the transcript and broke the story Down Under. Within minutes of publication, copies were being faxed around the world. Now there was no reason for Fleet Street to hold back.

The conversation is said to have taken place between Camilla, who was at her family home in Wiltshire, while Charles was lying on his bed with a mobile phone in the Cheshire country home of the Duke of

Westminster, where he was a guest. The recording begins when the conversation is already in progress.

CHARLES: ...he was a bit anxious actually.
CAMILLA: Was he?
CHARLES: He thought he might have gone a bit far.
CAMILLA: Ah well.
CHARLES: Anyway you know, that's the sort of thing one has to be aware of and sort of feel one's way along with, if you know what I mean.
CAMILLA: Mmm. You're awfully good at feeling your way along.
CHARLES: Oh stop! I want to feel my way along you, all over you and up and down you and in and out...
CAMILLA: Oh.
CHARLES: Particularly in and out.
CAMILLA: Oh, that's just what I need at the moment.
CHARLES: Is it?
CAMILLA: I know it would revive me. I can't bear a Sunday night without you.
CHARLES: Oh God.
CAMILLA: It's like that programme 'Start the Week'. I can't start the week without you.
CHARLES: I fill up your tank.
CAMILLA: Yes, you do.
CHARLES: Then you can cope.
CAMILLA: Then I'm all right.
CHARLES: What about me? The trouble is I need you several times a week. All the time.
CAMILLA: Oh God, I'll just live inside your trousers or something. It would be much easier. (She laughs.) What are you going to turn into, a pair of knickers? It would be much easier. (They both laugh.) Oh, you're going to come back as a pair of knickers.
CHARLES: Or, God forbid, a Tampax. Just my luck. (He laughs.)
CAMILLA: You're a complete idiot. (She laughs.) Oh, what a wonderful idea.
CHARLES: My luck to be chucked down a lavatory and go on and on forever swirling around the top, never going down...
CAMILLA: Oh, darling.
CHARLES: ...until the next one comes through.
CAMILLA: Oh, perhaps you could come back as a box.
CHARLES: What sort of box?
CAMILLA: A box of Tampax so you could just keep going.
CHARLES: That's true.

CAMILLA: Repeating yourself. (She laughs.) Oh, darling. Oh, I just want you now.
CHARLES: Do you?
CAMILLA: Mmm.
CHARLES: So do I.
CAMILLA: Desperately, desperately, desperately. I thought of you so much at Yearly.
CHARLES: Did you?
CAMILLA: Simply mean that we couldn't be there together.
CHARLES: Desperate. If you could be here – I long to ask Nancy sometimes.
CAMILLA: Why don't you?
CHARLES: I daren't.
CAMILLA: Because I think she's so in love with you.
CHARLES: Mmm.

And on it goes. She tells him that she loves him 11 times; he tells her twice. She calls him 'darling' 18 times; he calls her 'darling' seven times. Her husband is referred to simply as 'A' or him. At one stage, she says: 'He won't be here Thursday, pray God.'

That assignation arranged, she begs him to get some sleep and to call her in the morning. Then they say goodnight to each other no fewer than 19 times. The final sequence goes like this:

CAMILLA: ...night, night.
CHARLES: Night, darling, God bless.
CAMILLA: I do love you and I am so proud of you.
CHARLES: Oh, I am so proud of you.
CAMILLA: Don't be silly, I've never achieved anything.
CHARLES: Yes, you have.
CAMILLA: No, I haven't.
CHARLES: Your great achievement is to love me.
CAMILLA: Oh darling. Easier than falling off a chair.
CHARLES: You suffer all these indignities and tortures and calumnies.
CAMILLA: Oh darling, don't be so silly. I'd suffer anything for you. That's love. It's the strength of love. Night, night.
CHARLES: Night, darling. Sounds as though you're dragging an enormous piece of string behind you, with hundreds of tin pots and cans attached to it. I think it must be your telephone. Night, night, before the battery goes. (He blows a kiss.) Night.
CAMILLA: Love you.

CHARLES: Don't want to say goodbye.
CAMILLA: Neither do I, but you must get some sleep. Bye.
CHARLES: Bye, darling.
CAMILLA: Love you.
CHARLES: Bye.
CAMILLA: Hopefully talk to you in the morning.
CHARLES: Please.
CAMILLA: Bye. I do love you.
CHARLES: Night.
CAMILLA: Night.
CHARLES: Night.
CAMILLA: Love you forever.
CHARLES: Night.
CAMILLA: Goodbye. Bye my darling.
CHARLES: Night.
CAMILLA Night, night.
CHARLES: Night.
CAMILLA: Bye, bye.
CHARLES: Going.
CAMILLA: Bye.
CHARLES: Going.
CAMILLA: Gone.
CHARLES: Night.
CAMILLA: Bye. Press the button.
CHARLES: Going to press the tit.
CAMILLA: All right darling. I wish you were pressing mine.
CHARLES: God, I wish I was. Harder and harder.
CAMILLA: Oh darling.
CHARLES: Night.
CAMILLA: Love you.
CAMILLA: Camilla yawns.) Love you. Press the tit.
CHARLES: Adore you. Night.
CAMILLA: Night.
CAMILLA: Night. (Camilla blows a kiss.)
CHARLES: Night.
CAMILLA: Goodnight my darling. Love you...

And finally Charles hangs ups.

Not only were people appalled at the Tampax exchange, they realized that they could not figure out Prince Charles at all. Here was a man who was married to one of the most beautiful women in the world, who was obviously besotted by a woman who, not to put too fine a point on it, needed ironing. She was a little older than Charles and a good 13 years older than his glamorous young wife.

If Charles had been cut in the mould of his great-great-grandfather Bertie, the public would have forgiven him for fooling around. If he had been seen out on the town with a supermodel on each arm, he would have got away with it. But no one could understand how he could cast aside a supermodel for a woman who, frankly, looked like one of the horses she liked so much to ride.

The sad truth was that Charles was no playboy prince, no lovable rogue with a heart of gold. He was like his mother, deeply middle class. He was a one-woman man. Unfortunately, that one woman was not Diana.

Again, people began to wonder where the Tampax tape had come from. The author and former MI6 officer, James Rushbridger, pointed the finger at GCHQ. A year later he was found hanged in his West Country home.

Next out of the woodwork was James Hewitt. In 1994, a 'novelized' version of the torrid love affair between Hewitt and Diana called *Princess in Love* was published by Anna Pasternak, a distant relative of the author of *Dr Zhivago* and former girlfriend of Hewitt.

Open warfare between Charles and Di continued on TV. Diana appeared on *Panorama*, where she admitted committing adultery and begged to be the people's 'Queen of Hearts'. She said she wanted to be a British goodwill ambassador to the world – despite the fact that, as consort to the heir to the throne, by admitting adultery she was also technically admitting treason. No one from Scotland Yard was sent to investigate.

Charles responded with an authorized biography and an extended TV interview with a sycophantic Jonathan Dimbleby. He, too, admitted adultery and having three separate affairs with the winsome Mrs Camilla Parker-Bowles. The battle of the documentaries was a draw. They both limped from the battlefield, licking their self-inflicted wounds.

Diana then threw herself into a charm offensive. She was seen very publicly doing good works. There were plenty of photo opportunities showing her with sick children. And, in front of the world's TV cameras, she began a campaign against land mines. This blew Charles off the front pages completely.

Diana then won a £15-million divorce settlement, but was forced to drop the title 'HRH' in the process. Even a publicized affair with England rugby captain, Will Carling, which lost him his wife, failed to dent her popularity.

Then she shot herself in the foot. She began a serious affair with Dodi Fayed, son of Harrods' boss Mohamed Fayed. This was a dangerous move. Mohamed Fayed's business methods had long been a source of criticism and he had been refused a British passport. Although Dodi Fayed himself listed his profession as 'movie producer', he was better known for his activities on the casting couch than for those behind the lens. The newspapers referred to him more accurately as 'millionaire playboy'.

Dodi wooed Diana on his yacht on the Côte d'Azur. Their love blossomed in front of the telephoto lenses of the paparazzi, for the delectation of tabloid readers world-wide. Meanwhile, Charles seized the opportunity to walk out the freshly divorced Camilla, laying on her 50th birthday bash. It seemed the scandal would never end. But end it did, tragically.

Mohamed Fayed revelled in the publicity that his son's royal affair afforded him. He bought the house in Paris where the last British royals to be ousted by scandal, Edward and Mrs Simpson, had spent their exile. It was rumoured that this was where his son and the exiled Princess of Wales would set up home, too.

But it was not to be. On the night of 30 August 1997, Dodi and Di enjoyed a romantic dinner at the Ritz Hotel in Paris where he proposed – although a Hollywood starlet was quick to say that Dodi was already engaged to her and produced a rock to prove it. The couple left the Ritz late that evening, apparently on their way to view their putative matrimonial home. On the way, the car they were being driven in smashed into a pillar in an underpass, killing them both.

Criticism of Di ended at that moment. Fears that the mother of the heir to the throne – and hence a future head of the Church of England – might marry a Muslim were put aside. No further mention was made of the fact that Di's marriage to Dodi Fayed would be opposed by the establishment because he was, shall we say, tinted. However, the idea that the powers that be were so against the match that they had the happy couple bumped off has spawned a lively new outlet for conspiracy theorists.

The press, perhaps guilty over its own role in the hounding of Di, now shot the line that the fairy-tale princess had died in the arms of her handsome young sheikh. When the Royal Family maintained their usual regal decorum, they were pilloried for being cold, old-fashioned and out of touch. The fresh, young, modernizing Prime Minister Tony Blair had to step in.

Nevertheless, the tabloid-reading public blamed the paparazzi for hounding Di to her death. Echoing public sentiment, the press were vilified from the pulpit by Diana's brother, the adulterous Earl Spencer, whose own messy divorce was already attracting the newspapers' scrutiny.

Slowly, Prince Charles turned the situation to his advantage. With Di dead, Charles now had no rival on the global stage. He was now 'keeper of the flame' – and the royal children. Even when Camilla emerged as stepmother-in-waiting, no one said a thing. Everything was going swimmingly.

But then, in an ill-judged move, biographer and journalist Polly Toynbee did an Andrew Morton, publishing *The Prince's Story*. The book told the story of the royal marriage from the Prince's side, seemingly with the collusion of, if not Charles himself, certainly those in his camp. When it came to the key issue – adultery – his defence was simply 'she did it first'. Suddenly, the longest running royal scandal of the 20th century showed that, even though its central, most glittering character had been written out, it still had legs.

## 2 ❖ Familias Horribilis

Even before the acrimonious divorce of the Prince and Princess of Wales, life had not been simple for Good Queen Bess. Throughout her long reign the Palace has been plagued with low-level scandal.

There were persistent rumours surrounding her husband, Prince Philip, Duke of Edinburgh, during the 1950s and 60s, when he showed a distinct partiality for the company of actresses and night-club 'hostesses', and would often spend long periods of time travelling the world, away from his wife. Despite finding himself on the fringes of the Profumo affair, his name was kept out of the papers. He did his public duty, maintaining a suitably feisty profile with his remarks about foreigners – although Greek-born himself – and the need for the people of Britain to 'get their fingers out'. Apart from serving as an officer on a British warship during World War II, it could be argued that he has never had what one might describe as a proper job.

However, he did not get caught with his hand in the cookie jar, so his aristocratic disdain for the conventions of the marriage bed should pass without comment. Even the revelation that his sisters had all married high-ranking Nazis – one of whom, as a pilot in the Luftwaffe, had bombed

Britain during the War – was made little of by the press. And no one even mentioned the fact that his father, Prince Andrew, lived with a French widow, Madame Andrée de la Bigne, on her yacht in Monte Carlo.

Sailing rather closer to the wind was Lord Louis Mountbatten – born Battenberg – who was Prince Philip's 'Uncle Dickie', too. He arranged for the young Philip Schleswig-Holstein-Sonderburg-Glucksberg to become a British citizen and, in the process, gave him the more manageable surname, Mountbatten – his own adopted sobriquet.

During the 1930s and 1940s, Mountbatten was a member of a rather fast set, whose members included a number of Hollywood movie stars, such as Douglas Fairbanks. Mountbatten's wife, Edwina, was notoriously promiscuous, counting among her lovers the jazz singer 'Hutch', the father of modern India, Pandit Nehru, and Nada Milford Haven, a prominent lesbian.

Mountbatten's love of uniforms caused a little gossip around the mess. He also boasted of being the first man to have a zip in the fly of his trousers. 'A minute can be as costly as an hour,' he would joke to his servants.

However, in the 1950s, scandal was to focus on the Queen's younger sister, Princess Margaret. At 14, she developed a school-girl crush on the dashing 29-year-old RAF fighter pilot, Group Captain Peter Townsend, who had been appointed air equerry to her father, the King. He lived with his wife in a house in the grounds of Windsor Castle.

No one took her amour seriously, but in 1947, Princess Margaret seized her opportunity. The King opposed Princess Elizabeth's proposed marriage to Prince Philip and wanted to put their love to the test. He arranged for them to be apart for three months. The two princesses were to accompany him on an extended tour of South Africa. Captain Townsend would be accompanying the royal party, but his wife would have to stay at home.

Margaret was now 16 and this exotic voyage presented her with endless opportunities to throw herself at the handsome young war hero, and her youthful infatuation turned into an enduring love.

Townsend's marriage was already on the rocks, but Margaret had to wait four long years before she heard the joyful news that he was suing for divorce on the grounds of his wife's infidelity with a royal portrait painter. Meanwhile, Margaret had been dating the American entertainer, Danny Kaye – who it was later revealed had had a gay affair with actor Laurence Olivier – and John Profumo, the soon-to-be-disgraced politician.

Although Townsend had sought the King's advice over the divorce, the King was less than happy when he found the young captain carrying his daughter upstairs.

'But, papa, I ordered him to,' Margaret protested.

George VI died in February 1952. When Queen Elizabeth acceded to the throne, Princess Margaret moved out of Buckingham Palace. Her new quarters were to be in Clarence House and Margaret asked Townsend to help her choose the decor there, believing that one day it would be their home.

In December, Townsend's divorce was finalized and they began to spend a lot of time together. Margaret checked with the Queen's private secretary, Sir Alan Lascelles, that there was nothing constitutional to prevent her marrying the innocent party in a divorce. He reassured her that everything would be all right, provided they wait for a decent interval to elapse.

For that to happen, the lovers would have to be discreet. But the tiniest slip blew all their plans out of the water. At the coronation, Margaret was seen talking to Townsend. While she was doing so, she leant forward and brushed a loose thread from his uniform. Trivial though the gesture might be, it was seen as the act of a woman in love.

The reputation of the British press had been badly damaged by keeping quiet about the romance between Edward and Mrs Simpson, which led to the abdication crisis, while the foreign press had been reporting the affair in detail. It was not going to happen again.

The day after the coronation, breakfast tables across the nation were regaled with torrid tales about the young Princess and her dashing divorcé. The Prime Minister Winston Churchill had been damaged by his support for Edward during the abdication crisis. He, too, had learnt his lesson. He exuded sympathy for the young couple, and gave them reason to believe that one day they would be able to marry. Then he posted Townsend to Brussels for a year as air attaché. Meanwhile, the Queen Mother whisked Princess Margaret off on a tour of Rhodesia.

Townsend's tour of duty in Brussels was extended to two years, then to three. Occasionally, he managed to slip back to England for a tryst with Margaret. The couple continued to believe that, sooner or later, they would be allowed to marry. But for the moment, they were told the time was not propitious.

By the time she was 25, Princess Margaret would be able to marry without the Queen's consent. However, with the deadline fast approaching, the government delivered the killer blow. If she married Townsend, it said, she would be stripped of her royal titles, lose the money she got from the Civil List and, perhaps, be forced into exile. To press home the message, Margaret was sent on a lavish, all-expenses-paid tour of the Caribbean, a place she had longed to visit. This was the sort of thing she would be giving up.

Despite the opposition of the government and Parliament, Princess Margaret felt she could count on the support of her sister, the Queen. However, despite Margaret's support when George VI had taken against his marriage to Princess Elizabeth, Prince Philip turned against Captain Townsend. With few prospects in life outside his position as the Queen's consort, he had most to lose if Margaret's marriage caused any damage to the standing of the Royal Family.

Nevertheless, the young couple still had the support of the people. When Captain Townsend arrived at Clarence House from Brussels for one last week with Princess Margaret, there were cries of 'Good luck, sir' from the crowd outside.

Later, when Margaret was spotted driving through the East End of London, a woman shouted: 'Go on, marry him.'

But the support of the people was not enough. The last act of their doomed love affair was a wild round of drunken parties. Both Princess Margaret and Captain Townsend knew that if they defied authority and went ahead and got married in spite of everything, they would both be ruined.

On Monday 31 October 1955, Princess Margaret issued a statement that read simply: 'I would like it to be known that I have decided not to marry Group Captain Peter Townsend. I have been aware that subject to my renouncing my rights of succession it might have been possible for me to contract a civil marriage. But mindful of the Church's teaching that a Christian marriage is indissoluble and conscious of my duty to the Commonwealth, I have resolved to put these considerations before any others. I have reached the decision entirely alone, and in doing so I have been strengthened by the unfailing support and devotion of Group Captain Townsend. I am grateful for the concern of all those who have constantly prayed for my happiness.'

And that was the end of that.

Townsend's name only surfaced again in the press on his death in June 1995. He had married a young Belgian woman who looked remarkably like Princess Margaret. They had settled near Paris and raised three children together.

But Princess Margaret's name was frequently in the papers and often associated with scandal. She enjoyed drinking and socializing with a group who became known as the 'Princess Margaret set'. Her name was linked to that of Billy Wallace. Rumour had it that they were just about to announce their engagement when Billy jetted off to Nassau where he had a fling with a Bahamian girl. After a huge row, Margaret dropped him.

She was also 'just good friends' with Colin Tennant. But when he married, she found herself attracted to the young photographer who was taking the wedding photos. His name was Anthony Armstrong-Jones.

At the time, he was living with the Oriental model, Jacqui Chan, but she moved out when Princess Margaret began making regular night-time visits to his shabby Rotherhithe studio in London's then unredeveloped docklands.

The powers that be could not quash her wedding plans again, even though there were persistent rumours about Armstrong-Jones's sexual predilections. These were revived when he asked known homosexual, Jeremy Fry, to be his best man. His second choice was Liberal politician Jeremy Thorpe, who fell later in a homosexual scandal.

Armstrong-Jones was given a peerage and, as Lord Snowdon, he married Princess Margaret in Westminster Abbey on 6 May 1960 in the first royal wedding of the television era.

By all accounts, the marriage was passionate but, after they had had two children, the passion showed itself in flare-ups and other displays of temperament. In 1966, while he was away on assignment, Margaret began an affair with one of her husband's friends, Anthony Barton, a married man with two children. Regretting the fling, she called Barton's wife to apologize and, fatefully, Margaret also told her husband.

Their marital difficulties soon became very public. At a charity ball, he spent so much time dancing with one girl that Margaret was forced to cut in, eventually telling the girl to 'run along home now'. She would also burst into his studio unannounced.

'Never come in here without knocking,' he would shout.

By then, Margaret was rumoured to be carrying on with Derek Hart and Dominic Elliot. And she and the royal photographer Lord Lichfield were said to be 'kissing cousins'. Then there was a tragic affair with society pianist, Robin Douglas-Home. When he committed suicide, a number of embarrassing letters from her were found.

Princess Margaret and Lord Snowdon began to lead increasingly separate lives. She spent much of her time on the Caribbean island of Mustique where, on a plot of land given to her by Colin Tennant, she had built a holiday home.

Snowdon retired to his country cottage in Sussex. He would often visit his neighbour, the Marquis of Reading, who had a very pretty daughter. When it became clear that Snowdon had taken the 22-year-old Lady

**The marriage of Lord Snowdon and Princess Margaret on 6th May, 1960**

Jacqueline Rufus Isaacs as his lover, the Palace put pressure on him to break off the affair. There followed a succession of other attractive women.

In retaliation, Margaret took up with one of Colin Tennant's friends, Roddy Llewelyn. He looked like a younger version of Snowdon and was 17 years her junior. When not in residence at her villa on Mustique, he lived in a hippie commune in Wiltshire. She visited him there, wearing old clothes and looking, according to the locals, like a farmer's wife. Other commune members commented on the distinct royal 'squawk' they heard coming from Llewelyn's room at night-time. One placed a tape recorder outside their bedroom door in the hope of capturing it on tape. In fact, Llewelyn had shared a flat with a gay friend before meeting Margaret and had said that he always found the physical side of the relationship difficult.

Things came to a head when Snowdon celebrated his 44th birthday in a London restaurant without his wife. The public disquiet this caused forced Margaret to break it off with Llewelyn. A sensitive lad, he went to stay in the family home in Barbados alone. Soon after he was found unconscious and was flown back to Britain with a doctor at his side, making great pictures for the tabloids.

In 1976, Margaret took another holiday on Mustique. This time, a **British** journalist managed to sneak on to the exclusive island with a camera. He snapped Margaret and Llewelyn together, sipping drinks at a beach-side bar.

The pictures appeared in the *News of the World*. Revelations about their life together in Wiltshire followed. The commune members, it was said, smoked marijuana. In the House of Commons, a Member of Parliament described Princess Margaret as 'a wayward woman'.

Something had to be done. On 19 March 1976, Kensington Palace issued a statement saying: 'HRH the Princess Margaret, the Countess of Snowdon, and the Earl of Snowdon have mutually agreed to live apart.'

Lord Snowdon was in Australia at the time, making a TV documentary with attractive production assistant Lucy Lindsay-Hogg. He made a tearful appearance on TV, begging his children's understanding.

Then in 1978, Princess Margaret broke scandalous new ground. She did the unthinkable – unthinkable certainly in royal terms at that time. She divorced her husband, sending him packing with a six-figure settlement, more than enough to set up home with his new wife, Lucy Lindsay-Hogg. It was the first of what would become an avalanche of royal divorces. Roddy Llewelyn also went on to find a beautiful new bride, Tania Soskin, leaving Princess Margaret along with her booze and her fags.

Once freed from sexual scandal, Princess Margaret made a gaffe worthy of Prince Philip. During a fund-raising tour of America for the Royal Opera House, she was heard to remark that the Irish were 'pigs'. She apologized, saying she was referring only to the terrorists who had blown up beloved Uncle Dickie in 1979. Cheers turned to jeers. Her life was threatened. Since then, she has kept a low profile.

PRINCESS Margaret's divorce was still hot news when Prince Michael of Kent, until then the invisible man of the Royal Family, plunged the Windsors into another scandal. He married a divorcée who was both a foreigner and a Catholic. Her name was Marie-Christine von Reibnitz, but she quickly became known as Princess Pushy.

She was born in Czechoslovakia in 1945; her family fled before the advancing Russian army with all their worldly possessions in a handcart. In Vienna, her parents split. Her father fled to Mozambique, while Marie-Christine and her mother emigrated to Australia.

In the 1960s, Marie-Christine arrived in London, where she threw herself into the social scene. In 1971, when she was 26, she met and married Old Etonian Tom Troubridge, a merchant banker. He was a good catch, but she could do better. At a dinner party, she found herself seated next to Prince Michael of Kent, who was then an officer in the Royal Hussars. Romance blossomed.

Marie-Christine divorced but, as a good Catholic, she also applied to have her marriage annulled. The wedding was set to take place in Vienna in June 1978. But two days before the service, the Pope refused an annulment. The elaborate ceremony in an ancient church had to be cancelled. Instead, they had to make do with a perfunctory civil ceremony at the local town hall.

Although the royal couple were granted a grace-and-favour apartment in Kensington Palace, there was a good deal of tension between Princess Michael and the other royals. They called her 'Our Val', short for Valkyrie, because of her Germanic good looks. While she felt that her in-laws looked down on her, others in the family remarked, with irony, that Princess Michael was 'too good for the likes of us'.

The newspapers picked up on this tension and began satirizing her attempts to become a real royal. But then the real scandal broke. On 15 April 1985, the *Daily Mirror* revealed that her father had been a member of the SS.

At first, Princess Michael denied it and threatened writs. But documents in the Imperial War Museum proved it to be true. The Palace issued a curt statement, saying: 'Princess Michael confirmed tonight that it is true her father was a member of the SS. It came as a total shock. There will be no further statement from the Princess.'

But matters did not end there. The Nazi-hunter Simon Wiesenthal pointed out that her father's Nazi Party membership number showed that he had joined the party early in the 1920s, and he had joined the SS in 1933. She was forced to go on television and admit that she had known that her father was a member of the Nazi Party, but had not known about his membership of the SS. She insisted that his membership must have been 'honorary' and that somewhere there was a document that exonerated her father.

During the search for this document, the newspapers unearthed records showing that Prince Philip's brother-in-law, Prince Christoph of Hesse, had been a high-ranking SS man himself. This line of enquiry had to stop and, although Simon Wiesenthal pointed out that there was no such thing as an honorary member of the SS, documents were quickly found showing that Baron von Reibnitz had not been involved in any atrocities.

Even so, scandal has continued to dog Princess Michael of Kent. When she began a literary career in 1986, she was immediately accused of plagiarism, an allegation she stoutly rejected. *The News of the World* also reported that she had been spending a great deal of time with Texan multi-millionaire Ward Hunt and her name was linked with Elizabeth Taylor's ex-partner, Senator John Warner.

MEANWHILE, the Queen had been having troubles of her own. On the morning of 9 July 1982, she awoke to find 32-year-old unemployed decorator, Michael Fagan, in her bedroom. He was not there to harm her, he said. He had simply dropped by for a chat.

It was not the first time he had been in the Palace. A month earlier, he had scaled the railings, eluded the guards, the guard dogs and the high-tech security system, and had shinned up a 50-foot drainpipe to an open window. He had squeezed himself, in only to be spotted by a chambermaid, who had screamed. Inside, Buckingham Palace is like a rabbit warren and Fagan had quickly disappeared into the maze of corridors. After examining the priceless works of art on the walls, he had broken into a storeroom, stolen a bottle of wine and made off into the night.

Fagan did not have much of a home life to return to. He was not a good provider and his wife had left him, taking the kids. Their final row had been so tumultuous that the police were called. Alone in his East End squat, Fagan began to feel sorry for himself and had decided to spill out his troubles to the Queen.

Early in the morning of 9 July, he went back to the Palace. This time, gaining entry was even easier. He found a ground floor window open. Inside, he found himself in the room that houses the royal stamp collection, worth an estimated £14 million. Unfortunately for him, the inner door was locked, so he climbed out of the window again. There was scaffolding on the building outside. This afforded him easy access to the window of the office of Vice-Admiral Sir Peter Ashmore, Master of the Queen's Household and, as such, the man in charge of security at the Palace. Fagan forced it easily.

On this occasion, the Palace security had not failed completely. Fagan had tripped an infra-red detector, but the police guard had dismissed it as a false alarm and switched it off.

Fagan took a leisurely tour of the state rooms and in the throne room 'tried them on for size'. A maid who saw him did not consider this suspicious and failed to report it.

Eventually, he stumbled into the Queen's bedroom, but thought that the figure on the bed could not be Her Majesty because it was too small. When he opened the curtains to take a closer look, he disturbed her. According to Fagan, the Queen sat bolt upright in shock and ordered him to get out.

'I think you are a really nice woman' was Fagan's opening conversational gambit. The Queen grabbed for the phone and yelled down it. Then she jumped out of bed and bolted out of the door.

Fagan sat on the bed crying. He said he could hear the Queen shouting and shouting, trying to raise the alarm. A full six minutes later, a housemaid turned up and effected a citizen's arrest. Fagan did not resist. He sat quietly until, eventually, the police turned up.

The Palace issued a statement stressing the Queen's bravery. Although she does not smoke, she had gained the intruder's confidence by asking for a cigarette, it said. Then she listened calmly, while he told her his troubles. The Palace said that he was carrying a menacing shard of glass from an ashtray he had broken in an ante-room and she feared that he was going to slash his wrists. But her regal bearing soothed him. After a cursory court hearing, Fagan ended up in a mental hospital.

The real scandal here was the lax security at the Palace, which took a hammering in Parliament and the press. But, of course, the British people were more interested in the fact that the Queen was sleeping alone. Prince Philip had long since moved into a separate bedroom.

With shenanigans in the Palace very much in the news, a 38-year-old homosexual prostitute from Yorkshire called Michael Rauch tried to sell his story to the papers. He claimed to have had an affair with Commander Michael Trestrail, the 51-year-old personal bodyguard to the Queen. He had been with the Royal Protection Group for 16 years and only months before had passed MI5's screening procedures.

When the allegations were put to him, Commander Trestrail confessed at once and resigned. An inquiry was set up, which quickly ruled that Palace security had not been compromised. Although Trestrail had been gay since he was a teenager, he had maintained a double life by abstaining from sex for long periods. Then, every so often, he would binge on orgies with male prostitutes. Each time he had been vetted he was on a period of abstinence. That was how he had slipped through the net, the inquiry concluded.

But Trestrail was not the only gay in the Palace. Christopher Irwin, a royal butler of 11 years' standing, caused a right royal scandal when he revealed that a large proportion of the Palace staff and the Queen Mother's staff were homosexual. The younger ones, he said, were involved in bedhopping orgies.

Three royal servants, including the flunky who walks the Queen's dogs, were arrested for importuning and, in 1992, three footmen were caught having a gay sex romp in one the Palace's huge Victorian baths.

Security was still so lax that drugs were freely available in the royal quarters. And the vetting procedures had not improved either. Irwin himself had 29 criminal convictions, for drugs, theft and assault, and he had once served dinner to Charles and Di stoned out of his head.

Drugs and sex parties would last until dawn. When the guest had left a royal banquet, the staff piled into the food and wine. There would be a race to sit in the Queen's seat. The waitresses and maids were just as wild. After one state banquet, one girl whipped off her top and performed an impromptu striptease.

The drink problems at the Palace hit the front pages again in 1991, when one of the staff fell off the roof after a Christmas party. And the Queen's 83-year-old Clerk of the Royal Kitchens was caught by the *News of the World* visiting a prostitute.

EVEN after the capture of Michael Fagan, intruders seemed to come and go at will. Stephen Gould was sentenced to three months' imprisonment after breaking into the Palace for a second time. When challenged, he claimed to be Prince Andrew.

This was not a bad ploy as Prince Andrew has brought down more than his fair share of scandal on the Royal Family and blazed the way for the break-up of Charles and Di with his disastrous marriage to Sarah Ferguson.

The Duke of York's loutish behaviour first hit the headlines when he was 21. He had been sent on an official tour of America and took with him Sandi Jones, a willowy blonde he had picked up in Montreal. His demeanour was so boorish that the American press called it: 'The most unpleasant royal visit since they burned the White House in 1812.' The British media immediately dubbed him 'The Duke of Yob'.

'Randy Andy' assiduously cultivated his playboy image. One morning, Carolyn Seward, former Bond girl and one-time Miss UK finalist, was seen leaving the Palace. He escorted 21-year-old model, Gemma Curry, to Princess Margaret's 50th birthday party. After a fling with 32-year-old actress Finola Hughes, who left England for a career in the American soaps, he took up with 31-year-old model Katie Rabett. The Palace took a dim view when nude photographs of Katie turned up in the tabloids.

*Dynasty* star Catherine Oxenburg and Carolyn Herbert, daughter of the Queen's racing manager, Lord Porchester, were both in the picture briefly. Then Andrew topped it all with a very public affair with topless model, Vicki Hodge.

Hodge had a holiday home in Barbados. When Andrew's ship, *HMS Invincible*, docked there, Hodge tried to put the paparazzi off the scent by arranging for her friend Tracey Lamb to be seen with him. But Vicki was no shrinking violet. Afterwards, she earned £40,000 from the Sunday papers for her blow-by-blow account of their love romps.

According to her own account, Vicki discovered why all his earlier affairs had been so brief. Andrew, it seems, was a sprinter, not a marathon runner. One ex-lover, it seems, had advised Andrew to distract himself by counting. Unfortunately, Andrew could only could out loud, which Vicki found a trifle disconcerting.

But 37-year-old Vicki was a woman of the world and knew how to handle the situation. In Barbados, she put Andrew into intense training and, according to her account, he left the Caribbean a man not a boy.

Which was just as well, because his next lover was 25-year-old American soft-porn star Koo Stark. The tabloids had a field day, running explicit pictures from her extensive career in soft-porn movies that had begun with her first full-frontal role at the tender age of 17. London cinemas dusted off their old reels and the capital's movie buffs could once again enjoy such steamy classics as *Emily* and *The Adolescent*.

At the time, Britain was engaged in the Falklands War and Prince Andrew was sent to the South Atlantic as a helicopter pilot. The affair with Stark was allowed to continue. It was seen as good for morale, if not morals. They wrote to each other almost every day, then holidayed together at Princess Margaret's villa on Mustique. But once hostilities were over, his parents put their foot down. However convincing she was in no-holds-barred sex scenes, they did not think she was up to playing the role of the Duchess of York. That was to go to someone even less suitable, Sarah Ferguson.

However rebellious and independent Prince Andrew seemed to be on the surface, he knew which side his bread was buttered. He ended his 18-month affair with Koo without so much as a phone call. He simply told the Palace switchboard that he was not taking any of her calls.

Andrew was now 25 and, in the eyes of the firm, as the Royal Family like to call itself, it was time for him to think about getting married. They had seen him at a party at Windsor during Ascot week feeding profiteroles to a bouncy redhead. She was the daughter of Prince Charles's polo manager, Major Ronald Ferguson and, as such, was considered suitable material.

Her romantic history had not been too chequered. Her mother had run off with handsome Argentinian polo player, Hector Barrantes, and she had been brought up by Major Ron's second wife, Susan Deptford.

Fergie had first fallen in love with city banker, Kim Smith-Bingham, when she was 19. He had introduced her to ex-racing driver Paddy McNally. McNally had a home in Verbier, one of Fergie's favourite ski resorts. Fergie adored his jet-setting life style and, despite their 22-year age difference, they became lovers.

She played mother to his two sons, Sean and Rollo, and the relationship lasted four years. It ended when Fergie gave McNally the ultimatum 'marry me or else'. He chose the 'or else'.

Fergie was still going out with McNally when she became a close friend of Princess Diana. She visited her frequently at Buckingham Palace, in the hope of bumping into Andrew. McNally even dropped her at Windsor the day she consumed Prince Andrew's profiteroles to such great effect. The invitation had come from Diana herself.

Given the nod by the Queen and the Duke of Edinburgh, Andrew and Fergie became inseparable. In February 1986, they announced their engagement. They married in July.

The press was already hard on the case. It scrutinized her life style in Verbier and was soon publishing stories to the effect that Fergie was the first royal princess to walk up the aisle in a less-than-virginal state. Nevertheless, her outgoing, fun-loving demeanour endeared her to the public. The newspapers reported that she and Diana had gatecrashed Andrew's stag night, dressed as policewomen. No one doubted whose idea it was.

The marriage began passionately enough and their public kissing and pawing embarrassed friends. Prince Andrew even delayed a naval manoeuvre by spending two hours in his cabin with his bride, feigning seasickness.

However, the public began to get unsettled when, in 1988, she took off on a seven-week tour of Australia just seven weeks after the birth of her first daughter, Princess Beatrice. By the time she came back, it was said, the child thought her nanny Alison Wadley was her mother.

The trip also drew attention to the fact that the Duchess's fun-loving nature resulted in a love of holidays, especially if they were at the taxpayer's expense. The press dubbed her 'Her Royal Idleness'. And criticism grew of the £5 million squandered on the Yorks' vulgar and ostentatious home, Sunninghill, a 50-room, red-brick monstrosity in the middle of Berkshire. It was compared to the Ewing family home in the soap opera, *Dallas*, and was dubbed 'South York'.

Her father, Major Ron, added an element of farce to the growing scandal when he was caught leaving the Wigmore Club, a London massage parlour where additional sexual services were provided.

In 1989, Fergie took eight holidays; in 1990 seven. It would have been eight but she was forced to cancel her Christmas trip to St Moritz when the Queen ordered her to turn up for the family festivities at Balmoral. In 1991, she had another seven, increasingly leaving her ever-loving husband behind.

Polls showed that her junketing was damaging the standing of the Royal Family and the newspapers began to tot up how much Fergie's 'freebies' were costing the country. Her particular passion was skiing. One trip to the French Alps cost the taxpayer £55,000. Her royal duties occupied just four hours. Another three days were spent gallivanting with friends.

And it was not just Britain that was footing the bill. A private holiday Down Under cost the Australian government £100,000. She was also known for her shameless hints to travel agents and department stores. She accepted furs, gifts and airfares that cost thousands. It was all the same to her. A visit from the Duchess of York became a liability.

Taking a leaf from Diana's book, Fergie tried to cover her tracks with good works. She wrote a series of books about Budgie the Helicopter, the royalties from which were supposed to go to children's charities. It transpired that only 10 per cent of the royalties found its way into the hands of needy children. The rest of the royalties went to royalty. Fergie's secretary, Lieutenant Colonel Sam O'Dwyer, quit in protest.

The scandal continued when it was pointed out that her Budgie the Helicopter bore a remarkable resemblance to the creation of Arthur W. Baldwin, whose *Hector the Helicopter* was published in 1964.

Fergie remained blithely unconcerned about the criticism. Following the birth of her second daughter, Eugenie, she and Prince Andrew posed in their Sunninghill home for *Hello!* magazine. A sum of £250,000 reportedly changed hands. Although the Palace denied that the royal couple had actually been paid for the photos, nobody doubted that Fergie had got her hands on the money one way or another.

The Queen and Prince Philip ordered Fergie and Andrew to Sandringham where they were given a dressing down. It did no good. Fergie's outrageous behaviour on a transatlantic flight hit the headlines and more holidays, ostensibly alone, followed.

The press soon tumbled that she was often accompanied on these jaunts by 36-year-old Texan oil tycoon, Steve Wyatt. In January 1992, 120 photographs of Fergie and Wyatt sunning themselves beside various foreign pools were found in his London flat by a cleaner. What they showed was innocent enough, but it was enough to make Prince Andrew ask for a divorce. Hurt and humiliated, he looked to former lover Koo Stark for a shoulder to cry on.

The Queen ordered Fergie to stop seeing Wyatt, but the press caught her visiting his apartment in Cadogan Square twice more.

To make a show of being a reformed character, Fergie turned for therapy to Mrs Kortese, a Greek clairvoyant who worked under the name Madame Vasso. Bizarre stories of the Duchess sitting under a pyramid-like structure in the mystic's flat hit the press. Madame Vasso defended her methods and struck back with claims that the royal couple were still very much in love. They were just going though a bad patch, she said. Plainly her powers had failed her.

Fergie flew off to Florida to stay with notorious womanizer, 66-year-old Robert Forman, who confined his attentions to girls young enough to be his granddaughter. She then flew on to a month-long holiday in the Far East with her daughters and her 'financial advisor' Johnny Bryan, a close friend of Steve Wyatt. Bryan was dispatched back to Britain to discover what sort of divorce settlement Fergie could expect. He made it plain that unless the Royal Family came up with a satisfactory figure, Fergie would publish her memoirs. They offered £4 million.

Major Ron, now 59, seized the headlines again when his affair with glamorous 33-year-old horseman, Lesley Player was serialized in the Sunday papers. Fergie leapt to his defence, which hardly helped.

Fergie and her financial advisor, Bryan, were still pushing for more, when pictures of Fergie sunning herself topless while her children and two male bodyguards looked on were published in the *Daily Mirror*. Worse, Bryan was with her. He was pictured kissing and cuddling her, tucking her hair behind her ear, rubbing suntan lotion into her naked back and sucking her toe. Nowhere in the 50 pictures that the *Mirror* printed did he seem to being giving her financial advice. The game was up. They took the money and ran.

EVEN the tireless charity worker, Princess Anne, has brought some scandal to the Royal Family. Her father's daughter, she told press photographers to 'naff off' when they tried to snap her after she had fallen off her horse into a lake during the Badminton Horse Trials. Her frequent rudeness to the royal press pack earned her the reputation of being a spoilt brat.

Sadly, she was not blessed with good looks. Her affair with polo-playing commodity broker, Sandy Harper, ended when he ran off with model Peta Secombe. On the rebound, she met Captain Mark Phillips, who had earned the nickname 'Fog' at Sandhurst because he was thick and wet.

Obsessed with secrecy, they managed to deny any involvement for over a year. Then, in 1973, they married in Westminster Abbey in front of a world-wide TV audience of 500 million.

They had two children, but gradually drifted apart. She threw herself into a dizzying schedule of royal engagements, while he, out of his depth in the public eye, withdrew into private life.

The first nail in the coffin of their marriage came in 1985 when her ex-bodyguard, Peter Cross, began touting around the Sunday papers the story of his intimate relationship with the Princess. The asking price was £600,000. Phillips dismissed these 'hurtful stories' as 'fantasies'.

The following year, rumours spread that Princess Anne was having an affair with the actor, Anthony Andrews, one-time screen lover of Koo Stark. Andrews and his wife dismissed these stories as rubbish, but they served to further alienate Princess Anne and Mark Phillips.

Then, in 1989, four love letters from Princess Anne were stolen from the briefcase of the Queen's equerry, Commander Timothy Laurence. The contents were never revealed but they were said to be 'affectionate'.

Anne and Mark separated, but the Palace said that there were no plans for divorce. It was only then that stories about Phillips began to surface. First his name was linked with former Miss India and high-class hooker, Pamela Bordes, whom he had met at an equestrian weekend at Gleneagles. While Anne was away, he had invited her to stay at the royal couple's Gloucestershire estate, Gatcombe Park.

Then, with the prospect of getting a share of his £1-million divorce settlement, a 40-year-old art teacher in New Zealand called Heather Tonkin launched a paternity suit against him. She claimed that her six-year-old daughter, Bunny, was the result of a one-night stand with him in 1984. They had met at a party in Auckland and she had given him her phone number. Later that night, he had called her and asked her to visit him in his hotel. She had asked how she would recognize his room. He had said he would leave his riding boots outside the door.

Since then, Phillips had been making regular payments to Ms Tonkin as an 'equestrian consultant'. Now, she was reportedly after £300,000 or she would tell all. They made an out-of-court settlement.

After a discreet divorce, Princess Anne married Commander Laurence and, we are led to believe, are living happily ever after.

THE collapse of three of her children's marriages and a fire at Windsor Castle made 1992 an *annus horribilis* for the Queen. Plainly, what was needed was an old-fashioned royal romance. So Prince Edward, the Queen's fourth and youngest child, began being seen out with a girl.

However, it was going to take a lot of hard work to overcome the scandalous rumours that were already circulating about Edward. After quitting the Royal Marines in a miasma of publicity, he went to work at Andrew Lloyd Webber's Really Useful Theatre Company, where he was known as 'Barbara' Windsor. Even though he worked in the theatre, he showed little interest in show-girls and repeated allegations that he is gay have been ignored or parried, never denied. His very public relations with glamorous public relations girl, Sophie Rhys-Jones, continued for five years. Eventually, she put her foot down and, according to *The Sun*, issued the ultimatum, 'Wed me or dump me'. The result – another fairy-tale wedding, if you'll pardon the expression.

ONE royal wedding that was as far from a fairy-tale as you can get was that of Marina Ogilvy, daughter of Princess Alexandra and Sir Angus Ogilvy who had had their own nuptials televised in the 1960s. Stout monarchists, they have put the duty to their Queen and country first and have stayed out of the scandal sheets.

Their daughter, Marina, was cut from a different cloth. She hit the headlines when she started living with her boyfriend, leather-clad photographer Paul Mowatt. He claimed not to have known who she was when they had met at a party in 1987. It was only when she took him back to her dad's flat in St James's Palace that the penny dropped.

When Marina got pregnant, her parents insisted that she either had an abortion or got married right away by special licence. Marina refused both options and took her story to the tabloids. When she had visited a paediatrician in Harley Street to confirm the pregnancy, she said, she had discovered that an abortion had already been arranged for her.

Marina and Paul agreed to get married, but only after the birth of their child. The very public row continued. The newspapers even reported that the Queen was 'upset'.

Adding fuel to the flames, *The Sunday People* reported that Marina had once picked up painter and decorator Phil Filton and taken him back for a six-day sex romp at Kensington Palace.

The wedding eventually took place, not at Westminster Abbey but at St Andrew's Parish Church in Ham, Surrey. The press outnumbered the guests and apart from Princess Alexandra, who put a brave face on it, there were no other royals present.

The bride wore black – a tight-fitting crushed velvet number that must have sent shivers down her mother's back. The groom sported a silver earring and a pony tail. He was smart enough to renounce his Roman Catholic faith before the wedding, allowing Marina to keep her position in the succession. She is 24th in line to the throne.

And that was not the end of it. Soon after, Marina appeared in the newspapers in thigh boots and toting a gun. Next she was photographed in skin-tight leather with corgis at her feet and wearing an imitation crown. This was seen as a deliberate insult to the Queen, and her parents closed their doors to her. Marina ran to the press once more, although the public began to sympathize with her parents when she turned up at a wild sex and drugs party at Amsterdam Zoo, wearing a rubber dress from a prominent London bondage shop.

'There is absolutely nothing kinky about rubber,' she told the press. 'I'm just an ordinary person trying to live my life.'

BUT the biggest scandal concerning the current crop of royals hasn't happened yet – not in Britain at least. In the mid-1990s, American writer Kitty Kelley – who had already produced inflammatory exposés of Jacqueline Kennedy Onassis, Frank Sinatra, Elizabeth Taylor and Nancy Reagan – turned her attention to the Royal Family. Her book, *The Royals*, has not been published in Britain and it came out in America the very week that Princess Diana died, blasting it off the front pages.

One can only surmise that her book has not been published in the UK for legal reasons. British libel laws are much more draconian that those in the USA, so one has to tread carefully here. For example, it would be treasonous to make any suggestions about the sexual conduct of the Queen.

However, it is Prince Philip who particularly took Kitty Kelley's interest. He has had an extraordinary life. Although he was born Prince Philip of Greece, sixth in line to the Greek throne, his father was Prince Andrew of Denmark and his mother Princess Alice of Battenberg. His uncle was even expelled from Greece during World War I for supporting the Germans. Philip's mother had to be rescued by the Royal Navy and was taken to Corfu, then a British Protectorate. She gave birth to Philip on the kitchen table of a farmhouse that had neither electricity nor running water.

Philip was brought up largely in Britain, staying with his relative, the Marquis of Milford Haven, who was famous for his huge collection of pornography. During World War II Philip, then still a Greek citizen, joined the Royal Navy, but his uncle, Lord Louis Mountbatten, was already hatching plans to marry his nephew, an £11-a-week naval officer, to the girl who would one day become the richest woman in the world.

When Princess Elizabeth met Prince Philip, it was love at first sight. The British establishment were against the match, however, particularly because of Philip's Nazi ties. Philip showed remarkable sangfroid about their opposition and was seen drinking and dancing with other women in the West End, even while he was wooing the Princess.

Their three-month separation, engineered by her father, did nothing to dampen Princess Elizabeth's ardour and, as a royal prince, Philip of Greece could hardly be dismissed as an unsuitable husband. However, there were public doubts about the heir to the throne marrying a foreigner, so Philip naturalized. This lost him his royal title. The King, who was against the match, refused to give him another one and Philip only regained his title of 'prince' in 1957 after he had done his duty to the British throne by siring two heirs.

When the Queen acceded to the throne, Lord Mountbatten boasted that the House of Windsor was now the house of Mountbatten. Experts agreed. However, the Queen issued a proclamation that she and her children would continue to use the name Windsor. It was only with the birth of her third child, Prince Andrew, that she changed the family name to Mountbatten-Windsor.

By this time, Prince Philip had consolidated his position. This came about largely because of the Townsend scandal. The Prime Minister, Winston Churchill, had realized that if anything happened to the Queen while Charles was underage, Princess Margaret would take over as regent. So in 1952, he pushed though the Regency Act, making Philip regent in that eventuality.

Princess Margaret was miffed. Although she had backed her sister when Elizabeth wanted to marry Philip, Philip opposed her marriage to Group Captain Townsend. To get her own back, she dished the dirt on Philip. There was a lot to tell.

Persistent rumours linked Philip's name with Greek cabaret singer, Helene Corbet, who had two illegitimate children. Philip was godfather to both children and they went to his old school Gordonstoun, although Helene was a woman of slender means.

Stories also circulated about the novelist Daphne du Maurier and the actress, Anna Massey, a French cabaret star with whom he was said to have sired a daughter named Charlotte. All the stories have been denied with varying degrees of conviction. Photographs of Philip dancing the night away with actress Pat Kirkwood earned him a rebuke from the King. Princess Elizabeth was at home heavily pregnant at the time.

But the Queen ignored such tittle-tattle. Margaret repeating it only alienated the sisters further. The Queen, it is said, accepts that if Prince Philip needs to satisfy the sexual side of his nature elsewhere that is a matter for him, provided he is discreet.

Once or twice, he has sailed pretty close to the wind though. In 1956, Philip and his private secretary, Commander Michael Parker, spent five months gallivanting around the world. Parker's wife sued for divorce. The press speculated that the fairy-tale romance between the Queen and Prince Philip was over. The situation was resolved when Parker resigned and Philip returned obediently to the fold.

From then on, Prince Philip played closer to home. He joined an informal gentleman's association called the Thursday Club, which boasted among its members Dr Stephen Ward, a key figure in the Profumo affair. Ward committed suicide while on trial at the Old Bailey for living off immoral earnings. It was he who supplied the prostitutes Christine Keeler and Mandy Rice-Davis to the Secretary of State for War, John Profumo, and the Soviet spy, Yevgeny Ivanov. Ivanov later claimed that he had lodged with the Russian GRU, compromising evidence concerning Prince Philip.

None of it has ever been used. Philip, it seems, has the luck of the devil. If the meticulous muckraking of Kitty Kelley cannot besmirch him, nothing will.

# 3 ❖ Edward and Mrs Simpson

During their recent crises, the Royal Family's behaviour has been guided by one over-arching memory – that of the greatest scandal to hit the British throne this century, the Abdication Crisis of 1936.

For the British people it came like a bolt from the blue. As Prince of Wales, Edward had been popular. He had visited the front during World War I and genuinely seemed to sympathize with the plight of the unemployed during the Great Depression. For several years, he had been having a torrid affair with an American divorcée. He wanted to marry her and thought he would be able to when he came to the throne in January 1936.

The press barons were pillars of the establishment and, although foreign newspapers were full of the royal romance, nothing about the relationship was published in Britain. Sooner or later, the matter had to come to a head. The American papers were predicting that Edward would marry Mrs Wallis Simpson before his coronation in May 1937, so that she could be crowned Queen at the ceremony. But they had counted without the redoubtable Prime Minister, Stanley Baldwin, who was implacably against the match.

Over the years the waters have become muddied. Some say that the government opposed the marriage because Wallis Simpson was an American. Others think it was because she was a divorcée – twice over. Still others say it was because she was a commoner. And there are those who believe that Edward had already exhibited pro-Fascist sympathies and that the proposed marriage was simply an excuse to oust him.

The crisis was sparked by someone who knew nothing about the affair. The Bishop of Bradford, ironically named Dr Alfred Blunt, spoke out at the diocesan conference in 1936, condemning the King's playboy life style. Indeed, before he met Mrs Simpson, he had been a bit of a playboy and along the way it is said, sired two illegitimate children.

His first sexual experience was in a brothel in Calais during World War I where he said he found the prostitutes 'perfectly filthy and revolting'. That did not stop him going back for more in Amiens, or taking up with a courtesan in Paris.

On his return to England, he began walking out with Lady Sybil Cadogan, but was soon in love with Mrs Marian Coke, a married woman 12 years his senior. He seemed to have a thing about married women. One of his long-time lovers was Freda Dudley Ward, the wife of a Liberal MP. They met during a Zeppelin raid when she ran into a house where he was having dinner for cover.

The affair lasted several years but then, as now, there were plenty of other women, married and single, prepared to ease the libido of the heir to the throne. But in those days they did not kiss-and-tell in the newspapers. Besides, the owners of Fleet Street were peers of the realm and would not allow such things to be printed.

The Prince of Wales had a particular fascination for Americans. He visited America several times and set his cap at Audrey James, the daughter of an American industrialist. She rejected his advances when she was single but, once married, she had an affair with him that she recalled as 'merry but brief'.

Next came Lady Thelma Furness, the daughter of an American diplomat. Not only was she married, she was also a divorcée. At 16, she had eloped with a man twice her age. The marriage did not last. Once shot of her first husband, she snared Viscount Furness who was famous for his consumption of brandy and women.

Lady Furness accompanied Edward on a visit to Kenya in 1928 where, she said, she felt 'as if we were the only two people in the world'. In her diary she recorded: 'This was our Eden, and we were alone in it. His arms about me were the only reality; his words of love my only bridge to life. Borne along on the mounting tide of his ardour, I felt myself inexorably swept from the accustomed moorings of caution. Every night I felt more completely possessed by our love.'

Compare this with the Camillagate tapes, or Squidgygate.

The affair came to an end when she had a fling with Aly Khan, who had been trained in the art of delaying ejaculation in the brothels of Cairo

**Lady Thelma Furness arriving aboard the Queen Mary at Southampton**

when he was 18. He was so good at this that in aristocratic circles it was said that like Father Christmas, he only came once a year.

With competition like this, the Prince of Wales could not stand up. Thelma openly complained that Edward was a poor sexual performer and not very well endowed, scandalizing society by openly calling the heir to the throne 'the little man'. His deficiencies in the genital department had already been noted when he was at Osborne Naval College, where the other pupils called his private parts 'Sardines' rather than 'Whales'.

Ill equipped to satisfy women, he may well have experimented with men. The gay writer, Lytton Strachey, tried to pick him up once in the Tate Gallery, only to flee when he realized who his intended was. Later, Strachey wrote about it ruing what might have been.

When Dr Blunt spoke out, Edward had in fact been faithful to Mrs Simpson for several years. But Blunt's remarks at the diocesan conference breached the dam. The press pact was already under strain. Soon after Edward came to the throne, he began to put his marriage plans into action. First, he had to arrange a speedy divorce for Mrs Simpson. Her husband Ernest was found in the bedroom of a Thames-side hotel with a professional co-respondent, who rejoiced in the name of Buttercup Kennedy. When Lord Beaverbrook, the Canadian-born owner of the *Express* news-

**Edward, Prince of Wales**

paper group, heard that the divorce proceedings were to be heard at Ipswich on 27 October 1936, he called Mrs Simpson's solicitor and warned him that he intended to report the proceedings in the London *Evening Standard*. The solicitor told Beaverbrook that Mrs Simpson had no intention of marrying the King and that the notoriety their friendship had brought her was making her ill.

Beaverbrook bought it and, together with Lord Rothermere, owner of the *Daily Mail*, persuaded the rest of the papers to continue their code of silence on the matter. However, pressmen did turn up for the divorce hearings and were locked in the courtroom while Mrs Simpson made her escape. Two enterprising photographers tried to photograph her as she sped away in a car driven by the King's chauffeur, only to have their cameras smashed by the police. Nevertheless, while details of the divorce proceedings did appear in the papers, they were published without comment.

The American newspapers had a field day, of course. One ran the memorable headline 'King's Moll Reno'ed', after the Nevada's quickie-divorce capital, and they began calling Wallis Simpson 'Queen Wally'.

Parliament was getting restive, too. On 17 November 1936, Labour MP Ellen Wilkinson asked the President of the Board of Trade why two or three pages had been ripped from distinguished American magazines.

'What is it that the British public are not allowed to know?' she asked.

It was not until 3 December, when Dr Blunt made his remarks, that she got an answer. Although Dr Blunt later denied that he knew anything about the affair of Edward and Mrs Simpson, the newspapers assumed that he did. He was a senior churchman, an insider. The establishment, the press thought, were breaking ranks.

Now the whole thing was out in the open and the national debate raged.

'Why shouldn't the King marry his cutie?' asked Winston Churchill.

'Because England does not want Queen Cutie,' replied Noël Coward.

Stones were thrown through the windows of Mrs Simpson's London home. Letters and telegrams of abuse came in by the sack full. Terrified, she fled to the south of France, leaving Edward to face the furore alone.

Queen Mary, Edward's mother, was against the marriage instinctively. But Baldwin's opposition was more reasoned. The abdication of the King would cause a royal scandal, yet his marriage would cause a bigger one. The British Secret Service had already compiled a weighty dossier on Mrs Simpson's activities. It did not make pretty reading, especially if the papers got their hands on it.

Of Virginian stock, she had been born in Baltimore. Her first husband, navy flier Lieutenant Earl Winfield 'Win' Spencer had been an alcoholic and a sadist, who liked to tie her to the bed and beat her. He had numerous extramarital affairs with both men and women.

Wallis, for her part, had launched herself on the diplomatic scene in Washington, bedding the Italian ambassador and a senior Argentine diplomat, who was said to dance the best tango in DC.

In a belated honeymoon, Win took her on a trip to the Far East where together, and separately, they visited the brothels of Shanghai and Hong Kong. Wallis particularly liked watching girls performing lesbian acts and would sometimes join in threesomes without her husband.

It was in these famous 'singing houses' that Wallis learnt the ancient art of Fang Chung. The Chinese have been studying the erotic arts since the fifth century BC. Ancient Chinese Emperors would employ a mature woman as a sexual advisor to pick new wives and concubines for him, and to advise him as to how to satisfy the hundreds and sometimes thousands of wives and concubines he had. These women distilled their knowledge of sex and produced books.

Fang Chung is a method of relaxing a sexual partner. It involves massaging hot oil into their nipples, stomach and inner thighs. Only when the recipient is totally relaxed are the genitals caressed. Aficionados of Fang

Chung are said to be able to arouse even the most passionless of men by concentrating on the nerve centres and delicate brushing of the skin, and they learn to delay ejaculation almost indefinitely by firm pressure on the perineum.

Despite all Wallis's undoubted accomplishments in the erotic arts, Win decided that he was gay after all and moved in with a handsome young artist. This left Wallis free to practise her new-found techniques on a string of other men. These included a young American called Robbie, the Italian naval attaché Count Galeazzo Ciano, soon to be Mussolini's foreign minister, and American millionaire Herman Rogers. Together with Rogers' wife Katherine, they set up a *ménage à trois*. Wallis suffered a botched abortion that left her unable to bear children.

She met her second husband Ernest Simpson, a British subject, in New York. He, too, was married, but they quickly divorced their respective spouses and moved to London. Married life changed nothing. They were members of a fast set that included the Mountbattens and Lady Thelma Furness. Wallis went on a women-only holiday to the south of France with Consuela Thaw and Gloria Vanderbilt, who was having a lesbian love affair with Nada, wife of the Marquis of Milton Haven and lover of Edwina Mountbatten at the time. Consuela and Wallis shared a bedroom. And they went out together on the pull.

After Wallis was introduced to the Prince of Wales by Lady Furness, the two of them would often make up a foursome with Wallis's husband and Mary Raffray, Ernest Simpson's mistress. In 1934, Edward holidayed with Mrs Simpson in Biarritz. Mr Simpson could not join the party, so Wallis was chaperoned by her aunt Bessie.

In February 1935, Edward was photographed with Mrs Simpson leaving a lingerie shop in Kitzbühel, where they were enjoying a skiing holiday together. In May, the gossip came home to London when Edward danced with Mrs Simpson at his parents' Silver Jubilee ball.

In June, he told the British Legion that they should extend the hand of friendship to Germany. This was taken to indicate that he was pro-Nazi. Meanwhile, Wallis found a way to express her pro-German sympathies more directly. It was rumoured that she was having a brief fling with Hitler's ambassador to the court of St James, Joachim von Ribbentrop. But that did not stop her holidaying with Edward in the south of France and then on Corsica.

On 27 May 1936, the King invited Mr and Mrs Baldwin to dinner – along with the Mountbattens and the notorious swingers, the Duff Coopers – to meet Wallis. Baldwin was impressed with Wallis. He was also impressed by how much the King loved her. But he knew that a woman with Wallis Simpson's track record could not become Queen of England.

The British press respected the King's privacy when he set off on a cruise in the Adriatic with Mrs Simpson that summer, but the rest of the world's press and the newsreels followed every move. Many noted that her husband was nowhere to be seen. The Foreign Office was outraged when he paid an unauthorized visit to the Greek dictator, Ioannis Metaxas, who drove them through cheering crowds. Mrs Simpson was received like a queen. The couple also visited Kemal Ataturk, Turkey's dictator, and invited him on a state visit to Britain. All this was done without the knowledge of the British government or Parliament.

Baldwin bided his time and slowly public opinion turned against the King. He was due to open a hospital extension in Aberdeen, but cancelled and sent his brother instead, on the grounds that the court was still in mourning. However, Edward had already been seen at Ascot and had been on a Mediterranean cruise. Some noticed that the King was actually hosting a house party at Balmoral at the time and, according to the Court Circular, Mrs Simpson was on the guest list.

Not only was the King losing the support of the people, the Dominions were turning against him. They were following the King's romance in the American papers and were sending letters of protest to the government and prominent members of the establishment in London.

Baldwin put pressure on the King to halt Mrs Simpson's divorce proceedings. Edward refused on the grounds that it would be wrong to interfere in Mrs Simpson's affairs as she was 'just a friend'. From Edward's point of view, there could be no delay. As Mrs Simpson would have to wait six months after the *decree nisi* was issued before she got a *decree absolute* and could marry again, if she was to be by his side at his coronation in May, the divorce had to go ahead as planned.

Even friends counselled caution. He did not have to confront the matter now. Once he was crowned, he could introduce Mrs Simpson slowly and then, with the people on his side, marry her. He rejected this, saying that it would be like 'being crowned with a lie on my lips'.

Once Wallis Simpson was granted her divorce, nothing could prevent a constitutional crisis. In mid-November, Baldwin called a cabinet meeting to discuss what could be done. The government firmly rejected any marriage to Mrs Simpson.

Edward still believed that the situation could be saved. He set out for Wales where thousands of unemployed miners turned out to cheer and sing hymns of praise, in Welsh, to the man they still considered to be their champion.

Soon after, the press pact was broken and things moved fast. Edward withdrew to his country house, Fort Belvedere, near Virginia Water in Surrey, and spent hours on the phone to Wallis who was in Cannes. They had already discussed the possibility of a morganatic marriage, one that denied her and her heirs any position in the succession.

Edward put the proposal to Baldwin. Under the 1931 Statute of Westminster, to make any alteration to the succession required not only the approval of the British Parliament, but also the parliaments of all the Dominions. Under the King's instructions, Baldwin put it to them. They rejected it.

In Britain, it was not just the government that was against the marriage, but the Opposition was against it, too. Baldwin told the King that if he went ahead and married against the government's advice, he would resign and force an election over the matter.

With the press now free to discuss the matter, the King could get some sense of public opinion. The *Daily Mirror* issued a challenge on its front page.

'God save the King,' it said. 'Tell us the facts Mr Baldwin... The nation insists on knowing the King's full demands and conditions... The nation will give you its verdict.'

Others were not so equivocal. They mistrusted Mrs Simpson's hold over the King and her Nazi sympathies. It was rumoured that Mrs Simpson was blackmailing him; that Edward had punched his brother the Duke of Gloucester on the nose for criticizing the liaison; that the next in line to the throne, the Duke of York, was an epileptic; that American newspaper tycoon William Randolph Hearst had offered £250,000 for Mrs Simpson to file her divorce petition in America and name the King as co-respondent; and that the King was a closet Fascist. This last was not without foundation. He had refused to meet the exiled King of Abyssinia, ousted by the Italian invasion, when asked to do so by the Foreign Secretary.

Although there were, on balance, more papers against the marriage than for it, the embattled couple did not think that the situation was irretrievably lost. Mrs Simpson suggested that the King take a leaf out of the American president's book and go on the radio for a cosy 'fireside chat'. She felt sure that when his people heard the story of their romance from the King himself, they would back him.

Edward agreed, but he showed a draft to Baldwin, who pointed out that such an appeal to the people over the heads of the government was unconstitutional. Baldwin insisted that whatever the King did he should not divide the British people. The King offered to abdicate.

Wallis Simpson issued a press release, offering to withdraw from the situation. She even sent a message to the Prime Minister, offering to drop her divorce petition. But it was too late. The King had been outmanoeuvred by Baldwin. Even his one parliamentary champion, Winston Churchill, gave up after being shouted down in the House of Commons.

'Our cock won't fight,' said Beaverbrook.

On Thursday 10 December 1936, just seven days after the scandal had broken in the press, Edward signed the Instrument of Abdication, renouncing the crown of Great Britain and Ireland. He also resigned as head of state of the Dominions and as Emperor of India, and all the other titles and positions those posts entailed. He did, however, keep the £1 million settled on him by his grandmother, Queen Alexandra.

Alice Keppel, the last mistress of Edward VII, was dining at the Ritz when she heard the news.

'We did things much better in my day,' she said.

The following day, Edward was driven to Windsor where he broadcast to the Empire, explaining that he could no longer go on being King without the woman he loved. The whole world listened. People wept openly. Even tough New York cab drivers pulled over, amazed that the King of England would renounce everything for the love of a woman. This, everyone agreed, must be the greatest love story ever told.

Well, not exactly. Cynics have suggested that the tricks that Wallis picked up in the singing houses of China were deployed to such good effect that the thought of living without her was unbearable. She was also adept at fellatio and, it is said, had an operation to have her vagina tightened to help stimulate his undersized genitals.

Prominent socialite, Lady Ottoline Morrell, claimed Edward was also taking injections to make him more virile that were driving him quite mad. There was also talk of him being a foot fetishist, which Wallis ruthlessly exploited. She also acted as his dominatrix. One day in front of friends, she turned to Edward and ordered: 'Take off my dirty shoes and get me my shoes and bring me another pair.' To everyone's amazement, he did.

There was talk of elaborate nanny–child scenes enacted between them. Freda Dudley Ward also commented on this side of his nature.

'He made himself the slave of whomsoever he loved and became totally dependent on her,' she said. 'It was his nature; he was like a masochist. He liked being humbled, degraded. He begged for it.'

After the broadcast, Edward sailed into exile on board a Royal Navy destroyer. This was ironic as the prevailing joke was that Edward had resigned as Admiral of the Fleet, only to sign on as third mate on a Baltimore tramp.

In June 1937, Edward and Mrs Simpson married in France. No members of the Royal Family attended the ceremony and most of their friends stayed away. He was created Duke of Windsor. Although he retained his HRH, the Duchess was refused one. 'A damnable wedding present,' he called it.

But that was not the end of the scandal. In the run up to the War, Edward and Wallis paid a social call on Adolf Hitler. That Edward was sympathetic was beyond doubt. He encouraged friends to contribute to the Nazi cause and liked to speak German in private.

In 1937, he told a cheering crowd in Leipzig: 'What I have seen in Germany is a miracle.'

At the outbreak of hostilities he joined up but he was considered a security risk. When France fell, he sought refuge in Fascist Spain with friends who were openly pro-German. There was even talk that, should Britain fall, Edward would be restored to the throne as Hitler's vassal.

To get him out of harm's way, the government dispatched Edward to the Bahamas as Governor. Edward and Wallis became embroiled in illicit currency deals, making money out of the war. This all went disastrously wrong when one of Edward's friends, Sir Harry Oakes, who was also involved, was murdered. A relative of Oakes's was framed but, in court, was acquitted. No one has ever got to the bottom of the Oakes scandal.

Low-level scandal continued to follow the Duke and Duchess of Windsor for the rest of their lives. By the 1950s, there were rumours that Wallis had grown tired of Edward's cloying love and was seen everywhere with Woolworth heir, Jimmy Donahue.

Donahue was exclusively homosexual, but the rumour had it that Wallis was trying to convert him. Others said that it was the Duke who was sleeping with Donahue, although it was widely known that he despised all homosexuals.

Noël Coward, who moved in the same circles as the Windsors after the abdication, explained the situation.

'I like Jimmy,' he said. 'He's an insane camp but he is fun. I like the Duchess; she is the fag hag to end all fag hags, but that's what makes her likeable. The Duke... well, although he pretends not to hate me, he does because I'm queer and he's queer. However, unlike him I don't pretend not to be. Here she's got a royal queen to sleep with and a rich one to hump.'

The Duke and Duchess lived out the rest of their lives in Paris. The Duke never set foot in England again. But when he died in 1972, at the age of 77, his body was flown home. He was laid in state for two days in St George's Chapel, Windsor. Nearly 58,000 people filed past his body.

The Duchess accompanied the body and stayed, for the first time, in Buckingham Palace. After the chapel was closed to the public she was driven to Windsor, where she was greeted by Prince Charles and her old friend, Lord Mountbatten.

The Duchess of Windsor died herself 14 years later, in 1986. At the foot of her bed was a poem written by the Duke in his own handwriting. It read:

'My friend, with thee to live alone,
Methinks were better to own
A crown, a sceptre and a throne.'

# 4 ❖ Bertie, Prince of Wales

Scandal attended the life of Edward VIII's grandfather, Edward VII, every step of the way. When he was just 15, he was sent to Königswinter on the Rhine to improve his German. There he groped a serving wench and tried to kiss her. The Prime Minister, William Ewart Gladstone, that great reformer of fallen women, condemned his behaviour as 'this squalid debauch, a paltry affair, an unworthy indulgence'.

When the Prince of Wales – soon universally known as 'Bertie' – went up to Oxford, he began a life of drunkenness, gluttony and debauchery under the tutelage of the flamboyant aristocrat, Henry Chaplin, known to one and all as 'Magnifico'. At the sumptuous meals laid on by Magnifico's private chef, Bertie was regaled by stories of London life – the womanizing, the opium dens, the brothels, the boxing matches and the dog fights. Life in Oxford was tamer, but the story is told of Bertie and Magnifico meeting a peasant woman on a country road. They pulled her dress up over her head and stuffed a £5 note into her knickers.

After Oxford, Bertie was sent into the army. At just 19, he was posted to the Curragh, a military camp near Dublin. After a drunken mess party, his fellow officers decided that Bertie should lose his virginity. They put a naked young girl, an actress named Nellie Clifden, in his bed. Bertie enjoyed the experience so much that he began an affair with her.

Gossip about Bertie and his 'Princess of Wales' soon reached the ears of the Queen. She was appalled, especially as Nellie was also sharing her affections with Charles Wynn-Carrington. Prince Albert warned that if his son did not stop the affair 'the consequences for this country and for the world would be too dreadful'. He travelled to Cambridge to tell off his son in person, but there was an outbreak of typhoid in the city at the time. Prince Albert caught it and died.

To save him from himself, Bertie's marriage to the Danish Princess Alexandra of Schleswig-Holstein-Sonderburg-Glucksberg had already been arranged. Immediately after the wedding in 1863, Bertie and his bride moved into his own private residence, Marlborough House in Pall Mall. Freed from the constraints of Queen Victoria's court, which was still in mourning, the Prince began partying in earnest.

No one doubted that he loved his wife, but Bertie could not resist pretty women. Fortunately, Alexandra was happy to stay at home with the children while he gallivanted. Despite his love of gambling, sumptuous food, fine wines, good cigars and amorous adventures, Bertie was surprisingly popular. He turned the London social scene into one long round of banquets, balls and gala nights out. The only person he was not popular with was his mother, Queen Victoria, who still blamed him for the death of her beloved Albert. She kept up a constant barrage of letters condemning his debauched life style.

As well as savouring the high life, the Prince of Wales also enjoyed the low life. He visited brothels and illegal cockfights. Photography was still in its infancy, so Bertie could enjoy a discreet tryst with a lady of the streets in Cremorne pleasure gardens in Chelsea, or sex with a young woman in the back of a hansom cab without too much fear of discovery.

But, for the sake of discretion, it was easier for him to indulge himself abroad. Egypt was one favourite destination. He also enjoyed the debauched spa towns of Germany, particularly Marienbad. One prostitute travelled all the way from Vienna to sleep with him there. When she found that he was already occupied, she insisted that one of the other gentleman in his entourage enjoy her favours so that she could cover her train fare.

In Paris, Bertie became something of a legend. One brothel, Le Chabanais, kept a special chair for him where he sat while selecting his girls. The Duc de Gramont took him to visit Guilia Beneni, who proudly claimed to be the 'greatest whore in the world' and worked under the name of La Barucci. Breaching all codes of protocol, La Barucci turned her back on the Prince and pulled up her skirt to reveal her naked behind. When the Duc told her off, she replied: 'Well, you told me to show him my best side.'

When Bertie asked to see Cora Pearl, a prostitute from Plymouth whom Napoleon III had once paid £10,000 for a single night, she had herself served to the Prince on a silver salver. When the lid was removed, she was there naked except for a string of pearls and a sprig of parsley.

All this passed without comment in the press. But when Bertie took up with Hortense Schneider, an actress and singer so well known for distributing her favours to European royalty that she was known as *'Le Passage des Princes'*. *The Times* carried a report about this scandalous 'friendship'.

After that, Bertie decided that he must be more discreet. In France he began passing himself off as the Earl of Chester or the Duke of Lancaster. It did no good. His whiskers and portly figure were so well known that one night, when he visited the Moulin Rouge, one of the dancers yelled from the stage: 'Hello, Wales.' He smiled and bought champagne for the orchestra.

He had a long affair with the Princesse de Sagan, but her son grew jealous. One day, when he found the Prince of Wales's discarded clothes outside his mother's bedroom door, he threw them in a fountain. The Prince of Wales had to find his way back to his hotel in a pair of borrowed trousers that were much too small.

Back in England, the Prince used the Earl of Rosebery's London home for his afternoon's entertaining, later moving to the ultra-discreet Cavendish Hotel in Jermyn Street. The public largely tolerated his shenanigans with chorus girls and prostitutes, but it was a different matter when he was subpoenaed to appear in a divorce case.

The lady concerned was Harriet Moncreiffe, one of the eight beautiful daughters of Sir Thomas Moncreiffe of that Ilk. She had been a close friend of the Prince's before her marriage, at 17, to Sir Charles Mordaunt, the Conservative MP for South Warwickshire.

The year after their wedding in 1866, Mordaunt noticed his wife reading a letter from the notorious Bertie.

'I don't approve of your friendship with the Prince,' he said.

In 1869, Harriet gave birth to a daughter, who was almost blind. When Mordaunt tried to comfort his wife, she said: 'Charlie, I have deceived you. The child is not yours. It is Lord Cole's.'

The implication was that the child's eyesight problems were caused by syphilis caught from Viscount Cole, the third son of the Earl of Enniskillen.

Mordaunt was prepared to dismiss this admission as delirium. But then she confessed to sleeping with Lord Lucan, the man responsible for the disastrous Charge of the Light Brigade, Sir Frederic Johnstone, the Prince of Wales and others. The Prince, apparently, had made a habit of visiting her at home several times a week. Lord Cole and Sir Frederic Johnstone were friends from his Oxford days and took over as her suitors when Bertie's interest flagged.

Distraught, Mordaunt broke into his wife's writing desk to find a Valentine card from the Prince, along with one of his monogrammed handkerchiefs and a dozen letters. He also found letters from Lucan and hotel

**Hortense Schneider,
actress and singer**

bills made out to Johnstone, and he began divorce proceedings immediately.

Harriet fled to her father's home in Perthshire. There she was examined by an eminent physician who found no sign of syphilis. However, her emotional state had begun to deteriorate.

Her father petitioned the divorce courts, arguing that she could not be sued due to her mental condition. Mordaunt argued that she was feigning madness to save herself from public disgrace. The divorce petition was put on hold, but in 1869 a trial was ordered to determine Harriet's sanity. The Prince of Wales was summonsed. Both his wife and his mother were sympathetic. Queen Victoria wrote to the Lord Chancellor, seeking to have the heir to the throne excused the disgrace of appearing in the common divorce courts. Her letter read: 'The fact of the Prince of Wales's intimate acquaintanceship with a young married woman being publicly proclaimed will show an amount of impudence, which cannot but damage him in the eyes of the middle and lower classes, which is to be deeply lamented, in these days when the higher classes, in their frivolous, selfish and pleasure-seeking lives, do more to increase the spirit of democracy than anything else.'

However, the Lord Chancellor advised the Queen that there was no way the Prince of Wales could be excused. The Prince's own solicitor, Sir

George Lewis told Bertie: 'You must go into the witness-box. It is the only way to clear your name.'

Another way of handling the situation was to put some spin on the proceedings. Some of the Prince's letters were leaked to the newspapers shortly before the trial. They were, of course, 'unexceptional in every way', in the words of the Lord Chancellor. The judge also assured the Prince that he would be protected from 'improper questions'.

When the trial opened before Lord Penzance on 16 February 1870, Sir Frederic Johnstone and Lord Cole were cited as co-respondents, along with 'others' – generally thought to include the Prince of Wales.

Evidence was presented that Harriet had tried to kill her own child, had smeared herself with excrement, walked around the house at night naked except for stockings and a cloak and had tried to batter down the butler's door with a hammer. Mordaunt's barrister quickly conceded that Harriet was, indeed, insane.

But this was not the end of the case. Frederic Johnstone wanted to clear his name. This was unfortunate for Viscount Cole since extracts from Harriet's diary seemed to indicate that he was indeed the father of her child, conceived while her husband was away on a fishing trip in Norway.

The Prince of Wales was then called to the stand. He admitted a close friendship with Harriet Mordaunt. She had visited him frequently at Marlborough House. Then came the crucial question: 'Has there ever been any improper familiarity or criminal act between yourself and Lady Mordaunt?'

The Prince was emphatic.

'There has not,' he said.

Applause broke out in the court.

Johnstone then took the stand, where he was informed that Sir Charles Mordaunt had told his wife that the 28-year-old Johnstone was not married because he suffered repeated bouts of VD.

'A more untrue statement was never made behind a man's back,' Johnstone said.

When asked whether that meant that he had never suffered from venereal disease, Johnstone, later a Conservative MP, said: 'Certainly not. I have had my youthful indiscretions.'

The jury took less than 10 minutes to find Lady Mordaunt unfit to plead. But the damage had been done. After the trial, *Reynold's Newspaper* accused the Prince of 'bringing dishonour to the homestead of an English gentleman'. He was booed when he arrived at Ascot with Princess Alexandra, and a meeting in Hyde Park called for the abolition of the monarchy.

Sir Charles Mordaunt appealed the verdict and lost. Under the strain of the trial, Harriet's mental state deteriorated drastically and she was committed to a mental asylum, where she remained until her death in 1906.

Mordaunt returned to the courts to argue that his wife's mental state did not debar him from suing for divorce. A fresh trial was ordered, citing only Lord Cole as co-respondent. It was undefended. Mordaunt got his divorce and married a vicar's daughter who produced a son. Harriet's daughter recovered her eyesight, married a marquess and had five children.

The scandal did not cause Bertie to mend his ways. In 1871, the widowed Lady Susan Pelham-Clinton, wrote to him telling him that she was seven months pregnant. She went on to warn him: 'Without any funds to meet the necessary expenses and to buy the discretion of servants, it is impossible to keep this sad secret.'

Bertie gave her £250 and sent her to Ramsgate with his personal physician.

In 1875, Bertie was embroiled in another divorce scandal. During a royal tour of India, his companion Lord Aylesford received a letter from his wife, saying she was eloping with the Marquis of Blandford.

'Blandford is the greatest blackguard alive,' commented the Prince sympathetically, neglecting to mention that he, too, had enjoyed Lady Aylesford's favours.

Lord Aylesford dashed home to begin divorce proceedings. The families of both Lady Aylesford and the Marquis of Blandford tried to hush up the matter. When Aylesford refused to drop his suit, Blandford's brother Randolph Churchill asked the Prince of Wales to intercede. He refused, so Churchill went to Princess Alexandra and told her of her husband's involvement with Lady Aylesford. He had copies of their letters, which he threatened to make public if the Prince would not rally to his support.

Bertie was outraged. He challenged Churchill to a duel in France. This was ridiculous, and they both knew it. Duels were illegal and Churchill could hardly look forward to a comfortable future if he shot the heir to the throne.

The Queen rallied to Bertie's colours and Princess Alexandra went very publicly to meet her husband at sea off the Isle of Wight when he returned from India. That night, the royal couple made a great show of togetherness at the opera. Crowds that had been booing before, now cheered and clapped.

Ironically, Bertie's greatest popularity came with his very public liaison with Lillie Langtry, the Jersey Lily. The daughter of a clergyman, Lillie had been born on the island of Jersey, but she longed to get off it.

When she was 20, she saw a beautiful yacht in the harbour at St Peter Port.

'To become mistress of that yacht,' she said, 'I married the owner.'

His name was Edward Langtry. His family owned shipyards in Belfast. He was a passionless man, however, and the marriage was a disaster. When other men paid compliments to Lillie's stunning good looks, he said: 'You should have seen my first wife.'

Three years later, they arrived in London and the violet-eyed Lillie was the smash of the season. She was introduced to the Prince of Wales at a small supper party hosted by Arctic explorer, Sir Allen Young. The 36-year-old Prince was immediately captivated by the sensational figure of the pert 23-year-old.

Princess Alexandra was away at the time. When she returned, Bertie and Lillie were the talk of the town. They dined together openly and rode together in Hyde Park. In Paris, he kissed her in full view of everyone in the middle of the dance floor at Maxim's.

Lillie revelled in the notoriety that being a royal mistress gave her. She had her negligées trimmed with ermine. Society matrons such as Lady Cadogan would stand on chairs just to catch a glimpse of her. And she was so famous that she hardly dared venture out on the streets.

'People ran after me in droves,' she complained, 'staring me out of countenance and even lifting my shade to satisfy their curiosity.'

Although the whole world knew that Lillie was the Prince's mistress, the couple still managed to maintain a thin veneer of decorum. Bertie even managed to have Lillie and her husband presented to Queen Victoria.

Despite the popularity that his affair with Lillie gave him, the Prince still took up with the notorious French actress, Sarah Bernhardt. Lillie had other lovers, too, including Prince Louis of Battenberg, father of Lord Louis Mountbatten.

Her love affair with Bertie went on for five long years and Bertie only gave her up after the birth of her daughter, Jeanne-Marie, in 1881. This sparked a mucky divorce, which the Prince decided it best to stay out of. Nevertheless, he did not abandon her completely. When Lillie decided that she wanted to become an actress, Bertie persuaded the manager of the Haymarket Theatre to give her the lead in a charity performance of *She Stoops to Conquer*. The Prince's presence on the first night assured the success of her debut.

But Bertie was not the only member of the family to be embroiled in scandal. In 1886, the police raided a homosexual brothel at 19 Cleveland Street. When the owners of the brothel were arrested, they dropped the names of their aristocratic clients. These included the Prince of Wales's own son, Eddy, and the superintendent of his stables, Lord Arthur Somerset, along with the Earl of Euston.

The names of these high-born gentlemen were kept out of the subsequent trial, which earned the low-born brothel-keepers nine months' hard labour. However, Ernest Parke, the crusading editor of the *North London Press*, published the names of Somerset and Euston.

Somerset fled to France where he stayed until his death in 1926, but Euston sued for libel. He claimed that he had been given a flier advertising *'poses plastiques'* – that is, nude girls posing as classical Greek statues – at 19 Cleveland Street. Naturally, when he went there and discovered what was really going on, he was appalled and fled.

But that was not what one of the young boys, named John Saul, who worked at the brothel said. He said that Lord Euston had picked him up on the street and he had taken him back to Cleveland Street for sex. But Euston was 'not an actual sodomite', Saul said. 'He likes to play with you and then "spend" on your belly.'

The judge dismissed Saul as a 'loathsome object'. Parke went down for a year with hard labour. Lord Euston was appointed Bertie's aide-de-camp at his coronation in 1901.

Although Eddy's name was kept out of the proceedings, more scandalous rumours clung to his dissolute reputation. In 1888, it was rumoured that he was Jack the Ripper. It was also said that he murdered a baby he had fathered by a prostitute. Fortunately, Eddy died, probably of syphilis, before he could succeed to the throne.

In 1891, the Prince of Wales was summonsed to appear in court again – not in a divorce case this time but in what was known as the Baccarat Scandal, or the Tranby Croft Affair.

The previous September, Bertie had been invited to a house party at Tranby Croft, the country seat of Arthur Wilson, a wealthy Hull ship owner. Bertie had asked Wilson if he could bring his friend, Lieutenant-Colonel Sir William Gordon-Cumming, whom *The Sporting Times* described as 'possibly the handsomest man in London, and certainly the rudest'. He had a reputation as a sportsman, drinker and womanizer to rival Bertie's and often lent the Prince his house for assignations.

One evening they played baccarat. Sir William was seen to be cheating. One of the witnesses was the son of the house, Arthur Stanley Wilson. He alerted two of the guests, Berkeley Levett and Lycett Green, who also saw Sir William cheating. The following evening, they saw him do it again and word soon spread around the other guests.

**Alice Keppel**

When confronted, Sir William denied cheating, but everyone was eager to prevent a scandal that might embarrass the Prince. Sir William was told that if he signed a document promising never to play cards again, no more would be said. Otherwise he would be ruined. Sir William signed.

However, the next day Sir William discovered that the incident was the talk of Doncaster racecourse. In December, he received anonymous letters telling him that the story had spread as far as Paris and Monte Carlo.

As it seemed that his reputation was already in tatters, Sir William thought he had nothing to lose. He sued the Wilsons, Berkeley Levett, Lycett Green and his wife – but not the Prince of Wales – for slander. However, the Prince of Wales was called as a witness. He did not have much to say as he did not actually witness the cheating. But what shocked the public was the scale of his winnings, and losings, at baccarat. In a single night, they were more than a working man could expect to earn in a year.

The other witnesses were unshakeable. In his defence, Sir William claimed that he had signed the undertaking only to prevent a terrible scandal. In his summing up, the judge dismissed this, saying that no honourable man would sign a confession when he was innocent. The jury took less than 15 minutes to find the defendants not guilty. Sir William was ruined. He was cashiered from the army, blackballed from his clubs and ostracized from society.

However, the scandal did not reflect well on the Prince and the defendants were booed when they left the court.

The next day, Sir William married a 21-year-old American heiress, Florence Garner. She had stuck by him through the ordeal, maintaining for the rest of her life that the Prince of Wales had framed her fiancé over some other woman.

Bertie was unforgiving.

'The army and society are now well rid of such a damned blackguard,' he wrote to his son.

Although Bertie wisely gave up baccarat after the Tranby Croft Affair, he could not give up dangerous liaisons with women. His next affair, however, would not threaten to break as a scandal until after his death.

The woman in question was Frances Brooke, whom he called Daisy. She was beautiful, intelligent and rich. Bertie and Princess Alexandra had been the guests of honour at her magnificent wedding to Lord Brooke. She was just 18.

It was an aristocratic union. Although 'Brookie' loved his wife very much, he did not object when she satisfied her seemingly unquenchable sexual desires elsewhere. But Daisy was a jealous woman. When the wife of her lover, Lord Charles Beresford, fell pregnant, she wrote him a scalding letter. Unfortunately, this fell into his wife's hands and she threatened to make it public.

Hoping to avoid a ruinous scandal, Daisy turned to the Prince for help. He was very understanding, she said, and she was a woman who knew how to show her gratitude. From early 1891, he was a regular visitor to her home, Easton Lodge. She had a private railway station built nearby so he could reach her quicker on the royal train. They would meet for assignations in the summer house she had built in the gardens of the estate.

In London, they would be seen out together, dining in his favourite restaurants. They even went to church together. And, when they were apart, they would exchange passionate letters several times a week.

Her wealth was further increased when her father, the Earl of Warwick, died. She became Countess of Warwick, inheriting Warwick Castle and a vast fortune. At around the same time, she became a passionate socialist under the guidance of W.T. Stead, the idealistic editor of the *Pall Mall*

*Gazette*, and she began squandering her fortune on good causes.

She and Bertie inevitably broke up, as both had numerous new partners. After his death, her debts had mounted to some £100,000. With the help of the infamous journalist, Frank Harris, Daisy decided that her only way out was to publish the King's love letters. Their scandalous content would ensure a best-seller.

As soon as the Palace heard about the plan, she was hit with a writ. George V claimed that, as his father's son and heir, he owned copyright. Naturally, the courts were sympathetic to the new King's view and found in his favour. This kept the letters out of the public domain for another 50 years.

When Queen Victoria finally died, Bertie abandoned the name his father had given him – Albert – and decided to reign as Edward VII instead. He was far from popular, but he got lucky. The coronation was planned for 26 June, but Edward was struck down with peritonitis and almost died. Some 300 legs of mutton, 2,500 quails, snipe, oysters, prawns and sole poached in Chablis had already been prepared. This food was distributed among the poor of the East End, giving Edward VII a much-needed boost in public esteem before he was eventually crowned on 9 August.

His mistresses turned out in force for the coronation. A block of seats above the chancel was reserved for them. This was widely known as 'the King's loose box'. Noting this, Henry James, the American writer who became a British citizen, dubbed him 'Edward the Caresser'.

In Edward's declining years, there were two important women – besides his wife – in his life. One was Agnes Keyser, a middle-aged spinster, who mothered him. She bossed him about and would allow him to eat only the plainest of food. The other was Alice Keppel, the wife of George Keppel, a tall good-looking army officer who seemed flattered that the King should take an interest in his vivacious young wife. Alice was just 29 when the King met her. She was a great conversationalist and could hold her own with the highest in the land. The King would mischievously seat her next to the Archbishop of Canterbury at dinner.

The government used her as an intermediary with the King, and even Queen Alexandra praised her good sense. Edward and Alice holidayed each Easter together in Biarritz, but he still made time to visit Paris and Marienbad, alone. And there were always a number of society ladies that he would visit.

When Edward was dying, the Queen sent for Mrs Keppel so that she could visit him on his deathbed. After his death, the Keppels' home was plunged into mourning. Alice's two daughters considered the King their uncle and one of them asked her father: 'Why does it matter so much Kingy dying?'

George Keppel replied generously: 'Because Kingy was a very, very wonderful man.'

## 5 ❖ Mrs Brown

Although in our troubled times, politicians like to hark back to Victorian values, it was estimated in 1850 that there were 80,000 prostitutes in London alone, many of them underage girls sold into vice by parents who could not afford to keep them. And, although Queen Victoria is seen as a paragon of virtue, scandal was never far from her door.

Her father Edward, Duke of Kent, was so dissolute that his father, King George III, exiled him to Gibraltar. There he took a French mistress named Julie St Laurent and sadistically disciplined the regiment put under him. Posted to Montreal, he sentenced one soldier to 999 lashes. His unit rebelled. After a second rebellion in Gibraltar, he hanged three and brutally flogged dozens more.

Returning to London with his long-standing mistress, he ran up such enormous debts that they had to flee to Brussels. When his debts pursued him, he married Princess Victoria of Leiningen to put himself back in his father's good books. The King paid off his debts. His Madame St Laurent only found out about the match when it was reported in the Continental newspapers. They had been together for 25 years.

And the Duke of Kent was by no means the worst of them. His younger brother, Ernest, Duke of Cumberland, was said to have committed incest with his sister, Princess Sophia, in a mirror-lined room in St James's Palace. He was accused of attempting to rape the wife of the Lord Chancellor in her own drawing room, and Lord Graves slit his throat when he heard that the Prince was having an affair with his 50-year-old wife. The scandal sheets also said that he had killed a servant in a fit of rage, that his wife had bumped off her two previous husbands, and that the two of them planned to poison Victoria to put Ernest on the throne.

Princess Sophia gave birth to an illegitimate child, sired by an equerry at the Palace who was 33 years her senior. Her sister, Princess Augusta, fell in love with the King's equerry, Major-General Sir Brent Spencer. She never dared ask the King whether she could marry him. When she plucked up the courage to ask the Prince Regent, he forbade it. This did not stop them being lovers and they may have married in secret. Princess Amelia also fell for one of the King's equerries, a middle-aged philanderer named Charles Fitzroy who was descended from one of Charles II's bastards. They never married but she considered herself to be his wife and left everything she had to him when she died. Then there was Princess Elizabeth, who was rumoured to be pregnant while unmarried at the age of 16. She did not marry until she was 47.

George III's youngest son, Prince Augustus Frederick, married Lady Augusta Murray secretly in Rome, in direct contravention of the Royal Marriage Act. When she fell pregnant, they married again publicly in St George's Hanover Square. He used the name Mr Frederick Augustus. The marriage was ruled invalid and Prince Augustus was exiled. His wife's passport was seized to prevent her following him. However, using forged papers, she escaped and caught up with him in Berlin. For 10 years, they lived happily there until the lure of £12,000 and the Duchy of Sussex persuaded him to abandon her and return to England. He then sued for the custody of their children and married again, bigamously, to Lady Cecilia Buggin, the widow of a city grocer. Condoning the match, Queen Victoria created her Duchess of Inverness.

The Duke of Kent died less than two years after marrying. But in that period, Princess Victoria of Leinigen produced a daughter who would become Queen Victoria. The young Victoria knew of her father's murky past and sometimes referred to his former mistress as 'the old French lady' or 'the discovery of St Lawrence'. The misbehaviour of her uncles and aunts was simply overlooked, although she remained on friendly terms with her cousin, King Leopold of the Belgians, who was partial to feather boas and high-heeled shoes.

The scandalous behaviour of her widowed mother brought more shame to the young Victoria. She took as her lover the Irish upstart, Sir John Conroy, and made no effort to hide her physical familiarity with him in front of her impressionable young daughter. Together they tried to dominate the Princess, but when Victoria became Queen she banned Conroy from court.

Victoria became convinced that Conroy was using one of the Ladies of the Bedchamber, Lady Flora Hastings, as a spy. After Lady Hastings travelled back from Scotland with Conroy in 1838, her belly swelled and Victoria was convinced that she was pregnant by 'that Monster and Demon incarnate'.

Flora consulted the royal physician, Sir James Clark, a poor diagnostician, who quickly concluded that she was indeed pregnant. The other Ladies of the Bedchamber broadcast the fact. But when she was given a thorough examination, she was found still to be a virgin. The scandal had reached such proportions, however, that Flora's uncle Hamilton FitzGerald had to publish an open letter in *The Examiner*.

Once the public realized that Lady Flora was not pregnant but gravely ill, Queen Victoria's scandalous treatment of her made her very unpopular and she was hissed at by the crowds at Ascot. In 1839, this turned into a full-scale political scandal called the 'Bedchamber Crisis'.

When Victoria's prime ministerial favourite, Lord Melbourne – a two-time divorcé who once complimented Victoria on her 'full and fine bust' – fell from power, he was replaced by Sir Robert Peel, who insisted that she dismiss her gossiping Ladies of the Bedchamber. Victoria refused. In the street, mobs hurled abuse at her. They called her 'Mrs Melbourne', suggesting that the former Prime Minister was more than just an advisor. Eventually she had to give way.

When Lady Hastings died on 5 July 1839, it was found that the cause of the swelling was a tumour on her liver. *The Morning Post* described the Queen's behaviour in the affair as 'the most revolting virulence and indecency'.

Victoria's husband, the strait-laced Prince Albert, was not free from the

**Queen Victoria and John Brown - her 'personal highland servant'**

whiff of scandal either. His mother had outraged the good people of Saxe-Coburg-Gotha by having an affair with the court's Jewish chamberlain, who may have been Albert's real father. His parents divorced when he was five. His mother married an army officer and Albert never saw her again, while his father, in proper Hanoverian style, consoled himself with a series of mistresses.

Albert's brother took after his father and died of syphilis, but the young Albert prided himself on being a pillar of moral rectitude. He went to an all-male university and forswore contact with women.

As soon as she saw him, Victoria was bowled over by his looks.

'Albert's beauty is most striking,' she remarked.

At their third meeting, she asked him to marry her, while remarking that she was quite unworthy of him. He eventually consented, but warned that he would not be 'corrupted' by her.

Albert was good to his word. The first night of the honeymoon was strangely short, the diarist Charles Grenville noted.

'I told Lord Palmerston that this is not the way to provide us with a Prince of Wales,' he wrote.

Queen Victoria was a woman of robust sexual appetites, however, and she knew how to get the best out of Albert. She hung their bedroom at Osborne House with paintings of male nudes.

She hated getting pregnant, partly because Albert believed that sex was for procreation and not recreation. He would abstain for the nine months of the pregnancy and at least another three months after she had given birth. So she would have to go without sex for over a year. They had nine children in all. When Albert said that there should be no more, Victoria said: 'Can we have no more fun in bed?'

It was Albert who set the prudish standards that have become synonymous with the Victorian era. The Queen's maids were forbidden to entertain gentleman callers in the maids' parlour. Even their brothers were ushered into a special waiting room where their behaviour could be watched.

No lady with the slightest blemish on her character was allowed at court. One 70-year-old lady, who had eloped with her childhood sweetheart in her youth, was banned – even though the couple had led a blameless life ever since.

This lofty standard made scandals out of behaviour that would have passed unnoticed before. When one night, the Foreign Secretary Lord Palmerston blundered into the bedroom of Lady Blunt, a Lady of the Bedchamber, and tried to seduce her, Albert proclaimed that any man capable of such 'fiendish' behaviour should be debarred from high office. The public took a different view. Palmerston later won a landslide election after it was rumoured he had sired an illegitimate child at the age of 80.

When Prince Albert died in 1861, Queen Victoria was only 42. She went into prolonged mourning, ordering that his rooms at Buckingham Palace, Balmoral, Osborne and Windsor were to remain as they were on the day of his death. They were photographed so that when they were cleaned everything could be put back in exactly the same place.

She ordered that a picture of Albert be placed at the foot of her bed, wherever she slept. His nightshirt was to be laid beside her at bedtime and, in the morning, his hot shaving water was to be brought as if he were still alive.

Her withdrawal from public life was complete. This was a dangerous move with republicanism on the rise. People began to wonder what she was being paid for and mobs called for her to be overthrown. Even loyal newspapers, such as *The Times*, called her the 'Great Absentee', while the *Pall Mall Gazette* called her 'the invisible monarch'.

The Queen was quite clear about what she missed about Albert.

'What a dreadful thing this going to bed,' she lamented. 'What a contract to that tender lover's love. All alone.'

She brooded alone at Osborne, the home they had built together, and those around the Queen feared that she might become unhinged. She had to snap out of it. They sent for her carriage and favourite pony from Balmoral. They arrived in harness, led by her Scottish ghillie, John Brown, in bonnet and kilt. He was a giant of a man with a great shock of red hair. It is said that when she saw him she smiled – for the first time since Albert had died.

She hired him as her 'personal highland servant' and he was told to take orders from no one but herself. This piqued the Queen's equerry, General Sir Charles Grey, who was short with Brown. The Queen offered him an obscure posting in a remote part of India.

John Brown's salary was fixed at £120 a year – five times what he was earning at Balmoral. He addressed the Queen merely as 'woman' and told her off if she was dressed too lightly for the cold weather.

With John Brown's help, the Queen began to fulfil her public duties again. In 1866, she attended the state opening of Parliament for the first time since Albert's death. And he was with her when she reviewed the troops at Aldershot.

Punch magazine began calling her 'Mrs Brown' and published a spoof Court Circular detailing their activities. In September 1866, the Swiss newspaper Gazette de Lausanne ran a story from the special correspondent in

London, saying that Queen Victoria was pregnant and that she and Brown had married secretly.

The republican movement seized on these rumours to its own ends. A pamphlet saying that the Queen had hatched a morganatic marriage with Brown circulated. Cartoons showed him eyeing the empty throne. Brown was even blamed for the Queen's withdrawal from public life. It was said that she would rather spend time at Balmoral with her ghillie than attend to affairs of state.

Fearing hostile demonstrations, the government asked her not to appear in public with Brown. She refused to leave him at home, but the execution of Emperor Maximilian of Mexico – a remote relative by marriage – was used as an excuse to plunge the court back into mourning and cancel the Queen's public engagements. By this time, republican pamphleteers were claiming that she was diverting government money into her own private account.

Returning from a thanksgiving service for the Prince of Wales's recovery from typhoid at St Paul's Cathedral in February 1872, the Queen was confronted by a gunman who pointed a pistol in her face. Brown, who was on the box of the Queen's carriage, jumped down and barraged the man aside. He made a dash for it. Brown pursued and caught him. Instantly, Brown was a hero.

The would-be assassin was found to be deranged and the pistol did not work, but that did not matter. The tide of scandal had turned. The Queen had a special award – the Devoted Service Medal – struck and John Brown was awarded an annuity of £25 a year.

When John Brown died in 1883, at the age of 56, he lay in state in Windsor Castle for six days and his obituary in the Court Circular was longer than Disraeli's. His room at Windsor was given the same treatment as Albert's, until Edward VII came to the throne and turned it into a billiard room. Edward also had the statue of John Brown removed from the hallway at Balmoral.

Queen Victoria had already published a book dedicated to Brown. It was called *More Leaves from the Journal of a Life in the Highlands*. She began *The Life of John Brown*, but The Dean of Windsor read the manuscript and found it so scandalous that he threatened to resign if she published it. Eventually she gave in.

After John Brown's death, Victoria turned to her beturbaned Indian secretary, Munshi Hafir Abdul Karim, whom she called Munshi. Although he was still in his 20s, she gave him a cottage at Windsor and he had a staff of his own.

The government was concerned about their relationship and there were rumours that he was a spy. She was also told that it was deemed inappropriate to be on such intimate terms with a black man. She pointed out that since he was her subject, she could do what she liked with him.

After the death of Queen Victoria, when Munshi himself died, Edward VII had his papers burnt and all trace of him expunged.

# 6 ❖ The Delicate Investigation

Recent royal divorces have caused scandal, but they were tame affairs compared to the divorce proceedings of George IV and Queen Caroline, which went on for 52 days of detailed testimony before the House of Lords in 1820. This was bad enough in itself, but it was only one incident in the scandalous life of one of the most hated monarchs ever to sit on the English throne. When the King was crowned at the age of 50, the poet Leigh Hunt wrote in *The Examiner* that George was 'a violator of his word, a libertine head over heels in debt and disgrace, the companion of gamblers and demi-reps... and a man who has just closed half a century without one single claim on the gratitude of his country or the respect of posterity'. Hunt was fined £500 and jailed for two years for libel. Under English law, speaking the truth is no defence.

George IV began his life of dissipation with one of his mother's maids-of-honour when he was 16. The Queen admonished the boy for keeping 'improper company' in his rooms after bedtime. So he began an affair with an actress, Mary Robinson, who came to his apartments dressed as a boy.

The Prince promised her £21,000 on her 21st birthday. It was one of many debts he did not pay. So when they broke up she threatened to publish a number of highly charged letters he had sent her. The King had to recover them. It cost him £5,000, plus a pension of £500 a year. This 'shameful scrape' as his father, George III, called it, occurred when the Prince was just 17.

Soon after, wealthy divorcée Mrs Grace Elliot claimed that the Prince of Wales was the father of her daughter, whom she named Georgina in his honour, although the father could have been one of the two other men she was entertaining at the time.

George scythed his way through society ladies, as well as maids, cooks, prostitutes and actresses. At 18, he fell in love with the 'divinely pretty' Countess von Hardenburg, wife of the ambassador of Hanover. Her

**Queen Caroline of Brunswick**

husband only found out about the scandalous affair when he read about it in the *Morning Herald*. He wrote a curt note to the Prince. The Countess wrote, too, saying that she was ready to elope with him. In youthful confusion, the Prince confided in his mother, who cried a lot. After confessing, the Prince fainted. His father took the practical step of expelling the Hanoverian ambassador. Again, the King admonished his son for his 'follies' and begged him not to bring further shame on the family.

But that was what the Prince seemed determined to do. He teamed up with the radical politician, Charles Fox – whose future wife he had already seduced – to oppose his father's policies in Parliament. Not content with stirring up political trouble, he swished about London like a playboy, getting into drunken brawls in Vauxhall Gardens.

The King complained that there was something bad about him in the papers every day. *The Times* described him as a man who 'preferred a girl and a bottle to politics and a sermon'. Indeed, in church he would chat, eat biscuits and fool around with the other princes.

At the age of 23, he met and fell instantly in love with Mrs Maria Fitzherbert. He tried to stab himself when she refused his advances and she fled to France. He threatened to abdicate and emigrate with her to the newly independent United States of America. But she stood firm, only entertaining his propositions when he promised to marry her.

Not only was she unsuitable – like Mrs Simpson, she was twice divorced – marriage to Mrs Fitzherbert was illegal. In an effort to curb the

Hanoverian excesses of his offspring, George III had passed the Royal Marriage Act in 1772, preventing members of the Royal Family marrying without the sovereign's consent.

Worse, Mrs Fitzherbert was a Catholic, so marrying her was also illegal under the Act of Settlement of 1701. But the Prince of Wales went ahead and married her anyway.

Even the manner in which the ceremony was carried out was scandalous. George paid £500 to get an Anglican priest out of debtors' prison, who married them on the promise of a bishopric. George was not even discreet about it. He set up with 'Princess Fitz' quite openly and she bore him 10 children.

Even that was not scandalous enough for him. In his cups, he would attack her. On more than one occasion, she had to flee from his unsheathed sword. And he was constantly unfaithful to her.

A fresh scandal erupted when Lucy Howard bore him an illegitimate child and he paid £10,000 and a fine selection of jewellery to bed Anna Crouch, star of John Gay's West End hit, *The Beggar's Opera*. Her husband, a naval officer, demanded another £400 not to drag him through the divorce courts. George also left them a sheaf of passionate love letters, which assured them a healthy income for some time to come.

George's life never seemed complete if he was not making a fool of himself over an older woman. He began a very public affair with Lady Jersey. She was 40 and a grandmother nine times over, although, it has to be said, she did exercise considerable powers of seduction over both sexes.

The Prince was just 30 and he decided that Lady Jersey was the only one for him. He had a slight problem though. His excessive life style cost him a good deal more than the £50,000 a year his father gave him, although it was considered a fortune at the time. His stables alone cost him £31,000 a year and his gambling debts were legendary.

By 1791, his debts topped £630,000. He was now in the embarrassing position of being refused credit and Pitt's government showed no inclination to bail him out. Mrs Fitzherbert, once a wealthy woman, had to pawn her jewellery to stave of the bailiffs.

George III and Pitt cooked up a deal. The government would settle the Prince's debts, provided that he married and furnished the country with an heir. The pretty, intelligent, Louise of Mecklenburg-Strelitz was the favourite candidate. However, she did not get the all-important vote of Lady Jersey, who considered her too formidable a sexual rival. Instead the Prince plumped for the short, fat, ugly and smelly Caroline of Brunswick. She was considered 'excessively loose' even by the German standards of the time and a distinct odour followed in her wake, even though the British envoy sent to Germany to bring her to England persuaded her to wash herself and her underwear before they left.

Whatever charms she might have possessed were hidden beneath the unflattering gowns and heavy make-up that Lady Jersey, who had somehow inveigled herself into the position of the new Queen's Lady of the Bedchamber, persuaded her to wear. When the Prince first saw her, he said: 'Pray, fetch me a glass of brandy. I am unwell.'

For the next three days up to the wedding ceremony, he continued consuming brandy at an alarming rate. On the morning of the wedding, he sent his brother to tell Mrs Fitzherbert that she was the only woman he had ever loved. That did not stop him from leering drunkenly at Lady Jersey throughout the ceremony.

On the wedding night he was so drunk that he slept with his head in the fireplace. The following morning, however, he did his duty. To everyone's surprise, Caroline gave birth to a daughter, Princess Charlotte, nine months later.

The honeymoon was a surprisingly passionate affair, but only because George had had the foresight to take Lady Jersey along.

With the birth of Princess Charlotte, George considered that he had fulfilled his side of the bargain he had made with Parliament and told Caroline that he had no intention of sleeping with her ever again.

When the news broke, the public were overwhelming on the Princess's side. When George went out, mobs howled: 'Where's your wife?'

The King was also dismayed and once again chastised his wayward son.

'You seem to look on your union with the Princess as merely of a private nature,' he wrote, 'and totally put out of sight that as Heir Apparent to the Crown your marriage is a public act, wherein the kingdom is concerned.'

The Prince of Wales tried to smooth things over. He wrote to the Princess, explaining that 'our inclinations are not in our power'. He also reminded her of the importance of 'being polite'. Caroline asked the prominent politician, George Canning, what George meant by 'being polite'. Canning said that George was giving her permission to sleep with whomever she chose, provided she was discreet about it. Caroline immediately took advantage of this warrant and promptly slept with George Canning.

For his part, George dumped Lady Jersey and crawled back to his 'real and true love' Mrs Fitzherbert. He was received coldly. To worm his way back into her affections, George lost some of his considerable girth and began spending freely on his London home, Carlton House, and his Pavilion in Brighton, even though the Napoleonic Wars were putting a considerable strain on the public purse. Mrs Fitzherbert eventually took him back into her bed when the Pope sent confirmation that, in the eyes of the Church, she was the true wife of the Prince of Wales.

It was more than Mrs Fitzherbert could reasonably expect for the Prince of Wales to be faithful to her. He sired a string of illegitimate children and was happy to sleep with a number of French women, despite the state of war that existed between Britain and France at the time.

Mrs Fitzherbert, who was now in her middle age, was resigning herself to the fact that a man of George's inclinations would chase after pretty young women. But she was more than a little distressed when he sought out a series of grandmothers. When Napoleon heard that George was madly in love with the old and overweight Lady Hertford, he laughed uproariously at the news.

When George became Prince Regent, he dismissed Mrs Fitzherbert coldly with the words: 'Madam, you have no place.'

Mrs Fitzherbert and Lady Hertford had been thrown over for the portly Lady Bessborough, whom he begged to 'live with him publicly'. Her husband was made Lord Chamberlain and their son was also found a position in the royal household.

By this time the public were so used to George's excesses that such scandalous behaviour ceased to shock. However, new scandal was about to arrive from an unexpected quarter.

After the breakdown of the royal marriage, Caroline of Brunswick had moved to Blackheath. There, according to Lady Hester Stanhope, she had become 'a downright whore'. She was frequently 'closeted with young men'. In her front room, she had a Chinese clockwork figure, which, when wound up, made gross sexual movements and Caroline liked to dance around it showing off a good deal of her body.

Her partner in crime was Lady Douglas, who had been shunned by polite society for having an affair with her husband's commanding officer, Sir Sidney Smith. Not only did Lady Douglas take lovers whenever she felt like it, she also slept with Caroline.

When the two of them fell out, Caroline sent Lady Douglas's husband, Sir John Douglas, an obscene drawing showing his wife making love to Sir Sidney Smith. Rumours flew that a four-year-old boy in their circle named William Austin was her illegitimate son by Prince Louis Ferdinand of Prussia. This caused such a scandal that Parliament set up a Royal Commission to investigate the Princess of Wales's behaviour. It was called the 'Delicate Investigation'.

The commission investigated every sordid detail of the goings on in

Blackheath. Of particular public interest was her relationship with Captain Manby, a naval officer who was a frequent visitor. However, on the substantive charge that she had an illegitimate child, Caroline was exonerated and Lady Douglas, who had started the rumour, was found guilty of perjury.

In 1814, Caroline left England and started a scandalous progress across Europe. She began by dancing topless at a ball in Geneva given in her honour. In Naples, she had an affair with Napoleon's brother-in-law, King Joachim. In Milan, she took up with Bartolomeo Pergami, a former quartermaster in Napoleon's Italian army. They travelled around Europe, North Africa and the Middle East together as man and wife, before setting up home in Como.

With her own reputation in tatters, Caroline tried to ruin her daughter's, too. Charlotte had been strictly brought up by her maiden aunts in Windsor. But when she visited her mother, Caroline locked the young virgin in a room with Captain Hesse, who was said to be the illegitimate son of the Duke of York and one of Caroline's own lovers.

In 1820, George III died and the Prince Regent came to the throne as George IV. Caroline was now seen as a threat, a ready focus for public animosity towards the spendthrift new King. George IV offered her £50,000 a year if she promised to remain abroad. But Caroline now considered herself Queen of England and was determined to be crowned in Westminster Abbey alongside her husband.

She returned to England and was immediately arrested and arraigned before the House of Lords for 'a most unbecoming and degrading intimacy with a foreigner of low station' – Pergami. A Bill of Pains and Penalties was drawn up, which, George hoped, would dissolve their marriage on the grounds of adultery.

The matter was debated in lascivious detail by the House of Lords. Witnesses were called, including servants from Caroline's own household. They had seen Caroline an Pergami naked together. Pergami had been seen caressing Caroline's breasts and her inner thigh. They had slept together. He was frequently seen naked or semi-naked in her bedroom and was present when she took a bath. It seemed an open-and-shut case.

However, George had not taken into account the power of public opinion. Naturally, the public lapped up every juicy detail. But people also knew what the King had been up to. What was sauce for the goose was sauce for the gander, they thought. The Duke of Wellington was stopped by a mob in London, which shouted: 'God Save the Queen.'

'Well, gentlemen, since you will have it so,' said the Duke. 'God Save the Queen – and may all your wives be like her.'

Caroline herself found that she was cheered by crowds when she travelled daily from her new home in Brandenburg House, Hammersmith, to the Houses of Parliament. The crowds of her supporters there were so huge that a stout timber fence had to be built around the House of Lords. She frequently dozed off during the proceedings and, when she was asked whether she had ever committed adultery, she said only when she slept with 'Mrs Fitzherbert's husband'.

The hearings went on for 52 days and the Bill was passed with a majority of just nine. But the matter was becoming a cause célèbre. To save further embarrassment the government discreetly dropped it, rather than take it forward to the House of Commons.

One contemporary satirist wrote:

'Most gracious Queen we thee implore
To go away and sin no more;
Or if that effort be too great
Go away at any rate.'

But she wouldn't. And there was still the small matter of the coronation, which was scheduled for 19 July 1821. Caroline wrote to the Prime Minister, Lord Liverpool, asking what she should wear. He wrote back saying that she could 'form no part of the ceremony'.

She turned up anyway, dressed in a sheer muslin slip and accompanied by a large contingent of supporters. Arriving at the doors of the Abbey, she shouted: 'Open for the Queen. I am the Queen of England.'

The pages did as they were told, but a courtier bellowed to the guards: 'Do your duty. Shut the door.' And the doors were slammed in Caroline's face. Undaunted, Caroline sent the King a note asking for her coronation to be organized for the following Monday.

When news came of Napoleon's death, the King was told simply that his greatest enemy was dead. George replied: 'Is she, by God.'

Caroline did indeed die, just three weeks after the King was crowned. It was so convenient that a popular conspiracy theory of the time was that she had been poisoned. The King, it was noted, was 'gayer than might be proper to tell'. When her body was being taken to the dock, to be shipped back to Brunswick, there was a riot along the way in Kensington. Bricks were thrown and two protesters were shot by Life Guards. Caroline was buried in Brunswick Cathedral. The inscription on her coffin reads 'The Injured Queen of England'.

George IV continued his scandalous ways. He exchanged Lady Hertford for Lady Conyngham, who was the same age as Lady Hertford but considerably fatter. Rumours soon circulated that they were deeply in love and he was seen nodding, winking and making eyes at Lady Conyngham in Westminster Abbey, while the Archbishop of York was giving a sermon on the sovereign's duty to protect his people from 'the contagion of vice'.

He continued to be one of the most unpopular monarchs ever to sit on the throne of England. He had little influence with the government and Lord Holland admitted that they encouraged 'every species of satire against him and his mistresses'. On top of all his other vices, he became addicted to opiates.

When he died in 1830, his obituary in *The Times* said: 'There never was an individual less regretted of his fellow creatures.'

But perhaps he did have one redeeming feature. When he was buried, he had left instructions that a picture of Mrs Fitzherbert should be tied on a ribbon around his neck and placed on his heart. Although Mrs Fitzherbert had been estranged from him for many years, she wept when she heard of the King's instructions.

# 7 ❖ William IV and Mrs Jordan

William IV never expected to accede to the throne. He had two older brothers – George the Prince Regent and Frederick, Duke of York, who is commemorated in the children's nursery rhyme:

'The Grand Old Duke of York
He had ten thousand men,
He marched them up to the top of the hill,
And he marched them down again.'

This is a lasting tribute to his inept leadership of the British expeditionary force in Flanders in 1793.

However, unlike his older brother, Frederick did at least try to behave as his position befitted. While the Prince of Wales was living with Mrs Fitzherbert, Frederick did his bit to secure the succession. He married Princess Frederica of Prussia, but she proved barren. After that everything went off the rails.

First, he had an affair with Letitia Smith who, it was discovered, was simultaneously bedding highwayman John Rann. Then he took up with a bricklayer's daughter from Chancery Lane called Mary Anne Clarke, who was justly famed for her promiscuity.

But the real scandal broke after he dropped her for a Mrs Cary. Mary then took up with a Major Dillon and the MP for Salisbury, Colonel Wardle. The Duke was then Commander-in-Chief of the army. At Mary's behest, Dillon and Wardle accused the Duke of York of taking bribes to secure the advancement of officers.

There was a parliamentary inquiry. At the hearings, the Duke's love letters were read out – and quickly reprinted in the papers. Mary turned up to give evidence in a daring silk gown. Her manner was so coquettish and her answers so provocative that one distinguished Member sent a note offering her 300 guineas to have supper with him.

To Frederick's embarrassment, her story was backed up by one Elizabeth Taylor, a brothel-keeper from Chelsea. He was forced to resign his position in the army and was executed in effigy by mobs in Suffolk and Yorkshire. His love life was now such a public scandal that when people tossed coins, they no longer called 'heads' or 'tails'. Instead it was 'Dukes' and 'darlings'.

Mary then turned on Dillon and Wardle, claiming that they were in the pay of Frederick's younger brother, the Duke of Kent, Queen Victoria's father. Kent had offered her £10,000 to blacken Frederick's name, she said. She ended up in jail after libelling the Chancellor of the Irish Exchequer.

To be fair, the Duke of York learnt his lesson. After that, he chose his mistresses from his own class and was particularly close to the Duchess of Rutland until his death in 1827, three years before George IV, leaving no legitimate heirs.

William, Duke of Clarence, was cut from the same cloth as the Prince Regent. He was sent away to sea at the tender age of 13, after seducing two of the Queen's maids-of-honour. This was precisely the wrong thing to do. As his elder brother pointed out, the Royal Navy gave him plenty of opportunity to practise 'his natural inclination for all kinds of dissipation'.

But he did not confine his activities to foreign ports. On home leave, at the age of 15, he seduced his 14-year-old cousin Julia Fortescue. He was on the next boat out.

William mended his ways. He vowed no longer to debauch innocent women. But those who had already been debauched were a different matter. He spent a great deal of time trying to satisfy his seemingly unquenchable lust in the brothels of distant ports. On one spree he caused £700 worth of damage to a high-class whorehouse in Bridgetown, Barbados, run by a Mrs Pringle. He was particularly fond of the West Indies, and in Jamaica he made a vehement defence of slavery. It was said that this was because he could indulge his two principal passions, fornication and flogging, with the same unfortunate parties. Such things might be all right in distant colonies, but William caused a scandal by bringing his black concubine, Wowski, back to England with him.

His parents took charge of his moral welfare once more and sent him off to Hanover. This, again, was a mistake. There was more opportunity for vice within the narrow borders of that small German kingdom than in the whole of the British Empire. The women there, he found, were happy to have sex with him up against a wall or 'in the middle of the parade ground'. But they were all 'poxed as whores' and he longed for English girls 'such as would not clap or pox me every time I fucked'.

Back home in England at the age of 19, he fell in love with Sarah Martin, whose father quickly bundled her off out of harm's way. In Plymouth, he seduced the daughter of a ship's chandler. George III then shuffled him out to the colonies to avoid scandal, but he promptly got the wife of the Surveyor-General of Quebec pregnant.

On his return to England, his father gave him a bachelor flat in St James's Palace. This brought him under the direct influence of his brother George, the Prince of Wales, whom he quickly tried to emulate. He squandered his allowance of £12,000 a year on 'immorality, vice and dissipation' and bought a house in Richmond-upon-Thames, where he lived with a popular courtesan called Polly Finch.

Like his brother, William preferred older women and he set about wooing Elizabeth Sheridan, wife of the playwright Richard Brinsley Sheridan. She was a neighbour and 11 years his senior. This caused a little ripple of gossip, but William was now ready for a full-blown scandal.

Another neighbour at Richmond was the actress Mrs Jordan. Born Dorothea Bland, she was the daughter of an Irish stagehand. At 20, she had had an illegitimate child by a Dublin impresario. She had come to London where she was an overnight success in Garrick's *The Country Girl*, under the stage name Mrs Jordan.

During the 1780s, she became one of the most popular actresses in the country. Equally at home in contemporary comedy or Shakespearean tragedy, she was best known for her 'breeches parts' – her long and shapely legs making her perfect casting as a principal boy.

She became the mistress of theatre owner Richard Ford and had three more children by him. When William met her, Mrs Jordan was 30 and living with Ford in Richmond although he refused to marry her. William was 25 and set about a long campaign to seduce her. After 11 months, he wrote to his brother George saying: 'You may safely congratulate me on my success.'

Even *The Times* noted the development. 'That the Jordan has crossed the Ford is a matter no longer to be doubted,' it reported. 'The Royal Admiral has hoisted his flag.'

Mrs Jordan moved in with William and they set about producing 10 children over the next 20 years. However, life together was not going to be plain sailing. The French Revolution had left the position of the Royal Family vulnerable to criticism and the people were no longer happy to see their taxes frittered away on the sexual excesses of a bunch of wastrels.

Unfortunately, Jordan was a common expression for a chamber pot at the time. Cartoonists had a field day. The papers howled that he had already settled a fortune on her. In the light of the scandal, the King cut his allowance. She was accused of deliberately setting out to trap a wealthy man and of abandoning her children. The constant attacks in the press made her ill and unable to work. And when she did not appear on stage, it was said that the Prince was standing in the way of her career.

She complained that it was the sneers of the critics holding her back, and that without working she could not afford to keep her growing brood. The papers turned on her penniless prince:

'A Jordan's high and mighty squire
Her playhouse profits deigns to skim
Some folk audaciously enquire
If he keeps her or she keeps him.'

And if William could not keep her, *The Times* told her not to worry: 'There are certainly more fools than one in the world.'

Prince William called in lawyers to see whether anything could be done. Nothing could, so Dorothea took the matter into her own hands. Against the advice of her doctors, she staged a comeback in December 1791.

When she walked out on stage that night, the crowd was hostile. But in the face of their boos and hisses, she told the audience that she would never give up the stage for a man. Only illness could force her to do that. She then put herself in the audience's hands. As a woman who served the public, she said, she considered herself 'under public protection'.

The boos turned to cheers. It was a sensational coup, which completely overshadowed the play. Her triumph was so complete that even William's parents, the King and Queen, came to see her on stage. During the performance, a gunman loosed off a shot at the King. George III was unscathed and Mrs Jordan led the audience in a rousing rendition of 'God Save the King'. In gratitude, the King gave the couple estates in Bushy. Cartoonists showed them moving house with William pulling a pram with three babies in it, while a smartly dressed Mrs Jordan walked alongside reading a play.

Soon they became a picture of domestic contentment. But William was a Hanoverian, so it could not stay that way forever. By the time she was 50, Mrs Jordan had lost her figure and the Royal Family was putting pressure on him to put her aside. Desperate for money, William abandoned her and went on the hunt for a wealthy heiress.

The press, which had now grown used to the couple's unconventional relationship, saw this as an opportunity to renew the assault. One contemporary poem read:

> 'What, leave a woman to her tears?
> Your faithful friend for twenty years,
> One who gave up her youthful charms,
> The fond companion of your arms.'

Mrs Jordan was forced back on to the stage, but she no longer had the figure for breeches parts. She found herself landed with debts run up by her son by Richard Ford. When she turned to William's brothers for help, the Royal Family disowned her. The stress made her ill again. She fled to France to escape her debts, dying there alone and penniless. Even the sheets on her deathbed had to be sold to pay for her funeral.

William wooed a number of rich aristocratic women, unsuccessfully, and was rejected by a number of discerning princesses. When the Prince Regent's daughter, Princess Charlotte, died in childbirth in 1817, his marriage and the siring of an heir became a matter of importance. By then, William had fallen for the pretty Miss Wyckham and proposed to her. She accepted, but she was irretrievably vulgar. The Prince Regent was against the match and the government stepped in. Instead, William was instructed to marry Princess Adelaide of Saxe-Coburg and Meiningen, who was 'very ugly with a horrid complexion'. He had no choice.

To be fair, he did his best to sire an heir. Princess Adelaide gave birth five times, but none of her children survived infancy. Then she put William back in the scandal sheets again by taking as her lover the Lord Chamberlain, Lord Howe. It was even rumoured that she was pregnant by him.

In 1830, he came to the throne as William IV, known universally as 'The Sailor King' or 'Silly Billy'. Realizing how unpopular the Royal Family had become, he made a show of trying to clean up its act by banning décolleté dresses at court. However *The Morning Post* continued to complain at the sight of the King riding around London with Mrs Jordan's bastards in his carriage. And, to the end, there were persistent rumours that he had fathered yet another illegitimate child by one of Queen Adelaide's maids-of-honour.

George IV

# 8 ❖ The Badness of King George

That George IV – and for that matter William IV – turned out as badly as they did is little wonder. They came from bad stock. The poet Walter Savage Landor wrote savagely of the Hanoverian kings:

'I sing the Georges four,
For Providence could stand no more.
Some say that far the worst
Of all was George the First.
But yet by some 'tis reckoned
That worse still was George the Second.
And what mortal ever heard
Any good of George the Third?
When George the Fourth from earth descended,
Thank God the line of Georges ended.'

When the lesbian Queen Anne died childless, she left behind her something of a problem. Her half-brother James Edward, the Old Pretender, was enjoying the debauchery of the Italian courts, but he was a Catholic. Britain was staunchly Protestant and had ended the scandalous reign of James II when he had declared for Rome. So George, the Protestant Elector of Hanover, was invited to Britain to reign as George I.

He arrived with two hideous mistresses, Ehrengard Melusine von Schulenburg and Baroness von Kielmannsegg. England had seen nothing like it. Ehrengard was enormously tall while the Baroness, who was actually George's half-sister, was enormously fat. Horace Walpole recalled being terrified of her huge bulk as a child. 'The mob of London were highly diverted at the importation of so uncommon a seraglio,' he wrote. They called them 'the maypole and the elephant'.

To be fair, George had had to leave his attractive mistress, Countess von Platen, behind in Hanover, where she had borne him a child, while her husband milked the exchequer. But she was a Catholic. He also left behind his wife, Sophia Dorothea of Zell.

Like his father before him, George was a debauched man. He even shared a mistress with his father. Although his 16-year-old wife was a renowned beauty, he spent his time fooling around with all and sundry. After 12 years of neglect, his wife thought she deserved a little fun, too. So she took a lover, the handsome Swedish soldier, Count Philip von Königsmark.

George I

When George found out about it, he had Königsmark murdered and his body buried under the floor of her room. He divorced her on the grounds of desertion – she intended to elope with her lover, he said. Divorce on the grounds of adultery would have cast doubt on the succession. Sophia was then imprisoned in the castle at Ahlden for the remaining 32 years of her life.

Ehrengard von Schulenburg bore George three children and acted as hostess at royal functions. She was, said Walpole: 'As much Queen of England as any woman was.'

With two such odd creatures as 'the maypole and the elephant' holding sway in the royal household, all kinds of other women flocked to court to try their luck. Even mistresses of the three previous kings turned out. On spotting Louise de Keroualle, Duchess of Portsmouth, a mistress of Charles II and Elizabeth Villiers, Countess of Orkney, mistress of William III across George's drawing room, James II's mistress Catherine Sedley exclaimed: 'Who would have thought that we three whores should have met here?'

The biggest scandal of George's reign was not sexual, but financial. It was the 'South Sea Bubble'. The inspiration for the scam came from France, where a Scottish gambler called John Law had persuaded the Duc d'Orléans, then Regent, to open a bank that issued notes in lieu of gold. Against six million francs in gold, he issued 60 million francs in notes and believed that he had discovered the recipe for unlimited wealth, until a run on the bank finished him off four years later.

In Britain, the South Sea Company, which had been set up to transport slaves to the new plantations in South America, took note. Its director, John Blunt, realized that more money could be made in trading stock than in trading slaves.

First, he had to build confidence in the company. So, in 1718, he persuaded George I to become its governor. In January 1720, with the King's backing, Parliament passed a bill allowing the South Sea Company to take over the national debt, which stood at £50 million. Privatizing the national debt meant that the government would pay only four per cent, rather than five on its borrowing. Those who held treasury bonds, essentially the government's creditors, would be paid the same modest interest, but they would also be given a chance to convert their holdings into shares in the new company, which promised fabulous wealth to come.

Initially, an investor holding £10,000 in bonds would get one hundred £100 shares. But once the company floated and the share price rose to £200, say, £10,000 in bonds would get you 50 shares, leaving another 50 to sell on to another buyer. You could do this again and again, provided the share price continued to rise.

To start with, it worked well. Shares rose to £400. George I himself bought in, which boosted confidence in the company. But he was a shrewd player. He quickly sold his £20,000 worth of shares, realizing a profit of £86,000. And he maintained market confidence by giving John Blunt a knighthood.

Blunt became overconfident. He flouted the rules laid down by Parliament by issuing a further 20,000 shares only 12 weeks after the company was floated. A month later he issued another 10,000, but the share price kept on climbing. Money was coming in so fast that no one bothered to do anything with it. It seemed pointless to invest in any other enterprise when you had a money-making machine that generated wealth at such a rate.

Naturally, other shysters followed Blunt's example, launching all manner of harebrained schemes on the gullible public. One company's prospectus offered merely the chance to invest in an 'undertaking of great advantage but no one to know what it is'. The dividend it promised was £50 for every £1 invested. On its first day of trading, the company's director took in £2,000 and disappeared.

Blunt had the temerity to sue four rivals, on the grounds that they were trading without a royal charter, which Blunt had secured from King George. He won, but it was a Pyrrhic victory. Defeated in the courts, his rivals had to liquidate their assets. They did this by selling their shares in the South Sea Company. Major investors pulling out shook confidence. Share prices began to go down rather than up. The bubble burst and the whole enterprise collapsed. Shares plummeted from £900 to £190 when dealing was suspended. The Duke of Chandos lost £30,000 in a couple of hours.

The King's part in this could not be hidden. Von Schulenburg and Kielmannsegg had also made a fortune during the rise of the 'South Sea Bubble'. One day, they found their carriage surrounded by an angry mob.

'Good pipple, what for you abuse us?' Von Schulenburg cried out in imperfect English. 'We hef come here for your own goodz.'

'And our chattels,' yelled someone from the mob.

The King made plans to mobilize his troops in Hanover, but the riots he feared never materialized. As many people had made money out of the 'South Sea Bubble' as had lost it. Plainly, the rich had lost most since they had more to lose, but the redistribution of wealth the collapse produced had actually stimulated the economy.

George's English mistresses – which included among their number Lady Montagu, the Duchess of Shrewsbury and the Duchess of Bolton –

took bribes from those who sought favours from the King. At court one day, the Duchess of Marlborough spotted that Lady Montagu was sporting expensive new earrings and remarked: 'What an impudent creature to come with her bribe in her ear.'

'Madam,' replied Lady Montagu. 'How should people know where wine is sold unless a sign is hung out?'

Anne Brett, the Countess of Macclesfield's daughter, was given an apartment in St James's Palace. It was rumoured that George was going to create her a Countess in her own right. There was also much gossip about the King's interest in Lord Hervey's young wife. Despite these dalliances, George made little secret of the fact that he had come to England only for the gold.

When he heard that his wife finally died in November 1726, George showed his delicacy of feeling by going to the theatre. He left her body unburied for six months, until a French fortune-teller warned him that if he did not let his wife rest in peace in her grave, he would occupy it before her. A superstitious man, he headed off back to Hanover to attend to her burial, where he died of a stroke in 1727.

GEORGE I's son, George II, was little better. Although he was very much in love with his wife, Queen Caroline, he felt it was his kingly duty to take as many mistresses as he could manage. It helped the smooth running of the court and his mistresses were used to convey messages by the competing political factions.

One of his early mistresses, Molly Lepell, was a noted beauty and Lord Chesterfield celebrated the affair in verse:

'Were I king of Great Britain
To choose a minister well
And support the throne I sat on
I'd have under me Molly Lepell.

Heaven keep our good king from rising
But that rising who's fitter to quell
Than some lady with beauty surprising
And who should that be but Lepell.'

GEORGE was extremely crude in his advances to women and made no secret that he paid them well for their services. One evening at a ball, while ogling Mary Bellenden, one of his wife's ladies-in-waiting, he began counting the gold coins in his purse.

'Sir,' she said. 'If you count your money once more I shall leave.'

He continued counting, so she kicked over the pile of coins and stormed out of the room.

The plump and dowdy Henrietta Howard became his mistress for a mere £2,000 a year and the title Lady Suffolk. For her, it was a career move. She and her husband were so poor that she had had to sell her hair to a wigmaker to afford to come to court.

She was a lowly maid in Queen Caroline's bedchamber when she first started entertaining George. He would visit her apartment at precisely seven o'clock each night, even hovering about outside looking at his watch if he was a little early. He would stay with her for several hours. A courtier said that they spent their time talking, but Horace Walpole pointed out that she was deaf and George's tastes so indelicate that this could not possibly be the case.

The Queen got her revenge by forcing her maid to do the most humiliating of tasks. Henrietta's husband – whom she characterized as a 'wrong-headed, ill-tempered, obstinate, drunken, extravagant brute' – was little more understanding. Although he had risen to the position of Groom of the Bedchamber on the back of his wife's amorous exertions, he went to court to force her to return to her conjugal duties. The Lord Chamberlain issued a writ, allowing him to seize her. Only the offer of a pension of £12,000 persuaded him to back off.

Henrietta did not profit from the situation as much as she might have. She did not take bribes to bend the ear of the King. For this she won the admiration of Jonathan Swift and Alexander Pope.

When the King finally dropped her, after 20 years' service, Queen Caroline tried to revive the affair, concerned about whom her husband would chase after next – with good reason. He began an affair with their daughters' governess, Lady Deloraine, who was the wife of the King's son's tutor, Mr Wyndham. Lord Hervey complained that with this single act, George had made 'the governess of his two youngest daughters his whore and the guardian-director of his son's youth and morals his cuckold'.

The Prime Minister, Sir Robert Walpole, was afraid that the ambitious Lady Deloraine would use her position as the King's mistress to gain power over him. When she fell pregnant, Walpole asked her who the father was.

Lady Deloraine replied: 'Mr Wyndham, upon my honour, but I will not promise whose the next one shall be.'

Walpole turned to the Queen for help. She suggested that Lady Tankerville might be a 'safer fool' and Walpole put her 'in the King's way' at every possible occasion.

Like his father, George II went back to Hanover for a bit of rest and recreation every two years. His mistress there was Madame d'Elitz, a divorcée who reputedly had a thousand lovers. These included his father, George I, and his son, Frederick.

'There is nothing new under the son,' wrote one courtier, 'nor the grandson either.'

Queen Caroline was usually sanguine about her husband's affairs, but when he returned from Hanover with a portrait of the lovely Madame Walmoden, which he hung at the end of their bed, she was livid. She had already been treated to a graphic account of her seduction in a letter thoughtfully penned by the King himself. He was nothing if not a sharing husband.

He compounded the sin by asking her to arrange a visit by the notoriously promiscuous Princess of Modena as he felt 'the great inclination imaginable to pay his addresses to the daughter of the late Regent of France'.

But the Queen was rarely jealous, particularly when her husband found a 'sensible' woman to divert himself with. She told the Archbishop of York that although she 'was sorry for the scandal it gave others... for herself she minded it no more than his going to the closed stool'.

The King's trips to Hanover made him unpopular in Britain, particularly as the British taxpayer was expected to maintain his 'Hanover bawdy house in magnificence and enrich his German pimps and whores'. Even when the Scots rebelled in 1745, George insisted on going to see Madame Walmoden.

The outrage was such that a thin and spindly horse was let loose in London with a sign around its neck saying: 'I am the King's Hanoverian Equipage going to fetch his Majesty and his whore to England.'

A note was pinned to the door of St James's Palace, which read: 'Lost or strayed out of this house, a man who has left a wife and six children on the parish; whoever will give tidings of him to the churchwardens of St James's Parish, so he may be got again, shall receive four shillings and sixpence. N.B. This reward will not be increased, nobody judging him to deserve a Crown.' A crown was five shillings.

This worried the Queen, who wrote to the King in Hanover begging him to return urgently. His reply was full of further graphic details of his erotic encounters with Madame Walmoden and instructions to have Henrietta Howard's old apartments readied for her.

In fact, he returned alone. By this time the Queen was ill. While a surgeon was operating on her, her bowels burst.

'Here lies, wrapped in forth thousand towels,
The only proof that Caroline had bowels,' wrote Pope.

On her deathbed, Queen Caroline asked the King not to take another wife.

'No,' said George tearfully, 'I shall have mistresses.'

On that comforting note, Queen Caroline expired.

With the death of the Queen, Lady Deloraine moved in. This caused a political crisis.

Walpole wished that 'His Majesty had taken someone less mischievous than that lying bitch'. When the Duke of Newcastle suggested that they use the King's daughter, Princess Emily, as their intermediary, Walpole was scandalized.

'Does the Princess design to commit incest?' he asked. 'Will she go to bed with the father? Does he desire that she should? If no, do not tell me the King intends to take a vow of chastity or that those that lie with him won't have the best interest in him.'

Walpole's solution was to send for Madame Walmoden. He said he was 'for the wife against the mistress', but now he was 'for the mistress against the daughter'.

When Madame Walmoden arrived, she was created Lady Yarmouth and she supported herself by selling her influence with the King. Elevation to the peerage, for example, cost £15,000 a time. Although this may appear scandalous in itself, the fact that she cost the state nothing to maintain was widely praised and she was compared to Madame de Pompadour, the extravagant mistress of Louis XV, who was costing the French taxpayer millions.

'While Madame de Pompadour shares the absolute power of Louis XV,' wrote a French count. 'Lady Yarmouth shares the absolute impotence of George II.'

GEORGE'S son Frederick, the Prince of Wales, was not popular. He was criticized for his choice of mistresses, which included the Hanoverian mistress of his father and grandfather, Madame d'Elitz, and a chemist's daughter in Kingston.

'Like the rest of his race,' Walpole wrote, 'beauty was not a necessary ingredient.'

Frederick's own father, George II, described him as 'a monster and the greatest villain ever known'. His mother, Queen Caroline, claimed that he was impotent and had employed another man to father his children.

The great public scandal around Frederick concerned Anne Vane, a 'fat and ill-shaped dwarf' who, according to the Queen, had 'lain with half the town'. When she took up with the Prince of Wales, she was simultaneously sleeping with his best friend, Lord Hervey, and deliberately engineered a row between them to prevent them finding out.

When she fell pregnant, Frederick thought the child was his and set her up in a house in Soho Square. Hervey moved in with her and threatened to expose her unless she used her charms to persuade the Prince to take him back into his favours. Anne eventually confessed all, used Frederick's fling with a chambermaid as an excuse to dump him and ran off with Hervey.

The balladeers of the time had a field day satirizing these shenanigans. After marrying a 17-year-old beauty, Augusta of Saxe-Gotha, he confined his attentions to the elderly mother of 10, Lady Archibald Hamilton.

When he died suddenly, few mourned the loss. A contemporary epitaph caught the mood:

'Here lies poor Fred who was alive and is dead,
Had it been his father, I had much rather,
Had it been his sister, nobody would have missed her,
Had it been his brother, still better than another,
Had it been the whole generation, so much better for the nation,
But since it is Fred who was alive and is dead,
There is no more to be said.'

WITH Fred dead, his son took over when George II died, and reigned as George III. He was the first of the Hanoverian kings to speak English. This led him to dabble in politics, resulting in the loss of the American colonies.

His first act as King was to send Lady Yarmouth packing. She returned to Hanover with a strong-box containing £10,000, a bequest from George II. George III then put aside his love of beautiful women and dutifully married a plain princess from Mecklenburg-Strelitz. They had 15 children and George was much praised for his 'resolute fidelity to a hideous Queen'.

Then he set about cleaning up the Royal Family. It was an uphill battle. His uncle, the Duke of Cumberland – the infamous 'Butcher of Culloden' – had a penchant for actresses. There was scandal when he brought one to Windsor in a carriage, but sent her away on foot because she would not consummate his amorous demands.

George's brother, the Duke of York, a libertine, made a scandalous marriage with Mrs Clements, the widow of George's tutor and the illegitimate daughter of Walpole's brother. It ended in an even more scandalous divorce.

Prince Henry, Duke of Gloucester, liked to flaunt his mistresses by driving them around Hyde Park in an open coach. Just in case anyone should mistake him for any other 18th-century blade, he made sure that his royal coat of arms was prominently displayed. Even worse, he had a particular taste for married women. This reached its scandalous zenith when Lord

Grosvenor sued the Duke for committing adultery with his wife. Grosvenor won £10,000, which George III was forced to pay. He had only just coughed up when the Duke of York married his mistress, a young widow named Anne Horton, without the King's permission. George declared that his brother had the morals of a 'Newgate attorney' and resolved to have nothing further to do with him.

In an attempt to control the morals of the royal children, George III introduced the Royal Marriage Act in 1772. It stipulated that members of the Royal Family under the age of 25 could not marry without the sovereign's permission. In practice, one minister said in the House of Commons, it was the 'Act for the Encouragement of Adultery and Fornication'. It meant that the Prince Regent, for example, could marry without his father's permission, then put his wife aside when it suited him, claiming that the marriage had no validity in law.

The royal children were kept in baby clothes into their teenage years. Of George III's six daughters, three were never allowed to marry. Another two only married when in their 40s. Princess Charlotte married at 31, but her husband was the Prince of Württemberg who was obese. Napoleon remarked that he was so fat that the only reason for his existence was to demonstrate how far skin could stretch without breaking.

The strain of keeping his own sexual nature under control eventually proved too much for King George. In 1788, he went mad. His insanity manifested itself in him making scandalous suggestions to the respectable dowager Elizabeth, Countess of Pembroke. She was doubly mortified when the Archbishop of Canterbury asked her not to take advantage of a sick man's passions.

Renowned for his rustic passion, George III was nicknamed 'Farmer George'. His growing madness became widely known when it was reported that he had got out of his coach in Windsor Great Park to shake hands with an oak tree, believing it to be Frederick the Great. He recovered briefly, but in 1801 he relapsed. His final bout of madness overcame him in 1811. The Keeper of the Queen's Robes, Fanny Burney, wrote: 'He is persuaded that he is always conversing with angels.'

The poet Shelley's obituary was:

'An old, mad, despised and dying King;
Princes, the dregs of their full race, who flow
Through public scorn – mud from a muddy spring –
Rulers who neither see nor feel nor know
But leechlike to their fainting country cling
Till they drop, blind in blood, without a blow.'

## 9 ❖ The Lesbian Queens

In 1708, Queen Anne caused a scandal, not because she was a lesbian, but because she threw over her aristocratic lady love, Sarah Churchill, Duchess of Marlborough and forebear of Britain's great wartime Prime Minister, Winston Churchill, for a common chambermaid called Abigail Hill.

A scurrilous ballad of the time went:

'When as Queen Anne of great renown
Great Britain's sceptre swayed,
Besides the Church, she dearly loved
A dirty chamber maid.

O! Abigail that was her name,
She stitch'd and starch'd full well,
But how she pierc'd this mortal heart
No mortal man can tell.

However, for sweet service done
And causes of great weight
Her royal mistress made her, Oh!
A minister of State.

Her secretary she was not
Because she could not write,
But had the conduct and the care
Of some dark deeds at night."

Although, for political reasons, Anne had been married off to Prince George of Denmark, she was a life-long lesbian. George made the best of the situation and impregnated Anne 17 times. None of their offspring survived infancy and the disappointment drove her to drink. She became known to her subjects as 'Brandy Nan' and grew so fat that she had to be carried to her coronation in a sedan chair.

Anne and her older sister Mary, who also became Queen, were the daughters of James II and were brought up in an all-female household at Richmond Palace. At the age of 12, Mary had a crush on 20-year-old Frances Apsley, whom she referred to as 'my dear husband'. Their correspondence left nothing to the imagination. Mary wrote to Frances saying:

'I may, if I can tell you how much I love you but I hope that is not doubted. I have given you proofs enough. If not, I will die to satisfy you dear, dear, husband. If all my hairs were lives, I would lose them all twenty times over to serve or satisfy you... I love you with a flame more lasting than the vestals' fire. Thou art my life, my soul, my all that Heaven can give. Death's life with you, without you that I love you with more zeal than any lover can. I love you with a love that never was known by man. I have for you excess of friendship more of love than ever the constantest lover had for his mistress. You are loved more than can be expressed by your ever obedient wife, very affectionate friend, humble servant, to kiss the ground where you go, to be your dog on a string, your fish in a net, your bird in a cage, your humble trout...'

Although Anne had maintained a similarly heated exchange with Cecily Cornwallis, she moved in on Frances, too. But soon she tired of her and moved on to Sarah Jennings, who later married John Churchill.

At 15, Mary was heartbroken when she was sent to Holland to marry William of Orange. It was not a bad match. William was gay. A former pageboy named William Bentinck, whom he had slept with as a youth, had risen to be his closest adviser. William was also a soldier so he was frequently away, and Mary found herself surrounded by pleasing Dutch women. However, the couple were royals and had to do their duty. When he was in Holland, he would visit her chamber, Mary said, 'about supper time... [so] that I not tire him with multiplicity of questions, but rather strive to recreate him'.

When William finally got her pregnant, Mary wrote home to Frances admitting: 'I have played the whore a little; because the sea parts us, you may believe that it is a bastard.'

Like her sister Anne, Mary had several miscarriages and failed to produce a living heir.

To everyone's surprise, William took a mistress, Elizabeth Villiers, one of Anne and Mary's childhood playmates at Richmond. She was no beauty, especially when compared with the comely Mary, but William threw himself at her from the first time he saw her.

Elizabeth had been one of Mary's ladies-in-waiting when she had come to Holland in 1677. To discourage her mistress's husband, Elizabeth encouraged the attention of Captain Wauchop, a Scottish mercenary. It did no good. Soon she was entertaining William in secret. By 1679, the affair was the talk of Paris. When Mary heard the gossip, she waited outside Elizabeth's apartments and caught her husband creeping out at two o'clock in the morning. There was a blazing row, but William was sanguine.

'What has given you so much pain is merely an amusement,' he said.

**Queen Anne**

William Bentinck was put out, too. For William to take a wife, out of duty, was one thing; to take a mistress for pleasure quite another.

Mary took the matter in hand. She sent Elizabeth to England with a letter for the King. However, Elizabeth opened it on the way. In the letter, Mary had asked her father to detain Elizabeth. Instead of delivering it, Elizabeth went straight back to Holland.

She was met by Mary and Bentinck, who both told her she had to leave. But William heard of Elizabeth's return and forced Mary to take her back. She consoled herself with more long, passionate letters to Frances Apsley.

When James II was deposed, William and Mary went to England to take the throne. Elizabeth went, too. She settled in a house near Kensington Palace and was given a 90,000-acre estate in Ireland.

Supporters of James II tried to use William's scandalous entanglement with Elizabeth Villiers to their political advantage. They spread rumours that she was pregnant. William quelled the scandal by ordering the clergy to speak out against sin. He still maintained Elizabeth, however, until Mary's death in 1694. In a deathbed letter, Mary begged William to put away his mistress. In grief and remorse, he gave Elizabeth £30,000 a year and married her off to the Earl of Orkney.

William then resorted to his gay ways again, taking as his favourite the pageboy, Arnold Jooset Van Keppel. William Bentinck was once more put out.

Even while her husband was alive, Anne kept Sarah Jennings as her Lady of the Bedchamber and their passionate correspondence continued. Sarah married the soldier, John Churchill, who was frequently away at the wars. When he did return, however, she recorded that he 'pleasured her with his boots on'.

This marriage played a key role in history. During the Glorious Revolution of 1688, it was John Churchill who delivered Anne and her husband, Prince George, safely into the camp of William and Mary, thereby ending effective resistance in England.

Although John Churchill was rewarded with the title, Duke of Marlborough, Mary tried to prevent Anne bringing her lover Sarah Churchill to court. To get her own back, Anne took Frances Apsley, now Lady Bathurst, into her household.

When Anne became Queen, Sarah sought to control the court while her husband brought glory to England on the battlefield. But she could not control the new Queen's passions and quickly found herself supplanted by Abigail Hill, who used to visit the Queen for two or three hours at night when the Prince was asleep.

A fierce struggle broke out between Sarah and Abigail for the heart of the Queen. When this became public knowledge, a visiting French count was greatly amused by the way the British, who were so sophisticated in some ways, were shocked by 'that refinement of love of early Greece'.

It was suggested in the House of Commons that Abigail, who was now Mrs Masham, be fired from the royal household. But Abigail insisted that it was Sarah who should go. She got her way, but Sarah Churchill then threatened to publish her memoirs, including extracts from the Queen's letters. However, discrepancies in the accounts of the royal household were discovered and Sarah was blackmailed into silence.

Her position at court was taken by the redheaded Duchess of Somerset, who immediately caused fresh scandal when her young lover, Charles Königsmark, killed her husband. Jonathan Swift, a long-time supporter of Abigail's, wrote clumsily:

> 'Their cunnings mark [Königsmark] thou for I have been told
> They assassin when young and poison when old
> O root out these carrots [redheads], O thou whose name
> Is backwards and forwards always the same [Anna]
> And keep close to thee always that name
> Which backwards and forwards is almost the same [Masham].'

It was not until 1742, 28 years after Anne's death, that Sarah Churchill's memoirs were finally published. They caused a sensation.

## 10 ❖ Restoration Comedy

Charles II was one of England's most popular monarchs, partly because of his scandalous behaviour. He was known as 'Old Rowley' after a very well-endowed goat that was tethered on Tower Green. The aristocracy still remember him with pride. Twenty-six of the English dukes today can trace their ancestry directly to the illegitimate children of Charles II. He was also responsible for a number of marquises and earls.

His extramarital activities were widely known at the time, thanks to the rakish Earl of Rochester, who circulated a scurrilous poem about him. Explaining the King's popularity with the ladies, Rochester wrote:

'Nor are his high Desires above his strength,
His Sceptre and his prick are of a length.'

Nell Gwynne, the Drury Lane orange-seller, was his most popular mistress. He generously had her and other royal mistresses painted in the nude so that his subjects could share in his pleasure. He loved elaborate sex games and liked to maintain simultaneously a number of contrasting mistresses – a coy virgin yet to be seduced, an insatiable libertine, an elegant lady or a saucy actress. This kept his appetite whetted. And when that palled he relied on his trusted private procurer, Will Chiffinch, to scour London for highly attractive, nameless young ladies to pay nocturnal visits to his royal apartments. After 11 years of Puritan rule, it was all a breath of fresh air.

Charles had lost his virginity at the age of 15, during the Civil War, to Christabella Wyndham, a former wet nurse and wife of the royalist governor of Bridgewater. A year later, he sired his first bastard. He was in Jersey at the time, on his way into exile on the Continent. The mother was Margaret de Carteret, the daughter of a local aristocrat. The child went on to become a priest.

'During his exile, he delivered himself so entirely to his pleasures that he became incapable of application,' wrote the future Bishop of Salisbury.

Paris, particularly, was a delight for the young Prince, who was initiated into its ways by the Duke of Buckingham, who had honed his amatory skills in the promiscuous courts of Italy.

Just three months after his father, Charles I, was beheaded in Whitehall, the young Charles took up with Lucy Walters, whom the diarist John Evelyn described as 'a beautiful strumpet'. Indeed, the lady had a track record. She had fled England with her royalist lover, Colonel Sydney, who had promptly sold her to his brother. When that arrangement did not suit her, she had moved in with a man named Barlow and was calling herself 'Mrs Barlow' when she met Charles. She gave the exiled King a son, James, whom he made Duke of Monmouth.

By the time Charles went to Scotland to raise support for the Stuart cause in 1650, he already had a formidable reputation as a libertine. This was used against him as propaganda by the Puritans in England.

Lucy handed the Puritans another propaganda coup. In 1656, she travelled to England with another of her lovers and was arrested and deported as Charles's whore. He was forced to abandon Lucy, who died of syphilis and went to a pauper's grave.

Charles had three more bastards before he returned to England and 17 known mistresses, although there must have been many other casual encounters. Cromwell's spies reported back Charles's 'fornication, drunkenness and adultery'. But Puritans in England were no less shocked that he 'esteemed it no sin' to go to the theatre on a Sunday.

When Charles was proclaimed King in May 1660, he celebrated his first night back in England in the carnal embrace of the 19-year-old Barbara Palmer. She was known as 'the lewdest as well as the fairest of King Charles's concubines'.

Although married to Roger Palmer, she was the long-term mistress of the Earl of Chesterfield. Dedicated to her art, she had studied the banned works of Pietro Aretino, whose sonnets were illustrated with the 16 then-known sexual positions.

Although Samuel Pepys condemned Charles's court as 'nothing but bawdy from top to bottom', he had a soft spot for Barbara Palmer. He had erotic dreams about her and recorded his excitement at seeing her lingerie hanging out to dry. He wrote of her relationship with Charles: '[She] rules him, who hath all the tricks of Aretin that are to be practised to give pleasure – in which he is too able, having a large \*\*\*\*, but... as the Italian proverb says, "A man with an erection is in no need of advice".'

Exactly nine months after Charles was restored to the throne, Barbara gave birth to a daughter. She had two more daughters and two sons, all of whom Charles acknowledged as his own. In gratitude, he created her husband Earl of Castlemaine. Not that Barbara reserved her favours for the King or, for that matter, her husband. She continued to sleep with the Earl of Chesterfield, as well as the Earl of St Albans. She also took a series of other courtiers, who included the King's bastard son, Monmouth, and a Miss Hobart, who was another of the King's mistresses. Her conduct was so scandalous that the Lord Chancellor, Edward Hyde, refused to seal any document that bore her name.

Rochester summed it up:

'When she has jaded quite
Her almost boundless appetite...
She'll still drudge on in tasteless vice
As if she sinn'd for exercise.'

This was all very well, but the King had to marry. Lady Castlemaine drew up a list of suitable consorts. None of them were particularly enticing, but he picked the King of Portugal's daughter, Catherine of Braganza, because she brought with her a dowry of £360,000 and naval forces based in Bombay and Tangiers.

A devout Catholic, Catherine was less than thrilled at marrying a man who was, publicly at least, a Protestant. She had also heard of his reputation and swore to her mother that she would force Charles to put aside his mistresses. She failed, partly because Charles had made a vow of his own – to make Lady Castlemaine Lady of the Bedchamber to his new Queen.

When Catherine turned up in England, this arrangement caused much sniggering. The King compared the Queen to 'a bat'. The couple produced no heir, but not for want of trying. She miscarried twice. But, even though he needed to secure the succession, Charles steadfastly refused to divorce her. Although unfaithful, he was consistently kind and generous to his wife. Catherine, in her turn, came to accept her husband's mistresses.

Less than a year after his marriage, Charles fell in love with 15-year-old Frances Stuart. He did nothing to hide his affection and kissed her openly, in front of everyone. Her beauty was legendary. The King acknowledged it officially by having her pose for the image of Britannia that graced the penny piece for three centuries.

Frances refused to sleep with the King unless he married her, so Charles arranged a mock wedding, complete with ceremonial bedding. His friends set up a 'committee for the getting of Miss Frances Stuart for the King', but Lady Castlemaine knew how to handle the situation. She took Frances Stuart to her own bed and flaunted the fact in front of the King.

While Lady Castlemaine entertained other men, she also secured their advancement through her influence with the King. She maintained her influence, even though she made no secret of the fact that she was bedding others, because she kept a 'stable' of other young women to entertain the King.

One day, Charles stumbled across the then penniless young John Churchill making love to Lady Castlemaine.

'I forgive you,' he said to Churchill, 'for you do it for your bread.'

After all, Charles maintained that his personal motto was: 'God will never damn a man for allowing himself a little pleasure.'

More scandal followed when Lady Castlemaine seduced a tightrope walker named Jacob Hall in his booth at St Bartholomew's Fair. Then she had a baby by the footman who used to attend her in her bath, and demanded that Charles acknowledge the child as his own.

Her reputation was brought to an even wider public when an anonymous writer circulated 'A Petition of the Poor Whores to the Most Splendid, Illustrious, Serene and Eminent Lady of Pleasure, the Countess of Castlemaine'. In the spoof petition, poor working girls asked Lady Castlemaine for her help and advice in 'a trade wherein your Ladyship has great experience'. Other wits then penned a reply.

The King decided to spare her blushes and pensioned her off.

'All I ask of you, for your own sake, is to live so in future as to make the least noise you can,' Charles said.

He created her the Duchess of Cleveland and gave her a huge house befitting her new-found status. On the door she found an anonymous note, which contrasted her rich reward with those who had been punished for immorality. It read simply: 'The reason why she is not duck'd, Because by Caesar she is fucked.'

Nevertheless, she continued to scythe through new lovers, creating a political scandal by bedding the English ambassador to Paris. Rochester, as always, had the last word:

'Castlemaine I say is much to be admir'd,
Although she ne'er was satisfied or tired,
Full forty men a day provided for this whore
Yet like a bitch, she wags her tail for more.'

She provided one final scandal when, at the age of 64, she lost all her money by marrying a young bigamist named 'Beau Fielding'.

Charles took numerous other lovers, including one he shared with Rochester. A clergyman's daughter, she repented on her deathbed. Then there was Winifred Wells, who was said to have miscarried Charles's child during a court ball. The foetus dropped to the floor and she danced on. She was said to have 'the carriage of a goddess and the physiognomy of a dreamy sheep'.

During the Civil War, her family had been ardent royalists.

**Nell Gwynne, actress and mistress of Charles II**

'Her father having faithfully served Charles I,' it was said, 'she thought it her duty not to revolt again Charles II.'

Charles did not hide his amorous activities behind closed doors at court. One of his first acts following the Restoration was to reopen the theatres. Cynics suggest that this was so he could take advantage of the actresses – which indeed he did.

The first was Moll Davis, who played the guitar and was famous for a song called 'My Lodging, It is on the Cold Ground'. Contemporary wit John Downes remarked that Charles raised 'the fair songstress from the cold ground into the royal bed'. In fact, her private performance earned her a £600 house in Suffolk Street. They had a child together – Lady Mary Tudor – and Pepys dubbed Moll the 'most impertinent slut in the world'.

Moll was displaced by her friend, Nell Gwynne, who had grown tired of Moll's airs and graces. One night before an assignation, Nell spiked Moll's sweetmeats with a powerful laxative. When the King came round, he found Moll incapacitated with diarrhoea, so Nell stepped forward to provide the services her sick friend was unable to render.

Nell Gwynne was from lowly stock. Her father died in Oxford jail and Nell was brought up in a brothel in Drury Lane, where she and her sister prostituted themselves for half-a-crown. She became popular and boasted among her lovers the poet, John Dryden.

She also worked selling oranges outside the King's Theatre where Charles first saw her. Charles Hart, the great-nephew of Shakespeare, took her as his lover and put her on the stage. The King particularly liked her in breeches roles, and later paid for a special costume that would suddenly fly up and reveal her legs.

Her next lover was Charles Sackville, Lord Buckhurst, who was famous for making a sermon, stark naked, from the balcony of Kate's Tavern in Covent Garden, which he concluded by pissing on the crowd below. It was only then that she got around to Charles II – whom she called Charles III, as he was her third Charles.

Their affair was the talk of the town. She was, it was said, 'the indiscreetest and wildest creature that was ever in a court'. The Bishop of Burnet condemned the vulgarity of Charles's latest conquest, complaining that he 'never treated her with the decencies of a mistress but rather with the lewdness of a prostitute'.

Indeed, unlike his other mistresses, Nell was never rewarded with a title. Complimenting her on a new dress, Charles once said: 'You are fine enough to be a queen.'

'And whore enough to be a duchess,' she retorted.

However, she did secure titles for her 'little bastards', as she called them. Charles installed her in Pall Mall, conveniently close to St James's Palace. She asked for the freehold of a house as she had always provided 'her services free under the Crown'. Other than that she asked for just £500 a year to live on, although managed to prise £60,000 out of Charles in all.

One of the things she spent her money on was a custom-made silver bedstead with erotic engravings on it. One showed Lady Castlemaine with her tightrope walker; another showed one of the King's other mistresses, Louise de Keroualle, lying in a tomb with an Eastern potentate.

Nell Gwynne was popular because she was a London working girl made good, and she did not use her position to interfere in politics. An anonymous poet of the time summed up the situation:

'Hard by Pall Mall lives a wench call'd Nell
King Charles the Second he kept her.
She hath got a trick to handle his prick,
But never laid hands on his sceptre.
All matters of state from her soul she does hate,
And leaves to the politic bitches.

The whore's in the right, for 'tis her delight
To be scratching just where it itches.'

When the King did once ask for her advice, she told him to 'lock up his codpiece'. Even though Charles continued to fool around, Nell prided herself on the fact that she was 'but one man's whore'. And when Buckingham touched her up she rewarded him with a slap and she informed on him to the King.

During their four-year affair, Charles and Nell were recklessly indiscreet. Nell scandalized Newmarket when they went to the races there. She said loudly in front of a local alderman: 'Charles, I hope I shall have your company at night, shall I not?'

And in London, walking near her home in Pall Mall, the diarist John Evelyn reported hearing Nell and the King in 'very familiar discourse' over the garden wall.

During his affair with Nell Gwynne, Charles took another very public mistress. But Louise de Keroualle was not nearly so popular. She was French, Breton, and first came as maid to England with Charles's favourite sister, Henrietta Anne, who was married to the transvestite Philippe, Duc d'Orléans, the French king's younger brother.

Charles was immediately smitten and begged his sister to let her stay. Henrietta Anne refused, saying that she had promised Louise's parents that she would bring her home safely. She did so. Unfortunately, three weeks later Henrietta Anne died. But Louis XIV had heard about Charles's designs on Louise and sent her back to London, figuring it would do no harm to have a spy in the King of England's bed.

The innocent young Louise was not privy to the plan and stubbornly clung to her virginity, until the French ambassador explained that it was her patriotic duty to surrender honour for the sake of France.

The King staged another of his very public mock weddings at Euston Hall in 1672. There can be no doubt that Louise then succumbed. Nine months later, Louis XIV sent his congratulations on their first child. Louise was created the Duchess of Portsmouth and made Lady of the Bedchamber to the long-suffering Queen Catherine.

Nell Gwynne did not take kindly to the high-born Louise de Keroualle and mocked her in public. Although Louise was a great beauty she had a slight cast in one eye. Nell dubbed her 'Squintabella'. Nell also called her the 'weeping willow' because Louise was always bursting into tears and she mocked her aristocratic pretensions. When Louise appeared in mourning over the death of some upper-class cousin, Nell followed suit.

'Have you not heard,' she said, 'of the death of the Cham of Tartary?' More weeping followed.

'If she be such a lady,' said Nell, 'why does she demean herself to be a courtesan?'

Of course, Nell knew the answer. Louise was conspicuously attired in the latest French fashions.

'Why is it that the King of France does not send presents to me, instead of the weeping willow?' she asked the French ambassador.

Louise's allegiance to France was widely resented. When the Palace of Whitehall was refurbished, above the door of Louise's lavish new apartments a sign was left, which read:

'Within this place a bed's appointed,
For a French bitch and God's anointed.'

This discontent, especially over the fact that Louise was a Catholic, spread to the streets. One day, when Nell was approaching the royal apartments in her coach, a crowd surrounded her. Thinking the pretty young woman inside the carriage was Louise de Keroualle, they started shouting anti-Catholic abuse. Nell stuck her head out of the window and yelled: 'Pray good people be civil, I am a Protestant whore.'

If this was not bad enough, in 1675, one of Charles's Continental lovers, Hortense de Mancini, the Duchess of Mazarin, turned up in England with a parrot and a black pageboy named Mustapha in tow. During Charles's exile the two had had a passionate affair. Afterwards, she had married the Duke of Mazarin, who turned out to be a religious fanatic. Next, she had become the mistress of the Duke of Savoy. But when he died, his widow strongly advised that she absent herself from the principality, so she headed for England.

In her youth, Mazarin had been a great beauty and the French ambassador to the court of St James reported that he had never seen anyone who 'so well defies the power of time and vice to disfigure'. Soon he was reporting that 'Madame Mazarin is well satisfied with the conversation she has had with the King of England'.

Nell Gwynne was also delighted. She wore weeds and staged a mock funeral for Louise de Keroualle's ambitions.

However, the public were not happy that he had taken a second foreign mistress.

'Why should he take another French whore,' went the contemporary rhyme, 'when one already made him poor.'

Again, none of these shenanigans were kept secret. A contemporary ballad ran:

'Since Cleveland is fled till she's brought to bed,
And Nell is quite forgotten,
And Mazarin is as old as the Queen,
And Portsmouth, the young whore, is rotten.'

Hortense took other lovers of both sexes including, very publicly, a visiting prince from Monaco. When one of her young lovers was killed in a duel, Hortense threatened to become a nun, which greatly amused the King.

Louise strayed, too, bedding the Moroccan ambassador. This finally convinced Charles that he was in love with her. He began kissing her very publicly, although he spent his evenings with Nell and his afternoons with Hortense.

The three women learnt to get on well enough, although Nell complained that the other two were dirty. She told the French ambassador that Louise wore filthy underwear, while Hortense wore none at all. To prove the point, she lifted her own skirts. She was right, the French ambassador conceded, Nell's petticoats were immaculate.

On 31 January 1685, John Evelyn gives us a last glimpse of Charles's scandalous court: 'I am never to forget the inexpressible luxury and profaneness, gaming and all dissolution and, as it were, total forgetfulness of God (it being a Sunday evening)... the King sitting and toying with his concubines, Portsmouth, Cleveland and Mazarin, etc.; whilst about 20 courtiers and other dissolute persons were at basset [forerunner of the gambling game faro] round a large table, a bank of at least two thousand in gold before them.'

Six days later, Charles died, imploring his brother James to 'let not poor Nelly starve'. James did indeed save her from the debtors' prison. But she survived only another two years. In that time, she did not take another lover on the grounds that she would not 'lay a dog where a deer had lain'.

Although she had contracted venereal disease from Charles, Louise lived another 50 years. James II gave her a small pension and, when she returned home, she was rewarded for the great service she had rendered to France.

IF CHARLES II was a scandalous womanizer, he was a saint compared to his brother James. But James, Charles said, was accursed by God. While Charles prized beauty in his mistresses, James slept only with 'unsightly wantons'.

Despite siring a phalanx of illegitimate children, Charles provided no legitimate off-spring, so his brother James became King James II. However,

Charles predicted that he would 'lose his kingdom by his bigotry and his soul for a lot of trollops'.

He was right. Although Charles kept quiet about his faith, James's very public espousal of Catholicism sparked the scandal that would lose him his throne. He was already inured to scandals surrounding trollops.

When James returned to England with Charles at the Restoration, Anne Hyde, daughter of the strait-laced Lord Chancellor, was already carrying his baby. Against his brother's advice, James then married the girl. The Earl of Sandwich remarked: 'That he doth get a wench with child and marries her afterwards, it is as if a man should shit in his hat and then clap it upon his head.'

When the scandal broke, the Lord Chancellor demanded that his daughter be taken to the Tower and executed. James's mother and his sister, Mary, rushed over from the Continent to prevent 'so great a stain and dishonour on the Crown'. Mary declared that she would never accept as a sister-in-law a woman who had once stood behind her chair as a servant.

James insisted that unless the family accept his new wife, he would leave the country and live abroad. But then, seeing the beauties who were flocking to the newly restored court, he began to have second thoughts about his plain and pregnant bride.

Five of James's friends stepped forward, claiming to be the father of the child. One claimed to have 'eased the pains of love' with her during a brief encounter in a water closet. Another said he would marry Anne Hyde to save James from a woman who was so plainly unworthy of him. James himself said that he had never married Anne, which was a palpable lie.

Charles stepped in to quell the scandal. He insisted that his brother 'must drink as he had brewed and live with her who he had made his wife'. James's friends were forced to retract their allegations and, two months after the birth of a sickly son, James admitted that he had been married to Anne all along.

Even though he was now married, James quickly developed the reputation of being 'the most unguarded ogler of his time'. And it did not stop at ogling.

As Lord High Admiral, James was Samuel Pepys' employer, so Pepys took a special interest in his activities.

'He hath come out of his wife's bed, and gone to others laid in bed for him,' Pepys wrote.

In response to her husband's infidelity, Anne developed an eating disorder and grew enormous. This did not end their marital relations. Although their son died, Anne gave birth to two healthy girls, Mary and Anne, who both went on to become Queen. Six more children were stillborn.

James also impregnated a number of Anne's chambermaids and ladies-in-waiting. Some young women fled court to escape his advances, others were recalled by their mothers or their husbands. Lady Carnegy was one of the many who did not escape his attentions, but her husband deliberately contracted venereal disease to exact his revenge.

James openly fondled and kissed Lady Chesterfield until her husband withdrew her from court. A slew of other lovers followed, including Mary Kirke whom James shared with his nephew, Monmouth.

The 50-year-old royal poet, Sir John Denham, tried to turn a blind eye to the affair his 18-year-old wife was having with James. James was so taken with Lady Denham that, according to Pepys, he frequently took time off work to be with her. But Lady Denham was not content to be a secret concubine and followed James around like a dog on public occasions. Sir John became so distressed at being so publicly cuckolded that he complained to the King – to little effect.

One day, when he came upon the two lovers giggling over a guitar, Sir John took the instrument and smashed it on the ground. Soon after, Lady Denham died. Poison was suspected. The mob that turned up for her funeral turned so menacing that Sir John only escaped with his life by plying them with enormous quantities of wine.

James vowed never to 'have another public mistress'. It was a vow he conspicuously failed to keep since he quickly took up with Arabella Churchill, another of his wife's maids-of-honour, who bore him four children.

When James's wife, Anne, died six weeks after delivering one final stillborn child, there was again talk of poisoning. Within weeks, James was talking of marrying his 17-year-old mistress, Lady Bellasye, but the King put his foot down.

'It was too much that he had played the fool once; that was not to be done a second time, and at such an age,' Charles said. James was 40 by then.

James took his brother's advice, although it would have probably turned out better if he hadn't. A foreign princess was found for him – Mary of Modena. She was 15 and a rare beauty. James was quickly persuaded. Unfortunately, she was a Catholic and a very pious one, so pious that she had set her heart on becoming a nun. The Pope had to step in to convince her that marrying the heir to the British throne was a higher calling.

Anti-Catholic feeling was running so high in England that there could be no fairy-tale wedding in Westminster Abbey – St Paul's was being rebuilt after the Great Fire of London at the time. They were married by proxy.

Even though he was now married to the beautiful Mary, James continued seeing the scrawny Arabella and gave her another child. Then he took up with one of his new wife's maids-of-honour, Catherine Sedley. While Mary remained barren, Catherine quickly produced a daughter.

In 1685, when James finally came to the throne, Mary insisted that he get rid of Catherine, otherwise she would cause a scandal by taking her vows as a nun. Catherine protested. Under Magna Carta, she said, it was the right of every free-born Englishwoman to sleep with her King. She was created Countess of Dorchester and packed off to Ireland.

James was now seen to be under the sway of his Catholic Queen and became very unpopular. Charles II's bastard son, the Duke of Monmouth, raised an army against him. But the Monmouth rising was crushed. Monmouth himself was tried for treason and executed. The famous executioner, Jack Ketch, bungled the job. He took five swipes of the axe to dispatch the prisoner. Even then his head was not fully severed and Ketch had to finish the job with a knife.

Judge Jeffreys convened his 'Bloody Assizes' and sentenced 320 of Monmouth's followers to be hanged, drawn and quartered. Eight hundred were to be transported to Barbados and hundreds more to be flogged. This did little for James's popularity.

Catherine Sedley grew bored with Ireland and returned to London and the King's bed. Then what was seen to be a miracle happened. Queen Mary, who was thought to be barren, gave birth to a child. This raised a constitutional problem since Mary insisted that the child be raised a Catholic. James, too, came out publicly for Catholicism – a move that prompted the Bishop of Salisbury to enquire whether he had been seduced by a nun.

Plainly, it was unsustainable to have a Catholic as head of the Church of England, a Protestant church. Anti-Catholics declared that the Queen's pregnancy had been a sham. They said that she had padded her belly with cushions and that when it came to the time to give birth, an unknown infant had been smuggled into the bedroom in a bedpan.

An investigating council was set up. James's sexual conduct was discussed in 'a long discourse of bawdry... that put all the ladies to blush'. However, evidence that the child was legitimate was overwhelming. Nevertheless, the scandal brought James down.

Seven leading opponents of the King wrote to James's oldest daughter, Mary, and her husband, William of Orange, inviting them to take the throne. Not only were they Protestants, William was a noted soldier. The couple arrived with an army, and when James's younger daughter, Anne, rallied to her sister's cause James fled. He returned through Ireland with an army but was defeated at the Battle of the Boyne.

James blamed his defeat on letting himself go 'too much to the love of women'. He had paid dearly for it and he warned his son, James Francis Edward, 'the Old Pretender', against 'the forbidden love of women'.

He did not take his own advice, of course. He spent his long exile traipsing around the Continent with a long line of scrawny women in tow. Eventually, he ended up with the monks at La Trappe, who liked to dress in winding sheets and spend their time contemplating an open grave. Their cheery greeting was: 'We must die, brother, we must die.'

Catherine Sedley wanted no part in this. She remained behind in England where, being the daughter of a staunchly Protestant family, she received a pension from William for being a double agent in the struggle against James. At court though, Mary was cutting to her.

'Remember, Ma'am, if I broke one commandment with your father, you have broken another against him,' was Catherine's riposte.

THE Old Pretender, James Frances Edward, did not take his father's advice to stay away from 'the forbidden love of women'. Rather, he emulated his father's scandalous ways in the debauched Italian courts.

His son, Bonnie Prince Charlie, had public brawls with his Polish mistress, the Princesse de Talmond. In 1745, back in Scotland, Bonnie Prince Charlie met Clementina Walkinshaw who bore him a daughter and followed him back into exile. He beat her and squandered her meagre inheritance on other mistresses. After 15 years, Clementina fled and took refuge in a French nunnery. Charles demanded that Louis XV send her back, but the French king took pity on her and refused.

At the age of 51, Bonnie Prince Charlie married the 19-year-old Princess Louise of Stolberg-Gedern. His beautiful young bride was thrilled at the prospect of marrying the Young Pretender, the tragic hero of the '45 Rebellion and the heir to the British throne. What she got was a fat alcoholic, so she took up with a young Italian poet named Vittorio Alfieri.

The Pretender grew jealous. One night he beat down her bedroom door and raped her. He was going to kill her but the servants stopped him. She fled to a convent and appealed to the Pope for protection. Eventually, the scandal died down. Bonnie Prince Charlie went back to the bottle and Louise and Alfieri lived happily together for the next 20 years.

## 11 ❖ Gay Times

There have been more than a few scandalous queens on the throne of England – queens in the homosexual sense that is.

William the Conqueror's son, William Rufus, made little secret of his sexual preferences, and scandalized the nation with the camp goings on at court. Here is a description from one disapproving cleric: 'Then was there flowing hair and extravagant dress, and was invented the fashion of shoes with curved points; then the model for young men was to rival women in delicacy of person, to mind their gait, to walk with loose gesture, and half naked. Enervated and effeminate, they unwillingly remained what nature made them, the assailers of others' chastity, prodigal of their own.'

William II died young in a mysterious hunting accident. Despite allegations that it may not have been an accident, there was little scandal surrounding his death. The people of England thought they were well rid of him.

The great hero, Richard the Lionheart, was also gay. He was warned by a prominent clergyman to leave off his unnatural practices and spend time with his lovely Spanish wife. But he left his marriage unconsummated and went dashing off to the Middle East with his rough crusaders.

His heterosexual brother, King John, took over but made so free with the wives and daughters of his barons that they made him sign the Magna Carta. His wife, Isabella of Angoulême, caused scandal when she took lovers of her own. John had them slaughtered and their bodies draped over her bed as a warning.

The most notorious homosexual to sit on the throne was Edward II, largely because of the nature of his death. While Edward was still Prince of Wales, his father banished his lover, Piers de Gaveston. When Edward took the throne, de Gaveston returned to become Earl of Cornwall and Keeper of the Realm. Naturally, Edward had to get married. He picked as his bride the 12-year-old Isabella of France and, so that Piers would not feel left out, Edward arranged for his marriage to Edward's young niece. At the royal wedding breakfast, Edward and de Gaveston made so free with their affections to one another that Isabella's uncles left in disgust.

Despite his marriage, Edward banned women from his court. Within nine months of his accession, the barons were demanding that de Gaveston be exiled again. Edward was too weak politically to resist. De Gaveston

**Edward II**

was banished, but Edward accompanied him to his ship and they kissed and caressed on the dockside.

De Gaveston tried to return two years later, but was banished again. The next time he returned secretly, but when he appeared openly at Edward's side during the Christmas festivities of 1311, the barons rebelled.

Edward and de Gaveston fled to Scotland where Edward begged Robert the Bruce for sanctuary. He refused. De Gaveston was captured and put to death. Edward went home to his wife, who seems to have offered some solace. Just five months after de Gaveston's death, she gave birth to the future Edward III.

Over the next nine years, Queen Isabella gave him three more children. Then Edward fell in love with Hugh Despenser, whose father had long been a court favourite. This sparked another rebellion. Isabella fled to France where she took a lover, Lord Roger Mortimer.

Edward demanded that Isabella return to his side. She refused to come back until he dropped his boyfriend. When he refused, Isabella claimed that her husband was dead and went into mourning. Mortimer then led a masterly military campaign against Edward. The elder Despenser was captured and put to death. Edward and Hugh tried to escape to Ireland, but the wind blew their boat back on to the Welsh coast. Hugh suffered the same fate as his father, while Edward was forced to abdicate in favour of his son and was imprisoned. Later, Edward was found dead in his cell. A red hot poker had been shoved up 'those parts in which he had been wont to take his vicious pleasure'.

When Edward III came to the throne at the age of 16, he avenged his father and had Mortimer put to death as a traitor. But the new King did not follow in his father's footsteps. He had four children by his wife and three by his mistress, Alice Perrers.

THE most flamboyant homosexual to sit on the throne of England was James I, who was also James VI of Scotland. His very birth was shrouded in scandal. His mother was Mary Queen of Scots. At the age of six she had been betrothed to the Dauphin and sent to France to be brought up in the debauched court of François I. There she was tutored by the Queen, Catharine de Medici, whose main educational goal seems to have been the corruption of her own children.

Mary married at the age of 16, but two years later the Dauphin died. She returned to Scotland, pursued by her lover, the poet Pierre de Chatelard. John Knox was outraged by the way that Mary would lean on Chatelard's shoulder and kiss his neck. Chatelard was executed after twice being caught in Mary's bedroom.

Elizabeth I of England tried to unload one of her own lovers, Robert Dudley, on her, but Mary secretly married Henry Stewart, Lord Darnley, who was said to be beautiful, beardless and, it was said, 'more like a woman than a man'. Although Mary liked his looks, she soon found that he was a syphilitic adulterer and a drunk.

Just four months after her wedding, Mary was caught 'playing cards' in a private room with the musician David Rizzio. Darnley and a group of armed men burst in. They grabbed Rizzio, who clung to Mary's skirts for protection. He was dragged from the room and hacked to death on the stairs.

There was uproar in Edinburgh and Mary and Darnley fled. Six months later, she gave birth to James. Darnley was soon plotting to kidnap the child and seize the throne. One night, in Mary's absence, there was a terrific explosion and Darnley's half-naked body was found in the garden. He had been strangled.

Suspicion fell on Lord Bothwell, who was tried but acquitted. Three months later, when Mary was on her way from Stirling Castle to Edinburgh, she was kidnapped and raped by Bothwell. However, once he had divorced his first wife, she married him. But in 1567, Mary was deposed in favour of her one-year-old son, who became King under the regency of James Stuart, Earl of Moray, one of the many illegitimate sons of James V.

Mary fled to England where she was imprisoned by her cousin, Queen Elizabeth I. Bothwell fled to Denmark where he died in prison in 1578. In 1586, Mary was implicated in a plot against Elizabeth I, tried and beheaded – despite the half-hearted protests of her son – at Fotheringhay Castle the following year.

Mary's son, James VI of Scotland, was brought up strictly. He was kept well away from nubile young girls and confined to an all-male court – with predictable results. The Earl of Holland had to spurn the young King's advances 'by turning aside and spitting after the king had sladdered in his mouth'.

**Mary Tudor, Queen of England**

James was just 13 when his colourful cousin, Esmé Stuart, turned up at court. Esmé was 30 and had just returned from the court of the flagrantly homosexual Henry III of France. Esmé immediately prostrated himself in front of the teenage monarch. The effect was electric.

'No sooner did the young King see him,' said an eyewitness, 'but in that he was so near allied in blood, of so renowned a family, eminent ornaments of body and mind, took him up and embraced him in a most amorous manner, conferred on him presently a rich inheritance; and that he might be employed in state affairs, elected him one of his honourable privy council, gentleman of the bedchamber and governor of Dumbarton Castle.'

He was also created Duke of Lennox. James's Regent, the Earl of Moray, had already been murdered. James had his new Regent, the Earl of Morton, arrested and executed, and Lennox became his closest adviser.

The courtiers who had accompanied Stuart from France were notorious for their drunkenness and their swearing, and the Scottish clergy complained that 'the Duke of Lennox went about to draw the King into carnal lust'. English diplomats also reported on the growing romance between the two young men. But what most concerned everyone was that Lennox had a Catholic wife whom he had left behind in France.

With English support, Scotland's Protestant lords kidnapped James and forced Lennox into exile. Lennox wrote that he would rather die than lose the King's love. James expressed his grief in passionate poetry, comparing Lennox with a little bird pursued by hunters, which he hoped he could save by hiding between his legs.

With Lennox gone, James consoled himself with a string of lovers. He was seen to 'hang around' these young men's necks and kissed them quite openly. This was pretty brave, if not foolhardy, in a country where sodomy was a capital offence. In 1570, during James's reign, two men convicted of sodomy in Edinburgh were burnt at the stake.

James's homosexuality became a political problem when the rumour spread that James, like Elizabeth I of England, was of 'barren stock'. Something had to be done. He needed a queen. He began writing love letters and sonnets to 15-year-old Princess Anne of Denmark. She sent him a portrait, which he hung at the end of his bed and looked at every night.

The marriage was arranged, but the ship on which she made the crossing was blown back to Denmark. James sailed to Copenhagen to get her. For political reasons, he wrote: 'God is my witness I could not have abstained longer.'

It took him four years to get her pregnant. Then they fell out over the upbringing of their son. To make his point, James wrote *A Satire*

*Against Woman*. In it, he expressed his true feelings. Here is a sample:

> 'Even so all women are of nature vain
> And cannot keep a secret unrevealed
> And where as once they do conceive disdain
> They are unable to be reconcealed.
> Fulfilled with talk and clatters but respect
> And often times of small or no effect.'

James continued to do his duty. The Queen gave birth to two more sons and four daughters. But James's preference for his own sex persisted. In 1603, when, on the death of Elizabeth I, James acceded to the throne of England, he went south with a smooth-faced young man named James Hay, who was officially Master of the Royal Wardrobe.

Hay fell out of favour after making free with England's treasury and was married off to the daughter of a peer. On the morning after his wedding, he and his bride found the King clambering into bed with them.

Hay was replaced by Philip Herbert, who was similarly married off when James grew tired of him. Next came Robert Carr, a handsome young Scottish pageboy who was thrown from a horse at a jousting competition. The King rushed over to check whether he was injured and immediately put him in the care of the royal physicians. During Carr's convalescence, the King visited him every day and even tried to teach him Latin. Some said that his time would be better spent teaching the young Scot to speak English.

When he was fully recovered, Carr became a Gentleman of the Bedchamber and the two of them were inseparable. Their relationship was not 'carried on with discretion sufficient to cover less scandalous behaviour'. They were seen kissing and fondling openly at the theatre, leaving little doubt as to what they got up to when they were on their own. Not that it mattered so much now that they were south of the border. In England, the attitude to homosexuality was less Draconian. In the 45 years of Elizabeth's rule and the 23 years of James's, only six men in the Home Counties were indicted for sodomy, and only one was convicted, even though London itself was awash with the vice. Nevertheless, it was still considered shocking for the King to flaunt his sexual preferences so openly.

The scandal grew when James created Carr Lord Rochester. The ambitious young man then sought further advancement by wooing Lady Essex. But her husband, who had been away for four years, suddenly turned up. Carr pressed the King to grant Lady Essex a divorce, while she defended her honour with potions she had bought from a magician. They seem to have worked. In 1613, her marriage was annulled on the grounds of impotence.

Rochester and Lady Essex were then married. At the ceremony, the bride wore her hair loose over her shoulders to symbolise, disingenuously, her virginity. As a wedding present, James created Rochester Earl of Somerset.

But that was not the end of the matter. Lady Essex was even less of a virgin than she pretended. She had a former lover called Thomas Overbury, who opposed Rochester's relentless ambition. Rochester used his influence with the King to have Overbury arrested and imprisoned in the Tower, but when he was found dead, poisoned, James had no choice but to have his former lover, Rochester, and his wife arrested.

There was rioting when the newly weds went on trial. Copious evidence implicated Rochester, at least, in the crime. They were both sentenced to death, but James, for old times' sake, commuted the sentence to imprisonment at his pleasure. They served seven years in the Tower. Rochester never saw the King again.

By this time, James was well provided for by young men eager to advance themselves. One political faction even sought to win the King's favour by employing the Countess of Suffolk to find young men for him. She spent her time curling their hair and perfuming their breaths, ready just for the royal pleasure.

The Queen had disliked Rochester. She had sought to curb his influence by pushing forward a candidate of her own. This was George Villiers, whom Bishop Goodman described as the handsomest man in England. Few disagreed, although some pointed out that he was somewhat effeminate.

He was also the protégé of James's former lover, Philip Herbert, but it was the Queen who secured him his position as Gentleman of the Bedchamber. James was soon hopelessly in love.

James called Villiers Steenie, after St Stephen who, according to the Bible, had a face that glowed like 'the face of an angel'. He referred to him in his letters as both 'wife' and 'husband' and told the Privy Council that he loved him more than any other man. Villiers was rewarded with the title Earl of Buckingham and an advantageous marriage. There was no doubt in anyone's mind that James loved Buckingham in the way that he had loved Rochester.

'The love the King showed was as amorously conveyed as if he had mistaken their sex and thought them ladies; which I have seen Somerset and Buckingham labour to resemble, in the effeminateness of their dress,' wrote one eyewitness.

When James died, it was rumoured that Buckingham had poisoned him, after growing tired of the ageing King's sexual demands. He certainly had plenty of opportunity as he had nursed the King through his final illness. James's death did Buckingham no harm either. He was already tight with James's heir, his son who became Charles I. Charles was submissive, narcissistic and effeminate. As a youth, he was jealous of his father's lover, but by the time James died he, too, was calling Buckingham 'Steenie'. In letters, he addressed him as 'sweetheart' and the two were constant companions. Francis Bacon remarked how nice it was that Buckingham could 'ease the heart of both father and son'.

Before James's death, rumours spread that 'Baby Charles' was 'sterile'. The problem had to be solved once more by a rapid marriage. James sent Charles off to Madrid to woo the King of Spain's daughter, the Infanta Maria.

Buckingham was sent along to keep Charles out of trouble. While they were away, James wrote to them saying: 'I wear Steenie's picture on a blue ribbon under my waistcoat, next to my heart.'

Instead of keeping Charles out of trouble, Buckingham precipitated it. He put out the nose of their go-between, Count Olivares, by arranging an assignation with his wife. The Countess sent a prostitute in her place, but negotiations were blocked. Charles, who mistakenly believed that he had made a good impression on the Infanta, took matters into his own hands. He climbed over the palace wall at the Casa Del Campo and caught her without her chaperone. The Infanta responded to this bold advance with a loud scream. She ran and told her father that she would rather become a nun than marry the future King of England. The situation turned so nasty that Charles and Buckingham had to be rescued by the Royal Navy. But back in London, James, Charles and Buckingham closeted themselves in the King's private chambers and, for four hours, peels of laughter could be heard echoing down the hallways.

James dispatched envoys, including his former lover, James Hay, now Earl of Carlisle, to woo other princesses. But Charles I solved the problem himself when his father died and he came to the throne. He married 15-year-old Henrietta Maria of France by proxy.

When she arrived in England the couple were cordial enough, but things did not seem to be going so well in the bedroom. Soon, the court was worried that there might be no heirs.

Buckingham tried to solve the problem. He tried to pass the benefit of his advice to the Queen via Henrietta Maria's Lady of the Bedchamber, Madame St Georges. But she refused to interfere in such delicate matters and was sacked.

The solution to the problem arrived via a more round-about route.

Buckingham had been having an affair with the beautiful and experienced Lady Carlisle, wife of James Hay. He had even prevailed on the King to send Hay away on a diplomatic mission so that he could seduce her.

When Buckingham's wife found out, he tried to pass Lady Carlisle on to the King. He refused the offer, but made her a Lady of the Bedchamber. Lady Carlisle then proceeded to impart everything she knew about the ways of love to the young Queen. Within weeks, Henrietta Maria was pregnant. She and Charles had nine healthy children, and several more stillborn.

Of course, the great scandal of Charles I's reign was not sexual, it was his high-handed attitude to Parliament, which tried to curb his excesses. He alienated them when he purchased a collection of paintings he could ill afford. And when they opposed him, he tried to have five Members of the House of Commons arrested. The Civil War ensued. After five years, his forces were defeated by the Puritans under Oliver Cromwell.

Charles was imprisoned on the Isle of Wight, where he was comforted by Jane Whorwood. The wife of the royalist leader of the City of London, she had come to him with half of the £1,000 he had raised for the royalist cause. Charles kept her as a courtier in lieu of the other half.

During his imprisonment Charles wrote at least 16 letters to her. On 26 July 1648, six months before he died, the doomed King wrote to 'Sweet Jane Whorwood' to meet him in his room as if by accident. He outwitted his guard on numerous occasions to see her and, in his last letter to her, he spoke of the 'great contentment' she had brought to him.

Sentenced as 'a tyrant, a traitor, a murderer and a public enemy', Charles died on the scaffold outside the banqueting hall in Whitehall. Unrepentant to the end, he warned the axeman that he would 'forgive no subject of mine who comes to shed my blood'.

## 12 ❖ Virgin Sovereign

Elizabeth I was the Virgin Queen, or so she said. In 1559, she asked Sir John Mason to tell the House of Commons to erect 'a marble stone which shall declare that a Queen lived and died a virgin'. No such stone was ever erected. The reason was that throughout Elizabeth's reign there were a series of royal sex scandals that she only just managed to keep in check.

When she was just 16 there were rumours that she had been made pregnant by her guardian, the ambitious Thomas Seymour, husband of her father's widow Catherine Parr, who had once caught them in a passionate embrace.

When she came to the throne, Elizabeth showed little interest in men. Perhaps her father's philandering had put her off. Naturally, she was besieged with offers from foreign princes, eager to wear the English crown. Even Philip of Spain, widower of Elizabeth's half-sister Mary who was hardly cold in her grave, rushed forward with a proposal. But he was a Catholic. Elizabeth, the daughter of Henry VIII and Anne Boleyn, was a confirmed Protestant. England was now a Protestant kingdom and she was determined to keep it that way.

A year after she was crowned, Elizabeth began taking a romantic interest in Lord Robert Dudley. They had been born on the same day in September 1533 and had been imprisoned in the Tower together during much of Mary's reign.

In 1559, the year that Elizabeth declared that she would live and die a virgin, the Spanish ambassador reported that 'Her Majesty visits him in his chamber day and night'.

The problem was that Dudley had a wife. She stayed out of the way in Berkshire and it was rumoured that she had a 'malady of the breast'. Apparently, she was not long for this world and, when she died, Elizabeth intended to marry Lord Robert.

Dudley's wife did die, but not of a malady of the breast. She was found at the foot of the stairs in their Berkshire home. Dudley was immediately suspected of murdering her. The Queen herself was implicated and she had no alternative but to send him away.

But she did not give up on the match. Slowly, she tried to rehabilitate him. Four years later, he was back in court and she created him Earl of Leicester. This was hardly calculated to dampen down the gossip.

'I am spoken of as if I am an immodest woman,' Elizabeth complained to the Spanish ambassador. 'I have favoured him because of his excellent disposition and his many merits, but I am young and he is young, and therefore we have both been slandered. God knows, they do us grievous wrong.'

With Leicester still out of the running, other men threw their hats into the ring. Sir Christopher Hatton, a handsome young lawyer from Northampton, wrote to the Queen with great passion. Those closer to home were soon unmasked as womanizers. One of them was Sir Walter Raleigh, who was frontrunner for a while, until he got Elizabeth Throckmorton, one of the Ladies of the Bedchamber, pregnant.

Leicester, too, developed a reputation as a ladies' man. Enemies spread the word that he would pay as much as £300 to sleep with the Queen's

**Queen Elizabeth I, The self confessed 'Virgin Queen'**

ladies-in-waiting. He bedded Lady Frances Howard, but broke off with her to seduce the Queen's beautiful cousin, Lady Douglas Sheffield. Her husband died mysteriously – poisoned by Leicester it was said – and she presented him with a son. To get her own back, the Queen entertained the advances of the Duke of Anjou, the King of France's brother and half her age. He was a devout Catholic and practising bisexual.

When that fell though, she began entertaining Anjou's younger brother, the Duke of Alençon. Finally, Leicester broke it off with Lady Sheffield and Elizabeth dropped Alençon. It was only later that one of Alençon's envoys pointed out that Leicester had dropped Lady Sheffield to take up with Lettice, Countess of Essex, another of the Queen's cousins and reputed to be the most beautiful woman at court.

Elizabeth sent Leicester off on a military campaign in Ireland and chastized Lettice for her disloyalty. But when Leicester returned, the affair continued. Then Lettice's husband died. Again, Leicester was suspected, and it was said that he was the real father of her children.

They married secretly in 1578, weeks before the birth of their first legitimate child. Driven half-crazy with jealousy, the Queen dragged Lady Sheffield in front of the Royal Councillors and tried to force her to admit that Leicester had secretly been married to her – making him a bigamist.

However, Lady Sheffield had since made a favourable match with Sir Edward Stafford and saw no reason to jeopardize her new marriage.

In 1579, Elizabeth invited the Duke of Alençon to England and fawned over him. She even allowed Leicester back into court so that he could witness their love-making. When Alençon fell ill, Elizabeth acted as nursemaid to her 'little frog', as she called him. The Puritan preacher, John Stubbs, thought this quite scandalous. He condemned Alençon as a serpent, come to seduce our English Eve and destroy the paradise that was England.

This did nothing to dampen Elizabeth's ardour and in 1581, when Alençon visited England again, she announced that she was going to marry him. But her ladies-in-waiting kicked up such a fuss that, the following day, she told him the wedding was off.

When Leicester died in 1588, Elizabeth was reconciled with her cousin, Lettice. When she returned to court, she brought with her her son, the Earl of Essex. He stepped into his stepfather's shoes and began to woo the Queen. It was a bold, if cynical move. Essex was young and handsome; the Queen was in her 50s. A bright auburn wig hid her thinning hair. Thick white make-up hid her wrinkles. Only by maintaining an unsmiling face could she hide her rotting teeth.

Essex knew the extent of the damage. Excitedly returning from an expedition one morning, he had impetuously pushed past the guards and barged into her chamber, before she had had time to put on her wig and make-up. He also had to contend with a court that was filled with young and scandalous distractions. Elizabeth sent her lady-in-waiting, Anne Vasavour, to the Tower after she gave birth to the illegitimate son of the Earl of Oxford. Later, Anne married, then had another illegitimate son by Sir Henry Lee. When he died, Anne married again, only to be fined £200 for bigamy.

When another lady-in-waiting, Mary Futton, was brought to court, her father asked Sir William Knollys to protect his innocent daughter. Sir William seduced the girl himself and promised to marry her when his wife died. In the meantime, Mary began an affair with the Earl of Pembroke. To meet her lover, Mary would steal away from court in men's clothing. The scandal broke when Mary fell pregnant. Pembroke refused to marry her and was sent to Fleet jail. Mary was sent home to the country in disgrace.

Essex himself secretly married the widow of Sir Philip Sidney. When Elizabeth found out about it, she was forgiving and allowed Lady Essex to be presented at court. But neither his wife's presence nor the censure of the Queen stopped him from bedding other ladies-in-waiting. His indiscreet affair with Elizabeth Brydges, daughter of Lord Chandos, was so scandalous that the Queen banished her from court. But she did not act quickly enough in the case of Elizabeth Southwell, who bore Essex's child.

The Queen was so jealous when Lady Mary Howard started throwing herself at Essex that she borrowed one of her dresses and wore it herself. It did nothing for the ageing Queen. When Essex was less than impressed, she confiscated the dress and condemned Lady Mary and all the other 'flouting wenches' of the court.

Essex's scandalous behaviour then developed a political dimension. He was charged with spreading sedition in Ireland, but Elizabeth merely had him censured in private, rather than put on trial for treason. This taught him nothing. With a small band of followers, he rode into London, intent on seizing the Queen. Forewarned, the Palace of Westminster was barricaded. Essex's following quickly dwindled. He was arrested and this time he was tried for treason and sentenced to death.

Even then he might have got away with it. The Queen had once given him a ring that, she had said, would absolve him from any crime. From his cell in the Tower, he sent it to her. But on the way, it fell into the hands of his old enemy, Lady Nottingham, who only passed it on to the Queen after Essex had been beheaded.

Of course, we cannot be sure that the relationship between Elizabeth and Essex was ever consummated. But we can be sure that the Virgin Queen was no virgin. She once said that she was 'of barren stock'. If she had not had sex with a number of men, how could she have known?

ELIZABETH'S half-sister, Mary, fared little better in love, but the main scandal in her reign was her propensity to burn Protestants, especially bishops. This earned her the epithet 'Bloody Mary'. Also, through her bad choice of a mate, she lost Calais, England's last possession in France.

Mary's reign began in scandal. The daughter of Catherine of Aragon, Henry VIII's first wife, she suffered the shame of seeing her mother divorced and her father repudiating the Catholic faith she had been brought up in. With the death of Henry VIII, her half-brother Edward VI, the son of Jane Seymour, took the throne. He died at the age of 16 – hardly enough time to get involved in any serious scandal. Not that he didn't try. After his betrothal in 1552 to Princess Elizabeth of France, he held a pageant in Greenwich called The Triumph of Cupid. He also fooled around with the 35-year-old Mary of Guise, the Regent of Scotland, and Mary, Queen of Scots.

With his death, Lady Jane Grey took over in a constitutional coup. She was only fifth in line to the throne. Like Elizabeth I, she had been brought up in Thomas Seymour's house and seems to have had a crush on the older man. When she blossomed into a young woman, he put about the rumour that he was going to marry her, possibly to discourage other suitors.

However, the ambitious Duke of Northumberland was not to be put off. He was Edward VI's chief adviser and the most powerful man in the land. He could do almost anything he pleased. But Edward was a sickly child and if he died, Northumberland's power would die with him. So he decided to marry Lady Jane Grey off to his witless son, Lord Guildford Dudley, and put the two of them on the throne. That way he would retain his influence.

There was a problem though. When Jane was told that she was to marry Dudley, she refused point blank. She protested that she was already promised to Lord Hertford. Her parents bullied and beat her until she agreed. Lord Hertford was placated by marriage to Jane's sister. In fact, Northumberland had arranged a series of marriages in order to secure his dynastic hold on the reigns of power. Katherine Dudley married Lord Hastings. Jane's 13-year-old sister, Katherine, married Lord Herbert and eight-year-old Mary was betrothed to her cousin, Arthur Grey. They were to be married as soon as she reached puberty.

Even so, nothing went smoothly. Although Jane's wedding was lavish, the bridegroom came down with food poisoning and was unable to consummate the marriage. By the time he had recovered, Edward was on his deathbed. Northumberland persuaded the young King to alter the succession in favour of Lady Jane and ordered that she be publicly 'abedded' by Dudley. Once this was done, Lady Jane went to take a rest cure at the Palace in Chelsea.

When Edward died, Lady Jane was proclaimed Queen. Her reign lasted just nine days. Mary swept to power. Jane and Dudley were arrested and tried for treason. She was sentenced to public burning; he to hanging, drawing and quartering.

Mary showed every sign of being merciful. But when she announced her intention to marry the Catholic King Philip II of Spain, the Protestants under Sir Thomas Wyatt rebelled. Although the rebellion was swiftly put down, Mary realized that Jane and Dudley posed a threat as long as they lived.

From his cell, Dudley asked to see his young wife one last time. She refused, although she did see his headless body as it was carried back from Tower Hill. Jane was then examined to see if she was pregnant before being taken to the block on Tower Green.

After observing the fortunes of her father's six wives, one might have thought that Mary would have had reservations about marriage. Indeed, when she first came to the throne, she surrounded herself with pretty young women and she resolutely stood in the way of any marriage plans they might have. One of them, Jane Dormer, slept in Mary's chamber and was often seen wearing the Queen's jewels.

But Mary had one major political ambition – to return Protestant England to the Catholic Church. To do that, she accepted the proposal of Philip of Spain.

This was no love match. When Philip arrived in Southampton in July 1554, he kissed all her ladies-in-waiting. Mary herself was 10 years his senior and plainly not to his taste. To Philip and his courtiers, English women were very loose and Philip made his intentions towards the Queen's maids very plain. However, when it came to Mary herself, his ardour was less than flaming. But, for the sake of the throne and the church, they went through the motions.

By September 1554 it was announced that Mary was pregnant. Spanish ladies flocked to attend her at Hampton Court. They waited and they waited. By Easter 1555, it was circulated that the date of conception had been miscalculated. By May, rumours suggested that she was not pregnant at all. The doctors and courtiers stuck valiantly to the official line throughout June and July. It was only in August that Mary was forced to admit that it was only air – not an heir – in her belly.

In disgust, Philip sailed back to Spain. Mary put a brave face on things in public but, in private, broke down and wept. She wrote to him often, begging him to return to her. He did in March 1557. But he wanted her, not as a bed mate, but an ally. Spain was at war with France. Philip wanted England to join in. The result: was the loss of Calais. Mary said that when she died, Calais would be found written on her heart.

Philip left England again in January 1558. Again, it was announced that Mary was pregnant. Indeed, her belly was swollen, but the swelling was caused by the dropsy that killed her later that year.

# 13 ❖ The Six Wives of Henry VIII

There have been few more scandalous monarchs than Henry VIII. He changed the religion of a kingdom in order to divorce his first wife and had two subsequent wives executed. With six wives he had the reputation of being a great stud. In fact, with two of them he was almost certainly impotent. He only married so much in an effort to secure an heir. At the time it was seen as a political imperative to avoid plunging England back into the 30 years of internecine feuding that had preceded his father's reign, which have come to be known as the Wars of the Roses.

**Henry VIII, one of the most scandalous monarchs**

Henry Tudor, Henry VIII's father, had won the Wars of the Roses by defeating Richard III at the Battle of Bosworth Field and was crowned Henry VII. A Lancastrian, Henry VII ended any further struggle by marrying the daughter of the other great rival dynasty, Elizabeth of York.

As a prince, Henry VIII was brought up chastely. A studious lad, he wrote the religious tract called *Assertio septem sacramentorum adversus Martin Lutherum*, a reply to Martin Luther's 95 theses nailed to the church door in Wittenberg that started the Protestant Reformation. As a result, Henry was awarded the title *Fidei Defensor*, or 'Defender of the Faith', by the Pope.

The first scandal of his reign centred on the marriage of his brother, the 15-year-old Arthur, to the 16-year-old Spanish princess, Catherine of Aragon. Arthur had died soon after and Henry was encouraged by his father to take an interest in Catherine. A marriage between the heir to the English throne and Spain was important for English foreign policy, so Henry VII pushed for a dispensation from the Pope to allow Henry to marry his brother's widow – which was technically incest – on the grounds that her marriage to Arthur had never been consummated.

Henry VIII came to the throne at 18 and, two months later, he married

Catherine. Although she was six years older than him, he genuinely loved her. They enjoyed hunting, hawking and making music together, and the grooms who escorted him from his bedchamber to the Queen's reported that he made the trip regularly.

For five years, he was faithful. In that time, Catherine produced a number of stillborn children, a son who lived just two months and a daughter, Mary. Then Henry's attention began to wander. At first, his attention alighted on Lady Anne Hastings. He used one of the Grooms of the Bedchamber, Sir Henry Crompton, as his go-between. But Sir Henry promptly seduced Lady Anne himself.

When they were interrupted by Lady Anne's husband, Sir George Hastings, Crompton claimed that he was making love to Lady Anne not for his own sake, but for that of the King. In the resulting scandal, Lady Anne was sent to a nunnery by her irate husband, and Henry banished her brother, the Duke of Buckingham, and Sir George's sister, Elizabeth, from court for spreading gossip. This did not prevent the news from reaching the ears of the Queen and the Spanish ambassador.

While the Queen remained vexed, Henry moved on to Jane Popincourt, the Flemish-born mistress of the Duc de Longueville, a French noble long held hostage in the English court. Her reputation was notorious. Louis XII personally crossed her name off the list of maids-of-honour who were coming to France with Henry's sister, Mary, saying that he would rather see Popincourt burn at the stake than attend his young bride.

Henry returned de Longueville to France to clear the way for his affair. And, when he tired of Jane, he gave her £100 to follow her lover. He had already transferred his affections to 18-year-old Elizabeth 'Bessie' Blount.

The daughter of a Shropshire knight, Bessie had come to court at the age of 13 when her dancing had brought her to the King's attention at a masque. The Queen was so taken by their performance that she had them repeat their *pas de deux* in her chamber by candlelight.

At 18, Bessie became Henry's mistress and, in 1519, she presented him with a healthy living son, Henry Fitzroy. Bessie was quickly married off to Gilbert Talboys, one of the wards of the Chancery. The happy couple were given Rokeby Manor in Warwickshire as a wedding present.

Later, Henry considered marrying his illegitimate son to Mary to secure the line – albeit incestuously – but Henry Fitzroy died of tuberculosis while still a teenager.

The next woman to bear Henry a child was Mary Boleyn, Anne's older sister. Both Mary and Anne had been maids-of-honour in the licentious French court, but Mary, it seems, had outperformed the local talent. An

Italian diplomat described her as the 'greatest and most infamous whore', while the King of France himself called her a 'hackney'.

Back in England, Mary was Catherine of Aragon's lady-in-waiting when Henry seduced her. Her compliant husband was rewarded with a knighthood. Henry named a ship in his new navy after her, but he dropped her without a penny when he grew tired of her.

Mary's father, Thomas Boleyn, was an ambitious man. It was said that he had even offered his own wife to Henry, who refused her, saying: 'Never with the mother.' Mary's younger sister, Anne, was more to Henry's taste. But Anne wanted nothing to do with him and proclaimed her intention to marry one James Butler.

However, fate – perhaps in the form of Thomas Boleyn – took a hand. Anne was picked to be one of eight ladies to take part in a masque at Cardinal Wolsey's London home, York Place. They were to represent Virtue and had to defend their castle against eight masked men, representing Desire, by dousing them with rose water and pelting them with fruit.

The outcome was predictable. After a few minutes of mock combat, Virtue succumbed. The ladies then danced with their assailants. When the gentlemen unmasked themselves, Anne found her suitor was none other than the King.

But Anne was not to be won over so easily. She took up with a married man, the poet Sir Thomas Wyatt, to protect herself from Henry's advances. Then she received a proposal from the Earl of Northumberland's heir, Sir Henry Perky. But, knowing the King's interest, Cardinal Wolsey put a stop to that match.

Henry stopped sleeping with the Queen and, in a series of passionate love letters, promised to make Anne his sole mistress 'rejecting all others'. This came as a bit of a shock to the court as Anne was no great beauty. She had an unsightly mole on her neck, which she hid with high collars, and she wore long sleeves to hide the tiny sixth finger that she had on each hand. But it was her pert young bosom that took the King's fancy – 'those pritty duckys I trust shortly to kysse,' he wrote. 'Ducky' is a medieval word for breast.

Anne still did not succumb. She did not want to suffer the short shrift that Henry had meted out to her sister Mary. But Henry was growing desperate to have a son and he thought Anne might provide him with one. He needed a legitimate heir, however, so he would have to marry her.

Henry began to contend that the dispensation the Pope had given Catherine to marry him had been obtained under false pretences. That was why God had cursed their union and it had failed to give him the son he craved. Henry persuaded the Dowager Duchess of Norfolk to testify

**128 THE WORLDS GREATEST ROYAL SCANDALS**

that Catherine had indeed slept with his older brother, Arthur. The marriage had therefore been consummated, making her marriage to Henry incestuous and illegal.

Unfortunately for Henry, the Pope was being held hostage by Catherine's nephew, Charles V, at the time and did not see it that way. All Cardinal Wolsey's attempts to seek an annulment failed. Anne, who was still sore at Wolsey for preventing her marriage to Sir Henry Perky, demanded his dismissal. Wolsey retired to York and died on his way back to London, summoned there to face a charge of treason.

Sir Thomas More took over as Chancellor, but he was against the divorce and wanted to fight what he saw as the Lutheran heresy. He was replaced by the ambitious Thomas Cromwell, who saw that the way to give Henry the divorce he wanted was for him to reject the authority of Rome and make himself head of the English Church.

After holding out for six years, Anne finally succumbed. By January 1533, she was pregnant. On 25 January, Henry and Anne were married secretly. In May, a new Archbishop of Canterbury, Thomas Cramner, presided over an ecclesiastical inquiry into Henry's first marriage, and on

Anne Boleyn, a surprising choice for the king due to her plain looks. She had six fingers on each hand

23 May a special Act of Parliament declared it null and void. At Whitsun, Anne was crowned Queen, and in September, she gave birth – to Princess Elizabeth. The Pope's response was excommunication. It bothered no one.

Disappointed at the birth of a daughter, Henry began indulging himself with other lovers. Anne herself complained to her sister-in-law, Lady Rochford, that Henry was neither skilful at love-making nor very virile. Nevertheless, she kept entertaining him in her bed in the hope that she would produce the male heir he so desperately wanted. Anne fell pregnant three more times – although she miscarried on each occasion. Anne blamed one of her miscarriages on Henry's dalliance with a pretty maid.

Anne turned for advice to her Lady of the Bedchamber, the sly Lady Rochford – whom Henry banished from court. In desperation, Anne tried to interest Henry in her own cousin, Madge Shelton. When Henry found out that Anne was trying to manipulate his love life, he dismissed Madge from court, too – after bedding her first, of course.

But Henry was slowing down. He suffered occasionally from bouts of impotence. To his doctors, he complained: 'I am forty-one years old, at which age the lust of a man is not as quick as in lusty youth.' This was in the days before Viagra.

Even so, Anne became pregnant again. Henry, then 44, was delighted. But the prospect of being a father again did not stop him from turning his attentions to Anne's maid-of-honour, the beautiful and nubile Jane Seymour.

In January 1536, Catherine of Aragon died and Henry held a joust to celebrate. During the action, Henry was thrown from his horse. He was stretchered from the tournament field and for two hours he lay unconscious. Anne suddenly realized how precarious her position was. If the King died without a son, England would be thrown back into civil war and she would be the first for the chop. Her anxiety triggered premature labour. She gave birth to a son – dead.

Rumours quickly spread that the foetus was deformed, a sure sign that she had been involved with witchcraft. When Henry revived, he denied paternity. In his eyes, the deformed foetus proved that his second marriage, too, was cursed by incest. After all, Anne's sister, Mary, had been his lover before their marriage.

With Catherine now dead, Anne was in a very vulnerable position. Henry could now simply declare that his first marriage had been legitimate after all. That would reconcile him with the Catholic Church, rid him of Anne and allow him to find a new wife.

Anne was also isolated. Those courtiers who had maintained a loyalty to Catherine called her 'the concubine' and 'the goggle-eyed whore'. In an attempt to find allies, Anne flirted. Enemies spread rumours that she had taken lovers. This played into Henry's hands. He encouraged the scandal by boasting that his wife had slept with a hundred other men.

'You never saw a prince, nor a man, who made a greater show of his cuckold's horns,' one observer said.

On 2 May 1536, Anne was arrested for adultery, incest and plotting to kill the King. Sir Henry Norris, a Gentleman of the Privy Chamber, the grooms Sir Francis Weston and William Brereton, along with a handsome young musician named Mark Smeaton were also arrested. The first three denied having sex with Anne, but Smeaton confessed, after torture. The four of them were found guilty of treason and paid a terrible price. They were hanged at Tyburn, cut down while still alive, castrated, disembowelled and, finally, had their limbs cut off. It was a gruesome way to go.

Anne's brother, Lord Rochford, was also arrested. The two of them were tried together in the Great Hall in the Tower of London. Their chief accuser was Rochford's wife, good old Lady Rochford, who alleged that her husband had always been in his sister's room. Other maids gave their own accounts of the 'pastimes of the Queen's chamber'. Lady Rochford also testified that there had been an 'undue familiarity' between brother and sister. The implication was that since Anne had been unable to produce the male hair Henry craved with Henry himself, she had tried to conceive one with other lovers. Her own brother lent a hand, as it were, because his position depended on being the brother-in-law of the current king and the uncle of a future monarch.

As evidence of incest this was less than convincing, but there was no crossing the King. The judge, who was Anne's own uncle, the Duke of Norfolk, shed a tear when he delivered the guilty verdict. For treason, the death sentence was mandatory. But whether they were to be burnt or beheaded was a matter for the King's pleasure.

Henry was merciful. Rochford was beheaded on Tower Hill. Perhaps in deference to the great love he had once had for Anne, Henry spared her the axe. He paid £24 to bring an expert swordsman over from Calais to dispatch his love on Tower Green.

Curiously, two days before Anne was executed, Henry divorced her. He had their marriage annulled on the grounds that she had previously been contracted to marry Sir Henry Perky. The annulment technically nullified the charge of adultery. And with no adultery there was no treason – and, thus, no reason to execute her. No one mentioned this to Henry. He was too busy having fun.

While Anne was preparing to die, Henry began a round of parties where he pursued any woman he found remotely attractive. He was now 45 and not in the best of health, but he compared his new-found freedom with a man who had disposed of 'a thin old vicious hack in the hope of getting soon a fine horse to ride'.

It did not take him long to find his new mount. On 13 May 1536, just 11 days after the death of Anne Boleyn, he married her pretty maid-of-honour, Jane Seymour. Although Jane had been in Henry's debauched court for several years, she was still reputed to be a virgin – a neat trick in a court where it was held 'a sin to be a maid'. As Queen, Jane imposed her modest demeanour on others. She forbade Anne Basset to wear 'French apparel' and insisted that she use 'chests', material that covered the plunging necklines.

Already, the rumour was that the King was impotent, but something about Jane must have inspired him. In February 1537, it was announced that the Queen was pregnant and on 12 October she gave birth to his long-awaited son, Edward.

Twelve days later, she died.

Henry was heartbroken. But now he had sired a Prince of Wales, he was eager to sire a Duke of York, too, a younger brother for the sickly Edward.

There was a problem though. Since there was now no Queen at court, most of the eligible young ladies-in-waiting were at home in the country.

The English ambassador to the Netherlands, John Hutton, was commanded to draw up a list of eligible women. These ranged from a 14-year-old lady-in-waiting to the Queen of France to a well-preserved 40-year-old widow. Hutton's recommendation, however, was the 16-year-old Duchess Christina of Milan. Henry was now 48.

However, Henry was interested in the current crop of French princesses and suggested a beauty pageant of five girls in Calais. The French ambassador said that if the princesses were to be paraded like ponies, why did His Majesty not go one step further – mount them in turn so he could pick out the best ride? The idea was dropped.

The artist Hans Holbein was sent to Italy to paint a portrait of Christina of Milan. Henry was impressed. The young lady was also experienced in the ways of love. At 13 she had been married to the Duke of Milan, who had died a year later. The wedding arrangements were set in hand, but the wily Lord Chancellor Thomas Cromwell was against the marriage. Politically, an alliance with Protestant Germany would be more advantageous.

Holbein was sent off again, this time to Germany, to paint a portrait of Anne of Cleves. The English envoy who went with him protested that Anne and her sister, Amelia, were so well covered that Holbein could see neither their figures nor their faces.

'Why, would you have them naked?' replied the Chancellor of Cleves.

Knowing which way the political wind was blowing, Holbein turned in an exceedingly flattering portrait of Anne. Henry did not find it displeasing and, bowing to the political exigencies, agreed to marry her.

It was noted that the King was very lusty at the time and, despite a gouty leg, he rode on horseback from Greenwich to Rochester to greet his bride. But when he set eyes on her, he was appalled by her ugliness and quickly dubbed her his 'Flanders Mare'. To make matters worse, she spoke no English.

After their first night together, Henry told Cromwell: 'I liked her before not well, but now I like her much worse.'

She was 'not as reported', he said. Her breasts were slack and droopy – he liked small pert ones like Anne Boleyn's – and other parts of her body were 'in such a state that one suspected her virginity'. She was apparently in such bad nick that Henry complained that never in her company could he be 'provoked or steered to know her carnally'.

Eight days later, he complained to his doctors that even though he had slept with his new wife each night she was 'still as good a maid... as ever her mother bore her'. And it was not his fault, he claimed. During the nights he had had a number of nocturnal emissions.

Anne was blissfully unaware of the problem. When Lady Rutland made discreet enquiries about the physical side of their marriage, Anne said: 'When he comes to bed, he kisses me and taketh me by the hand and biddeth me "Farewell, darling". Is that not enough?'

Lady Rutland tried to explain that a little more was expected of Anne if England was to have its Duke of York. But Anne would not listen. She regarded such talk as shameful.

Failing to get much stimulation from his new wife, Henry's amorous attentions quickly turned to Anne of Cleves's 18-year-old maid-of-honour, Catherine Howard, a cousin of Anne Boleyn. She was neither modest nor pious. She had been brought up in the crowded house of the Dowager Duchess of Norfolk in Horsham in Sussex, with numerous young relatives. There they had midnight feasts that often ended in communal sex.

Catherine took her first lover at 14. His name was Henry Manox and he was a young music teacher hired to teach her, ironically, the virginal. She later claimed that full sex had not taken place but he was persuasive and, she said: 'I suffered him at sundry times to handle and touch the secret parts of my body which neither became me with honesty to permit nor him to require.'

But when the family moved to Norfolk House in Lambeth, she met another young man named Frances Dereham. He set about seducing her and they were soon calling each other 'husband' and 'wife'.

'Frances Dereham,' said Catherine later, 'by many persuasions procured me to his vicious purpose and obtained first to lie upon my bed with his doublet and hose, and after in the bed; and, finally, he lay with me naked and used me in such sort as a man doth his wife many and sundry times, but how often I know not.'

They were not alone. Dereham would come to the maiden's chamber at night with Edward Waldegrave, where they would stay until dawn with their respective loves – Catherine and Joan Bulmer. According to Joan, Dereham and Catherine would 'kiss and hang by their bellies as if they were two sparrows'. Love tokens were exchanged and, in the dark, Joan heard a great deal of 'puffing and blowing'.

Catherine, despite her young years, was advanced. Joan said she knew 'how a woman might meddle with a man and yet conceive no child unless she would herself'.

Another member of the household, Katherine Tylney, later admitted

**Catherine Howard**

that on occasions she had joined Dereham and Catherine in what *The Sun* today would call a 'three-in-the-bed love romp'.

Catherine's behaviour was widely known, but her colourful past was quickly hushed up when Henry took an interest. He described Catherine as 'a blushing rose without a thorn' and a 'perfect jewel of womanhood'. He took her as his mistress, but the powerful Howard family had greater ambitions. They were Catholics and wanted to rid the realm of its Protestant Queen.

The diplomatic need for Henry's German marriage had passed. Thomas Cromwell now backed the King's desire to sire more children. He began to arrange for Henry a divorce from his 'Flanders Mare'.

A convocation of clerics was set up to investigate the validity of the marriage. Anne's blushes were not spared when she was asked to repeat her conversations with Lady Rutland in front of the committee. Henry's doctors were also called to give evidence. After the scandal of two very public divorce cases centering on incest, the people of England were treated to hilarious testimony concerning the King's inability to get it up. But this was just a foretaste of the even more juicy scandal that was to follow.

The clerics quickly found that 'there had been no carnal copulation between Your Majesty and the said Lady Anne, nor with that just impediment interceding could it be possible'. The King's inability to perform, they ruled, resulted from a troubled conscience concerning the fact that Anne of Cleves had previously been promised elsewhere. The marriage was quickly annulled.

Anne remained in England and hit the bottle. She took other, more virile, lovers. Rumour had it that she became pregnant twice and actually gave birth to an illegitimate child.

There was another impediment to Henry's marriage plans, however. Since Catherine was Anne Boleyn's cousin, marriage to Catherine was technically incest. The Archbishop of Canterbury, Thomas Cramner, quickly arranged a dispensation and the marriage went ahead. Catherine was already pregnant, but who was the father? Henry was fat, 50 and sick, and his waist had swelled out to a massive 54 inches. Nineteen-year-old Catherine had already shown her preference for younger, slimmer men.

Henry's court was soon packed with Catherine's adolescent playmates, including Joan Bulmer and Katherine Tylney. But, unfortunately, one of them had been overlooked. Her name was Mary Lassels. She had been one of the gentlewomen in the service of the Duchess of Norfolk, who had shared Catherine's communal bedroom at Norfolk House and had witnessed Catherine's youthful indiscretions. Egged on by her brother, a

Protestant who sought to end the influence of the Catholic Howard family, Mary spilt the beans to the Archbishop of Canterbury, Thomas Cramner.

Under torture, both Francis Dereham and Henry Manox admitted their sexual encounters with Catherine. Although he denied that he had known Catherine 'carnally', Manox admitted making advances to her in the small sacristy behind the altar in the Duchess's chapel. Both had ceased any sexual involvement with Catherine before she was married. However, it was revealed that Thomas Culpepper, a Gentleman of the King's Privy Chamber, had succeeded Henry in Catherine's affections.

Culpepper was one of Henry's favourites. According to the French ambassador, as a youth, Culpepper had shared the King's bed. Plainly, the Frenchman added mischievously, he 'wished to share the Queen's bed too'.

It was not the first time that Culpepper had been in trouble. Previously, he had raped the wife of a park-keeper in a secluded thicket, while three or four of his servants held her down. Henry had pardoned him for that offence. This time he showed no mercy.

Stretched on the rack, Culpepper claimed that Catherine's attendant, Lady Jane Rochford – who had given such eloquent testimony against Anne Boleyn – had 'provoked' him into a liaison. But even under torture, he continued to deny that he had ever enjoyed full carnal knowledge of the Queen. When questioned, Catherine also accused Lady Rochford of encouraging her to flirt and, like Culpepper, denied actual intercourse. Meanwhile, Lady Rochford condemned them both as adulterous, while simultaneously maintaining that she had no knowledge of the affair. Soon, the dungeons of the Tower of London were so full that the royal apartments had to be turned into a jail to accommodate the new influx of prisoners.

The trial was a juicy affair. It was Katherine Tylney's evidence that tipped the scales. She said that the Queen often strayed out of her chambers at night and ran up the stairs to Culpepper's room, where she stayed until two in the morning.

Dereham and Culpepper were both convicted of treason at the Guildhall and sentenced to be hanged, drawn and quartered. Both appealed for mercy. Culpepper's sentence was commuted to beheading. In Henry's eyes, Culpepper's had been the lesser crime. Dereham, on the other hand, had besmirched his bride by taking her precious virginity. He had to pay the full barbaric forfeit. Afterwards, both their heads were fixed on poles on London Bridge, where they were still to be seen, stripped of their flesh, four years later.

Catherine was stripped of her royal titles for a 'carnal copulation' with Dereham. She was indicted for having led 'a voluptuous and vicious life' and acting 'like a common harlot with divers people... while maintaining the outward appearance of chastity'.

On 13 February 1542, Catherine was beheaded on Tower Green, where her cousin Anne Boleyn had met her end six years before. She was followed to the scaffold by the conniving Lady Rochford, who was beheaded while the block was still wet with her mistress's blood.

News of the scandal spread far and wide. When the King of France heard about it, he was greatly amused by Catherine's misconduct. 'She hath done a wondrous naughty,' he declared. And he seized the opportunity to send Henry a sarcastic sermon on the 'lightness of women'.

It did no good. Henry had still not tired of the opposite sex. After Catherine's execution he attended a great supper with 26 women on his table and another 35 on a table nearby. One in particular caught his eye – Anne Basset, who had presumably now removed her 'chests'. She was 'a pretty young thing with enough wit to do as badly as the others if she were to try,' the French ambassador said.

But women were now getting a bit wary of Henry, in case Henry 'after receiving them to his bed should declare them no maid'. They shunned him. Soon he was so desperate he even considered taking Anne of Cleves back.

Instead, he turned to a woman whose virginity was not a question – the twice-widowed Catherine Parr. At 17, she had been married to a madman who had died in 1532. Then she had married Lord Latimer, who was a good 20 years her senior and only two years younger than Henry. For the 10 years of their marriage, Lord Latimer had been an invalid. While he was on his deathbed, she had fallen passionately in love with Thomas Seymour, Jane Seymour's dashing but unscrupulous brother. But Henry was already showing an interest.

Although her affections lay elsewhere, Catherine could not disobey the King and on 12 July 1543, she became Henry's sixth and final wife. It was clear that he had given up the idea of siring more heirs and Catherine was more of a companion than a bed mate. After four years of marriage, Henry died and Catherine married her sweetheart, Thomas Seymour, even though in the meantime he had proposed to both of Henry's daughters, Mary and Elizabeth, and to Anne of Cleves. Soon, Catherine fell pregnant and, while she was carrying the child, Seymour sought diversions elsewhere – notably with Catherine's stepdaughters, Princess Elizabeth and Lady Jane Grey.

Henry VIII has gone down in history as an oddity – a monarch who may have had more wives than mistresses. He was married six times. That remains a record for a King of England, but it is a pathetic score compared to the likes of Elizabeth Taylor and Zsa Zsa Gabor.

## 14 ❖ Camelot, It's Not

Even before the prodigious Henry VIII, the English royals have been mired in scandal. Just think about King Arthur. The tranquillity of the fabled Camelot was destroyed when one of the Knights of the Round Table, Sir Lancelot, had an illicit affair with Arthur's wife, Guinevere.

But there was a worse scandal to come. King Arthur was killed by Mordred, the son of his incestuous union with his sister, the enchantress Morgan le Fay.

King Ida, who reigned from AD 547 to 559, had 12 bastard sons. Ethelfrith, who died in 616, had five and Oswiu, who died in 670, just the one. Apparently, illegitimate daughters did not count in those days. That was changed in 786, when it was proposed that all children 'begotten by adultery or incest' should be allowed to succeed to the throne.

This admonition was obviously taken to heart by King Ethelbald, whose scandalous reign was condemned by St Boniface in 746 for being 'governed by lust'. It did no good. Ethelbald, King of the West Saxons from 858 to 860, married his own stepmother in order to maintain the alliance his father had forged with the Franks.

Ethelred the Unready, who reigned from 978 to 1016, was illegitimate. His mother, the concubine Aelgifu, is supposedly the mother of two other kings. There may, however, be some confusion over names. Ethelred's son, King Canute, who reigned from 1016 to 1035, was also supposed to be the son of Aelgifu. And, while trying to hold back the sea, Canute took time off to dally with a mistress named Aelgifu. Now she is not necessarily the same woman as the one who slept with his father and grandfather – though if we look at the case of Madame d'Elitz who bedded George I, George II and Frederick, Prince of Wales, we see that such things can happen in royal circles. But if it was the same Aelgifu, then she was clearly going for the record, because King Canute's son, Harold Harefoot, who reigned from 1035 to 1040, also had a mistress called Aelgifu!

Mindful of such things, Edward the Confessor was a pious man. This brought him – as well as a frustrated wife – canonization. He was succeeded by Harold of Wessex, who was trounced by a more scandalous candidate to the throne at the Battle of Hastings in 1066. Although the victor is known reverently in England as William the Conqueror, in France he is known as William the Bastard.

His father, Robert of Normandy, was a noted bisexual who one day spotted a strapping peasant girl called Helve, washing her clothes in a stream. He seized her and took her back to his castle. During her captivity, she bore him two children. Then, when he released her, she married Baron Heliun, the Vicomte of Conteville.

Robert of Normandy died leaving no legitimate heir, so William went to war with the other Dukes of Normandy to claim his birthright. This meant, by the time he came up against Harold, he was a seasoned campaigner.

Henry I, who reigned from 1100 to 1135, had 20 illegitimate children, but only one legitimate son, who died while trying to save his illegitimate half-sister, Maud, from drowning. Another illegitimate half-sister, Matilda, took his place on the throne.

Henry II's reign, 1154-1189, was marked by the murder of Thomas à Becket in Canterbury Cathedral. It is thought that Henry ordered the murder, although he claimed that when he said the immortal words, 'Who will rid me of this turbulent priest' – he was just thinking out loud.

However, Henry II was also involved in a sex scandal when he fell for the 'Fair Rosamund'. His wife, Eleanor of Aquitaine, was outraged at this, although she had a chequered past of her own. Her first husband had been Louis VII of France, but she had divorced him when she discovered that his love for his knights during their excursions on the crusades was not always platonic. Eleanor urged their two sons, Richard and John, to rise up against Henry, but they were defeated and Eleanor spent the rest of her days in jail.

Towards the end of his life, Edward III, who reigned from 1327 to 1377, took a mistress. This must have been something as a shock to the nation since Edward had an enduring marriage to Philippa of Hainault, whom he had wed in 1328 when he was 16 and she was 14.

His mistress was one Alice Perrers, a tiler's daughter from Essex. When the King became senile, she seized the opportunity to make herself a wealthy woman. She had already amassed more wealth than the Queen, when Parliament stepped in and banished her. Nevertheless, she managed to slip back into the country to throw herself weeping on the dead Edward's corpse – only to steal the rings from his fingers.

Richard II, who reigned from 1377 to 1399, married twice but had no children. He was gay and the opulence of his court led to the Peasants' Revolt in 1381. He foolishly legitimized the bastard sons of John of Gaunt, who turned against him, starting the Wars of the Roses. Richard was deposed, arrested and murdered in jail.

His successor, John of Gaunt's son Henry IV, the 'usurper' who reigned from 1399 to 1413, was a scandalous lecher. He was married twice, and it was said 'no woman was there anywhere... but he would importunely pursue his appetite and have her'. His son, Henry V, was the great warrior king who beat the French at the Battle of Agincourt in 1415. He was also said to have 'fervently followed the service of Venus as well as of Mars'.

Henry V's son, Henry VI, was more prudish, however. When a troupe of half-naked dancing girls were laid on to entertain him, he ran from the room crying 'Fy, fy, for shame'. This may have been because he was impotent. When his wife, Margaret of Anjou, announced that she was pregnant, he fainted. The court gossip was that the child's father was the Duke of Somerset, and the scandal surrounding his parentage helped Edward IV to seize the throne.

According to contemporary reports, Edward was 'licentious in the extreme'. He was not a very choosy lover. It was said: 'He pursued with no discrimination the married and the unmarried, the noble and the lowly.' However, he handed his women on to other courtiers once he had finished with them, often against their will. This was considered 'most insolent', but in his favour it was said that 'He took none by force' – not for want of trying. He tried to rape the widowed Elizabeth Woodville at knife point. She still refused him, saying she would rather die than give in. So he married her and they had seven children. Meanwhile, he took three new mistresses, who were said to be the 'merriest', the 'wiliest' and the 'holiest' in the land. The merriest, Jane Shore, was a great beauty.

'Nothing about her body you would have change,' wrote the saintly Thomas More. She herself was far from saintly. Her first marriage was annulled on the grounds of her husband's impotence and, when Edward died, she took up with his stepson, the Earl of Dorset.

Twelve-year-old Edward V succeeded his father in April 1483. His uncle, Richard, Duke of Gloucester, who was already thought to have been responsible for the deaths of Henry VI, his son Prince Edward and his own brother the Duke of Clarence, took the boy from his family to the Tower of London, which was then a royal palace. Edward's brother, Richard, Duke of York, was brought to join him. The two children disappeared, presumed murdered by Gloucester who seized the throne as Richard III. In 1674, when alterations were being made to the Tower, the skeletons of the two children were found. They were taken to Westminster Abbey where they were buried. Shakespeare painted Richard as one of the blackest villains of all time. But then Shakespeare was writing in Tudor times.

Still, mired in scandalous allegations surrounding the disappearance of the princes in the Tower was not the most auspicious way to begin a reign. But worse was to follow. One of the first victims of his regime was Lord Hastings. He was reputedly killed in the arms of the lovely Jane Shore who was still around. She was tried for immorality. This was somewhat hypocritical as Richard had fathered seven illegitimate children himself, perhaps indicating that he was not the ugly hunchback portrayed by Shakespeare. Jane's punishment was to walk through the streets of London barefoot, wearing only a white sheet. She was then imprisoned in Newgate. After that, her fortunes revived and she married Sir Thomas Lynom, Commissioner of the Welsh Marches.

After two years on the throne, Richard III paid for his usurpation with his life when he lost the Battle of Bosworth Field to Henry, who reigned as Henry VII. Jane Shore died in poverty in London. Sir Thomas More said that there was a moral to be drawn here. But since Jane had survived the reigns of Edward IV, Edward V, Richard III and 14 years into the reign of Henry VII, one can only wonder at what that moral might be.

## 15 ❖ The Raving Romanovs

It is not only British royals, however, who misbehave. Indeed, the most famous of all scandalous royals was Catherine the Great, who ruled Russia from 1762 to 1796.

From an early age, the German-born Catherine was a very sensual woman. She would lie in bed at night and masturbate with her pillow between her legs. At 16 she was married to her 17-year-old cousin, Peter, the German-born grandson of Peter the Great and heir to the throne of Russia. However, the marriage bed did not hold all the delights Catherine longed for. Peter was an alcoholic, impotent and feeble-minded. For him, bed was where you played with your toys.

For six years, Catherine contented herself with horse riding and voracious reading. But the Empress Elizabeth, Peter's aunt who was Russia's reigning monarch, wanted her to have children to continue the Romanov line. So, on an out-of-the-way island in the Baltic, Elizabeth arranged for Catherine, who was still a virgin, to be left alone with Sergei Saltykov, a Russian nobleman and accomplished womanizer.

After one night with Saltykov, Catherine could not get enough sex. Two miscarriages occurred in rapid succession. Then she went to term with

Paul, who was whisked away by Elizabeth and presented to the Russian people as heir to the throne.

Soon after, Catherine's husband Peter underwent an operation, which corrected a malformation of his penis and left him potent. He began taking a string of mistresses. However, he does not seem to have had sex with his wife, who by this time had had a second child by a young Polish nobleman named Count Stanislas Poniatowski.

'I do not know how it is my wife becomes pregnant,' Peter said.

He soon found out when he caught Count Poniatowski leaving their country home in disguise. He accused the Count of sleeping with his wife. Naturally, Poniatowski denied it. Peter then had Catherine dragged out of bed. She and Poniatowski were then forced to have supper with Peter and his latest mistress. Afterwards, Poniatowski was sent back to Poland in disgrace.

Catherine replaced him with an officer in the Horse Guards, Count Grigori Orlov, who soon got her pregnant. She managed to conceal her belly under the huge hooped dresses then in fashion. When she felt the child coming, one of her servants set his own house on fire to distract Peter, who never could resist a good fire. She had three children with Orlov. But they were always farmed out to servants as soon as they were born and only introduced to the royal nursery once no one could really be sure who they belonged to.

Catherine's infidelity drove Peter crazy and, when he came to the throne in 1761, he was determined to divorce her. But Peter was deeply unpopular. He made no effort to conceal his hatred of Russia and his love of all things German. Worse still, he worshipped Frederick II of Prussia with whom Russia was then at war. After just six months on the throne, Peter concluded a peace treaty with Frederick and was planning a disastrous war against Denmark.

Although Catherine had been born in Germany, too, she was much more popular than her husband. Dressed in a lieutenant's uniform, she rode to St Petersburg where Count Orlov was stationed. With the army behind her, she proclaimed herself Empress in Kazan Cathedral. Peter was arrested. He abdicated, but was murdered anyway eight days later by Orlov's brother, Aleksei.

Once on the throne, Catherine refused to marry Orlov, preferring to preserve the Romanov dynasty. He got his own back by seducing every attractive woman who came to court. He became a political liability when he bungled peace negotiations with the Turks. He capped that by seducing Catherine's 13-year-old cousin. Catherine kicked him out of court and he died mad, haunted by the ghost of the murdered Emperor Peter.

Catherine had already met the cavalry officer, Prince Grigori Potemkin. They had fallen instantly in love. This had so infuriated Orlov's brother that he beat Potemkin so hard that he had lost an eye. When Catherine's affair with Orlov ended, she planned to replace him with Potemkin but, after swearing his loyalty, Potemkin retired to a monastery. He refused to return to court until Catherine had sent away all her other favourites.

For two years they had an intense affair. The 35-year-old Potemkin loved to frolic in the royal sauna with the 43-year-old Catherine. However, these activities gave him an enormous appetite. He put on weight which turned the Empress off. However, Potemkin retained his position at court by selecting young men for her pleasure.

Although Potemkin was referred to as 'husband' by Catherine, he hand-picked handsome cavalry officers in their 20s for her. Candidates were first examined by Catherine's personal physician for symptoms of syphilis. Then their virility was tested by one of Catherine's ladies-in-waiting. When Ivan Rimsky-Korsakov, the grandfather of the composer, returned to Countess Bruce for extra tests, she was sacked and a more elderly virility tester was employed.

At least 13 officers passed this exhaustive selection procedure. News spread across Europe, and when Casanova heard of it he set off for Russia. But he was not even considered and contented himself by exchanging

**Catherine II, Empress of Russia**

'tokens of the tenderest friendship', swearing 'eternal love' to the beautiful and androgynous Lieutenant Lunin.

Aleksandr Dmitriev-Mamonov had to be excused duty, despite having passed the tests with flying colours. He had made one of the ladies of the court pregnant and had to marry her. This sent Catherine into a sulk, but she still favoured them with an expensive wedding present.

Those who had successfully passed through all the hoops were installed in special apartments below Catherine's, connected to hers by a private staircase. One thousand roubles would be waiting for them there. If a candidate proved satisfactory and a repeat performance was required, the 'emperor of the night' would be promoted to the rank of adjutant-general and given a salary of 12,000 roubles a month, plus expenses. One of her lovers said that they considered themselves 'kept girls'. When she was finished with a lover, he would receive a handsome golden handshake which in one case amounted to an estate with 4,000 serfs. This was a bit heavy on the public purse, but no one complained. Catherine was an autocrat.

Catherine continued this way until she was 60. Then she fell in love with 22-year-old Platon Zubov. This put Potemkin's nose out of joint as the ambitious Zubov became a rival for power.

The myth has come down that Catherine died when she declared that no man could satisfy her and she tried sex with a horse. The horse, it was said, was lowered on to her by crane. The crane broke and she was crushed to death. There is, however, no evidence to support this scandalous tale. She died at the age of 67, two days after suffering a massive stroke. No equine involvement was suspected.

CATHERINE the Great was succeeded by her son, Paul, who it seems suffered a mental illness. He was fearful of his mother and, during her reign, built up his own private army. Even after his own coronation in 1796, his paranoia did not disappear. He cut Russia off from the rest of the world, preventing citizens travelling abroad and banning all foreign music and books. Even the wearing of French hats, boots or coats was outlawed.

Failing to kneel before the tsar's palaces, even if you were on horseback or in a carriage, was an offence punishable by banishment. By the end of his reign, the suspicion of harbouring 'nefarious thoughts' led to a long term in Siberia. Four years after taking the throne, he was murdered by his courtiers, and his son, Alexander, who was one of the conspirators, was installed in his place.

THE last of the Romanov tsars, Nicholas II, was happily married to Queen

Victoria's favourite granddaughter, Princess Alix of Hesse. She had already turned down a proposal from the future Edward VII's son, Prince Eddy, heir to the British throne, as she had been madly in love with Nicholas since she first saw him when she was 12. With Victoria's blessing, Alix changed her name to Alexandra when she went to Russia to marry her tsar.

Their marriage was blissful until they discovered that the tsarevich, their eldest son Alexsei, was a haemophiliac. In their desperation, they turned to a strolling Siberian priest named Rasputin, who brought scandal to the Romanovs by trading his seemingly magical powers over the tsarevich's condition for political influence.

Rasputin was a pretty scandalous character from his beginnings in the Siberian village of Pokrovskoye. He was born Grigory Yefimovich Novykh in about 1872, only becoming Rasputin later – the name means 'the debauched one' in Russian. It was not wholly his fault. The local children would bathe naked in the pond and the young girls of the village apparently quickly picked him out for special attention because of his 13-inch penis. A further initiation into the world of sex came at the hands of Irina Danilov Kubasova, the pretty wife of a Russian general. She lured him into her bedroom where she and six of her maids seduced him.

After that, he joined a sect of flagellants named the Khlist, who believed that true mortification of the flesh came through sexual exhaustion. At 20, he married the long-suffering Praskovia Feodorovna who gave him four children. However, he was soon expelled from his village by a respectable priest and he took to the road with his wife and Dunia Bekyeshova, one of Irina Danilov Kubasova's maids who became his lifelong mistress. Together they wandered around Russia with Rasputin initiating hordes of other women into the rites of the Khlist in unrestrained orgies. His wife was not fazed by his numerous mistresses.

'He has enough to go around,' she said.

His doctrine of redemption through sexual release attracted numerous respectable guilt-ridden women, allowing many converts to enjoy sex for the first time. His unkempt appearance and peasant manners added to his attraction as a 'holy satyr'. As his biographer, Robert Massie, said: 'Making love to the unwashed peasant with his dirty beard and filthy hands was a new and thrilling sensation.' In fact, many of his lovers dowsed themselves in perfume beforehand as his body odour was so powerful.

By the time he reached St Petersburg, he had a powerful reputation as a mystic, a healer and a clairvoyant. In 1905, he was introduced at court. Soon after, he was called on to tend the tsarevich. It was found that he could successfully ease the child's condition – perhaps due to hypnosis.

While Rasputin remained a paragon of chastity and humility at court, outside he continued his scandalous ways. Women gathered in his apartment, eager for an invitation to visit his bedroom or the 'holy of holies' as he called it. Usually, he would be found in the dining room, surrounded by female disciples who took turns to sit on his lap while he instructed them on the mysteries of the resurrection. On one occasion, he gave a graphic description of the sex life of horses, then grabbed one of his distinguished guests by the hair and pulled her towards his bedroom, saying: 'Come, my lovely mare.'

He would often sing and they would dance wildly, collapsing in a swoon or being taken into the 'holy of holies' for a personal glimpse of paradise. One disciple, an opera singer, was so devoted to him that she would phone him to sing him his favourite songs. Attendance at his gatherings became so fashionable that cuckolded husbands would boast that their wives belonged to Rasputin.

People who tried to convey details of this scandalous behaviour to the Tsar's ears found themselves banished. But in 1911, Nicholas could ignore the rumours no longer when his prime minister drew up a long bill of Rasputin's offences. The Tsar expelled Rasputin from court, but he was soon recalled by the Tsarina, who feared for her son's life.

During World War I, Tsar Nicholas took personal command of his troops, leaving all other government business in the hands of the Tsarina and her personal adviser, Rasputin, who began making disastrous appointments. Rasputin also meddled in military affairs to catastrophic effect. To save Russia from his malign influence, several attempts were made on Rasputin's life.

His enemies were finally successful on 30 December 1916. A gang of conservative noblemen fed him poisoned cake and wine. As he fell into a coma, one of the assassins, Prince Felix Yussupov, a homosexual who had been rebuffed by Rasputin several times, took this opportunity to sexually abuse him. Then he shot him four times. While Rasputin was still alive, a second assassin pulled out a knife and castrated him, throwing his severed penis across the room. It was recovered later by a servant who gave it to a maid. (In 1968, she was still alive, living in Paris, and possessed a polished wooden box in which she kept what looked like 'a blackened, overripe banana, about a foot long'.) Rasputin was then tied up and thrown into the icy Neva river, where he finally drowned.

His assassination redoubled Alexandra's belief in autocracy. She cracked down hard on the Russian people, but within weeks of the death of the mad monk, the Romanovs were swept from power by the Russian Revolution.

# 16 ❖ Scandinavian Scandals

As well as getting on with it themselves, the British Royal Family have also been good at exporting scandal. A case in point was George III's sister, Princess Caroline Matilda, who was married at the age of 15 to King Christian VII of Denmark. Once ensconced in Copenhagen, she discovered that her husband was debauched and slowly going around the bend. So she took a lover and caused such a scandal that she had to be rescued by the Royal Navy.

It is not surprising that Christian went mad when you consider his upbringing. He was born in 1749. His father, Frederick the Good, was an alcoholic and incoherently drunk throughout most of his reign. Christian's mother, Queen Louisa who was a daughter of Britain's George II, died when he was three. Frederick married again, but his wife, Princess Juliana Maria of Brunswick-Wolfenbüttel, loathed her stepson. This was counterbalanced somewhat by Frederick who doted on the child, but only when he was sober enough to recognize him.

A fearsome martinet, Count Reventlow, was appointed as his tutor. He beat the boy unmercifully. Christian's one ambition was to finish his schooling so that he could travel around Europe and be as debauched as all the other crowned princes. He almost made it, but his father drank himself into an early grave when Christian was just 17.

Ruefully, he took up the reins of state. His first act as King was to appoint Count Reventlow as his Chamberlain. By that time he had become emotionally dependent on his tormentor.

Frederick the Good had already set up the marriage with Princess Caroline Matilda. Christian liked her portrait well enough, but he was in no hurry to marry. He was keen to sow a few wild oats. But when he started chasing ladies-in-waiting and chambermaids, his courtiers took fright. They were afraid that Christian might go off the rails like his father.

They sent for Princess Caroline Matilda. When Christian saw her in the flesh, he was impressed. She had a pretty face and an inviting figure, and he quickly forgot his objections to marriage.

But even though he had a queen, he was a king and he thought he should spread himself around a bit among his subjects. He and a few close friends began enjoying nights on the tiles in Copenhagen, when not a few

**George III**

pretty young women felt obliged to do their patriotic duty and give their all for king and country.

As well as indulging in wild bouts of womanizing, Christian began to drink heavily. He scandalized Denmark with his relationship with a notorious prostitute who worked under the name 'Milady'. The king would ditch his royal regalia and go out on the town with Milady. During their drunken sprees Christian liked to indulge himself in senseless vandalism and would hurl the grossest insults at anyone who tried to stop him. On more than one occasion he was beaten up. One night he and Milady wrecked a rival brothel; on another, he was pursued by a baying mob to the gates of the palace.

Things got worse when Christian furnished Milady with a mansion and created her Baroness. Something had to be done, so the courtiers forced the King to banish her to Hamburg, where she was kept under guard.

That put an end to one scandal, but those in the inner circles of court feared that another, worse one was about to follow. Christian had learnt Reventlow's lessons too well. Ugly rumours were now in circulation that the King was paying pageboys to beat him; whoever beat him the hardest got the most money. In one bizarre rite, Christian submitted himself to being 'broken on the wheel' with a royal favourite dressed as an executioner standing beside him reading his death warrant.

There was just one thing to be done. The King had to be sent abroad. His ministers thought he might sate himself discreetly in the courts of Europe, while they got on with the business of government. To keep an eye on Christian, they sent with him a Dr Johann Struensee as his personal physician.

To ensure the maximum discretion – and the maximum fun – Christian travelled under a number of pseudonyms. His first stop was Germany, then he moved on through the low countries to Calais, where the royal yacht was waiting to carry him to England.

The moralistic George III did not fully grasp the purpose of the trip. As Christian travelled from Dover to London, George laid on a reception at Canterbury hosted by the Archbishop. Christian remarked that the last time a Danish king had entered Canterbury he had burnt it to the ground.

In London, Christian adopted the pseudonym Mr Frederickson and set about bedding as many whores as he could. In the 18th century, London was full of prostitutes and a man could get anything he wanted for a few pence. Mr Frederickson would dangle purses full of bright golden guineas in front of them. There was no way Struensee could restrain him.

The Dowager Princess of Wales, Caroline Matilda's mother, was shocked. So was George III. After a hugely expensive two-month orgy in London, George and Struensee persuaded Christian to leave.

Next stop was Paris, where Christian threw himself into another round of sexual excess. But it was soon clear that the exertion was telling on his health, particularly his mental health.

After six months on the road, Struensee managed to pry him away from the pleasures of Paris. When Christian returned home he seemed a changed man. He held himself with more dignity and bearing and he was kind and considerate to the Queen. His ministers were relieved that the rest cure had worked.

It did not last long. Under the influence of his old friends, he began drinking and womanizing again. But this time it was worse. He refused to attend to any matters of state and it was clear that he was slipping into idiocy.

Struensee saw his chance. He managed to persuade his mistress, Madame de Gabell, to seduce Christian. That way, he thought, he would be able to control the King. Unfortunately, Madame de Gabell was a moral woman. The ethical dilemma that this arrangement put her in was too much for her and she died.

Cursing his luck, Struensee suddenly spotted a better opportunity. He seduced Queen Caroline Matilda. Together with the Queen Mother, they relieved Christian of the bothersome business of government, leaving him free to give himself up to his pleasures full-time.

All went swimmingly, until Caroline Matilda started appearing in public dressed in men's clothing. Tongues began wagging as to who was wearing the pants in the royal household. But it was Struensee who made the fatal mistake. Unusually for a usurper, he was basically a modern liberal. He instituted much-needed municipal and judicial reform, but foolishly he also established freedom of the press. The first thing the papers started printing was stories about the scandal in the palace.

The Dowager Princess of Wales, Caroline Matilda's mother, arrived in Copenhagen and tried to persuade her daughter to flee to England. Caroline Matilda pretended that she did not speak English and refused. The Dowager Princess left empty-handed.

As the scandal grew, Denmark became dangerously politically unstable. The nobility, particularly, objected to Struensee, a humble doctor, setting himself up as a backroom monarch. But the Queen Mother knew which side her bread was buttered on. One night in January 1772, while Struensee and Caroline Matilda were out dancing, Juliana Maria went to see Christian. She persuaded him that his wife and Struensee planned to kill him and got the feeble-minded King to sign a warrant for their arrest.

They were seized and Struensee was tortured to death. Caroline Matilda was tried for adultery and found guilty. Her marriage was annulled and she was imprisoned. George III sent a British fleet to rescue her. Fearful of letting the scandal reach the shores of Britain, the already unpopular King George had her taken to Hanover, where she died three years later, at the age of 23.

Christian ruled, in name at least, for another 16 years, first as the puppet of the Queen Mother, Juliana Maria. Then, after 10 years of her less-than-benevolent rule, Christian's teenage son, Frederick, staged a palace coup and installed himself as Regent.

NOT that the Scandinavians were not up to creating royal scandals of their own. In the 17th century, Sweden produced the brilliant and vivacious Queen Christina, who liked to wear men's clothes, refused to marry, gave up the throne and gallivanted around Europe getting into all manner of trouble.

When she was born on 8 December 1626, she was so hairy and cried in such a deep voice that her father King Gustavus was told that she was a boy. Gustavus was killed in battle in 1632 when Christina was six. Her mother withdrew to a room hung in black and slept with Gustavus's shroud at her side, under a gold casket containing his heart. This left the young monarch in the hands of five regents and surrounded by male courtiers, who supervised her education. She had no opportunity to develop an interest in feminine pursuits and instead loved to hunt reindeer on horseback in the snow. She rode at such a pace that no one could keep up with her, and she would often stay out in the biting cold for up to 10 hours at a time.

At the age of 18, she took the oath as King of Sweden. There had never been a reigning Queen before. She quickly mastered the art of statesmanship. She also had a great thirst for knowledge. Sleeping only four hours a night, she spent little time on her toilette and dressed in Hungarian riding outfits of a distinctly masculine cut.

Christina developed a passion for her lady-in-waiting, the beautiful Ebba Sparre, but she married Count Jacob de la Gardie, leaving Christina seething with jealousy. Just when everyone had concluded that she was a lesbian, Christina fell in love with the Count's brother. She heaped honours on him and everyone assumed they were lovers. Eventually, however, she sent him away.

Other suitable suitors were suggested, but Christina fell out with her government over her refusal to marry.

'Marriage would entail many things to which I cannot become accustomed,' she told them. 'I really cannot say when I will overcome this inhibition.'

To make things worse, she was planning to convert to Catholicism. The French, she had concluded, had much more fun than dour Scandinavian Protestants. To that end, she abdicated in favour of her cousin who became Charles X. The abdication did not just take the form of signing a legal document resigning the position of monarch. There was a bizarre ceremony where she was stripped of her coronation robe and royal insignia. Then she had to lift the crown from her own head.

Christina had already stripped the palace in Stockholm of its furniture, which she had sent to Rome where she intended to settle. She set off via Denmark, dressed as a man and calling herself Count Dohna. In tow was the lovely Ebba Sparre. In Brussels, Christina declared herself a Catholic and threw herself into a round of parties. The scandal sheets happily chronicled her sexual misadventures, which grew so outrageous that she was dubbed the 'Queen of Sodom', and the Swedish government threatened to cut off her pension.

In 1655, Christina was welcomed in Rome by Pope Alexander VII as a prize convert. But Christina soon became an embarrassment. She had converted for fun, not piety. She made fun of the Church's holy relics and spoke to her friends in a loud voice during Mass.

Settling in the Palazzo Farnese, she hung the walls with extremely indelicate pictures and had the fig leaves removed from all the statues. She introduced Ebba as her 'bedfellow' and told everyone that her mind was as beautiful as her body.

However, in the evenings, Christina would change out of men's clothing and into more alluring attire to entertain leading churchmen. Cardinal Colonna fell in love with her and the Pope had to send him away from Rome to avoid a public scandal. Christina herself was in love with Cardinal Azzolino, although the two of them managed to be more discreet.

She began dabbling in politics, which quickly made her unpopular, so she quit Rome for France where she received a royal welcome. She stayed at Fontainebleau with her two Italian courtiers, the Marquis Monaldesco, her chief equerry, and Count Santinelli, captain of her guard. The two men loathed each other and vied with each other for the favour of the Queen.

Monaldesco had discovered that Santinelli had swindled Christina over a property deal in Rome. To bring this to her attention, he forged a series of letters, which also made references to her affair with Cardinal Azzolino and her intention of taking the throne of Naples.

However, Christina recognized his handwriting and summoned Monaldesco. She asked him what he thought the punishment for treachery should be. Thinking that she had been convinced by the forgeries and that the forfeit would be paid by Santinelli, he said 'Death'.

She agreed. On 10 November 1657, Monaldesco was summoned to the Galerie de Cerfs in Fontaineblcau and asked to read the letters. As he did so, he found the door barred behind him. Santinelli and two guards entered with daggers in their hands. Realizing he had been rumbled, Monaldesco threw himself to his knees and begged Christina for mercy. She merely asked Father Lebel, a prior who had been summoned from the nearby Mathurin Monastery, to prepare Monaldesco for his death. Lebel also begged her to show mercy, as did Santinelli. He said that the case should be taken before the Royal Courts of France. Christina refused and told him to make haste and do his duty, as she strode from the gallery. For the next 15 minutes, she heard Monaldesco's screams as they hacked him to death.

The French were appalled at what they saw as an act of barbarity. Christina's host, Cardinal Mazarin, advised her to make herself scarce so she fled back to Rome. She was little more popular there and the Pope asked her to live outside the Papal See. As a sweetener, he offered her an annuity and an adviser to oversee her financial affairs – one Cardinal Azzolino.

Meanwhile, a woman named Gyldener was passing herself off as Christina in Sweden. She got away with it for several months. When she was unmasked as a fraud, Christina demanded that she be put to death. Charles X was more merciful and jailed her for a month on a ration of bread and water.

As if Queen Christina had not caused enough royal scandals, she now decided to interfere in European politics. First, she called for the Christian nations to unite to smash Turkey. Then she called on France to help her drive the Spanish out of Sicily, as part of her plan to seize the throne of Naples. Nobody took any notice.

Then Charles X died and Christina thought it was time to return to Sweden. When she reached Hamburg, she received a letter making it plain that she was not welcome in her homeland. She took no notice. In Stockholm, the government had no option but to greet her with due respect and house her in the royal apartments. They even allowed her to use one of the royal estates. But when the locals complained that she was celebrating Mass there, the government had to ask her to leave.

Christina spent the rest of her life wandering aimlessly around Europe, growing fat, unpleasant and eccentric. She put herself up for the vacant throne of Poland but, reviewing her CV, the people of Poland chose the Duke of Lithuania for their monarch instead.

As her health began to fail, she returned to Rome where she died on 19 April 1689, with her faithful Cardinal Azzolino by her side.

# 17 ❖ Here Comes the Sun

The reputation for debauchery of Louis XIV of France, the Sun King, was despised and envied across the whole of Europe. However, he was not quite as bad as he was made out to be. Instead of exploiting any extramarital opportunity that presented itself, he practised serial adultery, maintaining one favourite at a time whom he replaced when his passion waned.

When he came to the throne in 1661, Louis XIV was married to the Infanta Maria Theresa, the daughter of Philip IV of Spain. Although the marriage was contracted in order to shore up a peace treaty between the two countries, Maria Theresa was deeply in love with her husband, which was a shame. She was short and swarthy and Louis found her dull in the extreme, preferring hunting, gambling and even the business of government to her company.

He began his reign with an affair with his sister-in-law, which was so scandalous that it almost brought down the monarchy. Then her turned to her lady-in-waiting, Louise de la Baume-Leblac, whom he created Duchess de la Vallière. She was the first of four long-term mistresses who bore him 12 illegitimate children in all.

La Vallière produced four. It was only then that the magnetic effect she had had on the king began to flag. He then fell for the beautiful Françoise Arthenais de Mortmart, Marquise de Montespan. The King was used to the routine of dropping around to the house he had bought La Vallière when he wanted sex. Being a creature of habit, he ordered de Montespan to move in with her rival. This was too much for La Vallière, who quit the court and went into a convent.

De Montespan was Louis's mistress for 12 years and produced seven children, whom Louis had legitimized. Like the offspring of Charles II in England, they formed the backbone of the aristocracy. She lost her position in the King's affections when the 18-year-old Duchesse de Fontages came to court with the specific intention of seducing the King.

De Fontages gave birth to a son who died after a month. Then she herself took ill. Poison was suspected. France was in the grip of what was known as the Age of Arsenic at the time. This had begun in 1673, when two priests told the Paris Police Commissioner, Nicholas de la Reynie, that they had heard a number of disturbing confessions from wealthy men and women. A number of them had admitted to murdering their respective husbands and wives. The priests would not break the sanctity of the confessional and name names, but de la Reynie decided to investigate the matter.

He began by trying to track down the suppliers of the 'succession powders' – so-called because they were usually used to ensure the succession of the poisoner. Suspicion fell on a fortune-teller named Marie Bosse. De la Reynie sent an undercover policewoman to consult the clairvoyant on the best way to deal with her troublesome husband. Madame Bosse sold her some arsenic and was arrested, along with her husband, her two sons and another fortune-teller named La Vigourex, who admitted sleeping with all the members of the Bosse family. A huge cache of poison was found in the Bosses' home. Facing torture, La Vigourex and the Bosse family provided a list of their clients. These included a number of prominent members of Louis XIV's court.

Plainly, this was a very delicate matter politically, but de la Reynie explained that although an investigation might embarrass a number of important courtiers, with the epidemic of poisoning that was going on, Louis might find himself the next victim. Louis set up a commission of inquiry.

Officially known as La *Commission de l'Arsenic*, it was known to those who appeared before it as *L'Affaire de la Chambre Ardente*, because de la Reynie, with theatrical flare, conducted the investigation in a room draped in black and lit solely by candlelight. In *La Chambre Ardente*, Marie Bosse and La Vigourex admitted they were part of a devil-worship cult headed by one La Voison – real name Catherine Deshayes.

Madame Deshayes was the wife of a failed haberdasher, who had set up in business making skin-cleansing treatments which, at that time, contained a lot of arsenic. Her experiments had led her to learn about chemistry and she had developed preparations that, she claimed, promoted 'inner cleanliness'.

As a sideline, Madame Deshayes worked as an astrologer. Her clients were rich and aristocratic. To lend weight to her predictions, she had developed a network of informants throughout French society. These were exclusively women and many, including La Vigourex, took pseudonyms.

As an astrologer, La Voison would predict that a woman's husband, say, was going to die suddenly. If the woman seemed pleased at the prospect, La Voison would then supply some poison to hasten the event.

The business was so profitable that La Voison could afford to pay £30,000 for a secluded house in a rundown area of Paris. It was hidden by trees and protected by a high wall. She lived there with her husband, now a successful jeweller, her 21-year-old daughter, Marie-Marguerite Montvoison, and their lodger Nicholas Levassuer – an executioner by trade.

De la Reynie put the house under surveillance. One of his agents, working undercover, overheard one of Deshayes's assistants in a bar drunkenly describing acts of devil worship. The police then picked up two people who had attended meetings at Deshayes's house.

Under interrogation, they said that Deshayes and a 66-year-old priest, L'Abbé Guibourg, regularly conducted Black Masses there. During the service, a naked woman would act as an altar table. She would lie in front of the altar with her legs splayed. The Abbé, wearing an alb with black phalluses embroidered on it, would rest the chalice and wafers on her body. He would intone the Catholic Mass with the words 'infernal lord Satan' substituted for 'God' and 'Christ'. A child would urinate in the chalice and the contents would be sprinkled over the congregation. Then the wafer would be pressed against the breasts and vulva of the woman. As he inserted a wafer into the woman's vagina, the Abbé would chant: 'Lord Satan sayeth "in rioting and drunkenness I rise again. You shall fulfil the lusts of the flesh. The works of the flesh are manifest – they are drunkenness, revelling, immodesty, fornication, luxury and witchcraft. My flesh is meat indeed."'

This was the cue for an orgy of indiscriminate sex.

The police raided Deshayes's house. In a pavilion in the garden, they found a room draped in black with an altar in it. The candles on the altar were made from the fat distilled from human flesh.

Deshayes's daughter, Marie-Marguerite, told the police that animals had been sacrificed and their blood drunk. Then, under intense questioning, she admitted that there had been human sacrifices too.

She described how, at one ceremony, the Abbé had said: 'Astaroth, Asmodeus, prince of friendship, I beg you to accept the sacrifice of this child which we now offer you.' Then Guibourg had held the child up by its feet and slit its throat. The blood had spurted into the chalice on the belly of the naked woman. The Abbé had then smeared the blood on his penis and the vagina of the woman, and had sex with her.

One of the children had been Deshayes's own goddaughter, Françoise Filastre. Others had been supplied by the inner circle of devotees or a compliant midwife. Madame Deshayes had had another sideline, as an abortionist, and had often supplied living foetuses ripped from her clients. Victims' entrails were distilled for occult use and the rest of their bodies were burnt in a stove.

It turned out that one of the worshippers was none other than the King's mistress, the Marquise de Montespan. Fearing that she was losing the King's favour to the young Duchesse de Fontages, she had attended three of the 'love masses' to try and win back his favour by acting as the nude altar table.

Catherine Deshayes and the Abbé Guibourg admitted to murdering hundreds of children over a career in Satanism that spanned 13 years. Some 150 courtiers were arrested for poisoning and sentenced to death, slavery in the French galleys or banishment. Madame Deshayes herself was burnt at the stake in 1680. However, the Marquise de Montespan returned, briefly, to favour.

She was eventually replaced – not by a ravishing beauty, but by the middle-aged governess the King had employed to bring up de Montespan's children. Her name was Madame de Maintenon and she had been born in prison. At 17, she had married the elderly poet, Paul Scarron. When he died, she was left penniless and went into a convent before being summoned to court as a governess.

Although she had once been a great beauty, the hardships of life had left her wrinkled and worn. When Queen Maria Theresa died, Louis married de Maintenon morganatically. She was the first and only one of his consorts to have any political influence over him. This proved disastrous.

She urged him to persecute France's Protestants, which led to their mass exodus and also provoked war with England, Spain, Russia, Holland and most of the rest of Europe.

THE court that Louis XIV established at Versailles was a synonym for scandal. Louis XIII had bought a hunting lodge there in 1624, buying up the entire village in 1632. When Louis XIV came to the throne in 1643 at the age of five, he found himself continually surrounded by intrigue. The solution to prevent his, he discovered in later life, was the magnificent court he built at Versailles, which employed some 22,000 architects, gardeners, craftsmen and labourers. Life there was tightly regulated, from the lever – the ceremony that attended the King getting up in the morning – to the coucher – which attended his going to bed at night. Meals were public ceremonies where courtiers had to remove their hats when speaking to or being spoken to by the King. Officers of the state, lesser royals, army officers and members of the nobility – numbering 15,000 in all – were required to attend court. With so much leisure time on their hands, the cream of society gave itself up to promiscuity and had little time to plot against the King.

Contemporary chronicler, Bussy-Rabutin, remarked: 'Debauch reigned more supremely here than anywhere else in the world. Wine-drinking and unmentionable vice were so fashionable that their evil example perverted the intentions of the virtuous, so they succumbed to the lure of viciousness.'

Even though noblewomen gave themselves freely, a lot of courtiers gave themselves up to homosexuality. This, too, was useful to the King, who could elevate lowly lovers by marrying them off to gay courtiers without running the risk that they might sleep with their husbands. Louise de la Baume-Leblac became the Duchesse de la Vallière, by marrying the notorious homosexual, the Duc de la Vallière. He once tried to seduce a visiting Italian lad named Primi Visconti by observing: 'In Spain, monks do it; in France the nobility do it; in Italy everyone does it.'

Court homosexuals formed themselves into a society, whose leaders were selected according to the size of their sexual organ. Bussy-Rabutin recorded an incident that took place in a brothel where 'they seized hold of a prostitute, tied her wrists and ankles to the bedposts, thrust a firework into the part of her body that decency forbids me to mention, and put a match to it.'

The resulting scandal meant more princes and noblemen had to be banished from court.

LOUIS XIV was succeeded by his great-grandson, Louise XV, who came to the throne at the age of five. At 15, he married the 23-year-old Princess Marie of Poland. She gave him 10 children in 10 years. Then she called an abrupt halt to their sex life, forcing the 25-year-old King to seek his pleasures elsewhere.

Louis's first scandalous liaison was with the four de Nesle sisters, who came to his bed one after another. Then, when his young mistress, the Duchesse de Châteauroux, died suddenly in 1744, came Jeanne-Antoinette Poisson, the cultivated wife of Charles-Guillaume Le Normant d'Étoiles. Madame d'Étoiles moved into rooms under the roof at Versailles and gradually became the King's firm favourite. He created her Marquise de Pompadour, although she is universally known as Madame de Pompadour because she was looked down on by the courtiers as a bourgeoise. Through her natural guile and an ability to make herself agreeable to everyone at court, she began to grow in influence. The King was shy and introverted and had trouble communicating with his courtiers. Madame de Pompadour became his private secretary and moved out of her attic into regal apartments. When she fell out of favour sexually, she maintained her influence by procuring an endless stream of other lovers for him.

She was a patron of the leading artists and architects of the day, and a friend of Voltaire's. She also acted as an agent for the Empress Maria Theresa of Austria. Madame de Pompadour's protégé, the Duc de Choiseul, reversed France's old alliances, realigning France with Austria against the German principalities and England. This led to the Seven Years War, which left France crushed in Europe and Canada in English hands. These defeats were laid at her door. This left her depressed and Madame de Pompadour died in the royal apartments soon after the end of the war in 1764.

Next Louis moved further down the social scale, taking as his mistress the illegitimate daughter of low-class parents – Jeanne Bécu, a hostess in a gambling house. She was the mistress of Jean du Barry, a Gascon nobleman. However, she could not become the king's official *maîtresse en titre* unless she was married to a nobleman. So Jean du Barry generously married her off to his brother Guillaume, the Comte du Barry. The King then moved her into apartments directly above his own in Versailles. The Comtesse du Barry then outstripped even Madame de Pompadour in extravagance. Every day, she bought new jewels and dresses, costing the French treasury the equivalent of £40 million over five years.

She also fancied herself as the equal of Madame de Pompadour in political intriguing. Although she allied herself with the faction that brought down the Duc de Choiseul, she succeeded in putting everyone's backs up – including those of Louis's heir and his chief minister. Nevertheless, thanks to Louis's dependence on her, she maintained her place at court. He only sent her away five days before his death as an act of penitence.

When Louis XVI came to the throne, he confined du Barry to a nunnery. Despite her humble origins, the Comtesse du Barry aided aristocratic émigrés after the French Revolution, was branded a counterrevolutionary and perished on the guillotine in 1793.

# 18 ❖ The Lubricious Ludwigs

Bavaria was the home of two of the greatest royal scandals of the 19th century. The first involved Lola Montez, the Spanish dancer who captivated Europe. Lola Montez wasn't actually a Spaniard at all. She was born plain Eliza Gilbert in Limerick, Ireland. When her mother tried to marry her off to a 60-year-old judge, the 18-year-old Eliza eloped with British army Captain James who was posted to India. The marriage was a disaster and her husband ran off with the wife of an adjutant. On the ship home, she met a Captain Lennox. By the time they docked in London, they were firm friends and they checked into the Imperial Hotel together. The result was the spectacular divorce case, *James v. Lennox*, reported in *The Times* of 7 December 1842.

Now penniless, Eliza decided to become an actress. She enrolled in a drama school run by Fanny Kemble, but Eliza was such an awful actress that Fanny persuaded her to try dancing instead. In June 1843, she appeared on the stage of the Haymarket Theatre in London, dressed as a flamenco dancer and calling herself Doña Lola Montez. Unfortunately, Doña Lola seemed to know few of the steps of her native Andalusia. But she had a wonderful figure, which brought her to the attention of a number of Continental impresarios. Doña Lola then toured Europe, happily bedding theatre managers to help keep her career float.

In Dresden in 1844, she met the Hungarian pianist and composer, Franz Liszt. Although initially he enjoyed her favours, he soon found that Lola was a pain. She pursued him remorselessly around Germany. More than once she turned up at Liszt's hotel and persuaded the manager to let her into his room while he was performing at a concert. He would return to find her naked in his bed. Once, he bribed a hotel porter to lock her in the room for 12 hours while he fled town.

Liszt realized that things had gone too far when she caught up with him at the gala dinner following a memorial concert in honour of Beethoven in Bonn. The guests of honour were King Friedrich Wilhelm IV and his Queen. Lola elbowed her way through the crowd, declaring that she was 'a guest of Liszt's'. Once inside, she leapt on a table, stripped off and gave an uninhibited display of her talent as a dancer. The guests were shocked and fled the banqueting hall. They got outside just in time to meet an incoming thunderstorm. The clouds opened and they all got drenched.

She then threw herself at Richard Wagner, who turned her down. But she managed to ensnare Alexandre Dumas, briefly. Another lover, a journalist named Dujarier, was killed fighting a duel over her. At the subsequent murder trial, Lola told the court that she should have taken her lover's place on the field of honour as she was a better shot.

King Ludwig I of Bavaria was blissfully ignorant of all this. He was a scholar and a poet. As a young prince, he had helped draft Bavaria's liberal constitution of 1818. When he came to the throne in 1825, he dispatched archaeologists to Greece and Italy to bring back to Bavaria the splendours of the Ancient World. Meanwhile, he became a patron of the arts, although he sent the German poet Heinrich Heine into exile after an artistic disagreement.

The conservative Austrian Foreign Minister, Metternich, had his worries about the left-leaning King Ludwig. He encouraged the Jesuits to move into Bavaria and, while Ludwig wrote his less-than-memorable verse, they turned the clock back to the Middle Ages. Despite his liberal sentiments, Ludwig did not object to this. He was a romantic and the medieval period held a gothic appeal for him. So things rubbed along well enough until 1846, when Lola Montez turned up.

She had been booked to perform at a Munich playhouse, but the theatre owner had torn up the contract when he saw her dance. Lola was determined to protest to the King, and forced her way into the palace. There was a scuffle and she burst into Ludwig's study, pursued by the royal guards.

When the King looked up from his desk, Lola pulled out a knife, slashed open the front of her dress and let the remnants fall to the ground. Ludwig was impressed – so much so that he asked the guards to leave, assuring them that he would be quite safe.

But safe he was not. Five days later, the 58-year-old Ludwig introduced the nubile young Lola to court as his personal adviser. He bought her a house in Munich and described her as his 'sultana'. Then he forced the theatre owner who had sacked her to stage a royal command performance with Lola as its star, and he created her Countess von Starhemberg.

Everything went swimmingly until Lola began to dabble in politics. She, too, was a liberal by nature. In her autobiography, Lola claimed to have single-handedly inspired the Warsaw uprising of 1830. Her story was that the Russian viceroy of Poland had conceived a violent passion for her. But she had turned him down on the grounds that he was the ruthless oppressor of the Polish people. In revenge, he had employed a claque to boo her on stage. The people of Warsaw were so outraged by this, she said, and so inspired by her gallant support against the Russian occupation, that they rose up in gratitude. Although this almost certainly bore no resemblance to the truth, she reminded Ludwig of the passions of his youth. She persuaded him to sack his Jesuit Prime Minister and to let her rule Bavaria by his side.

However, it was not the forces of conservatism in Bavaria that brought her down. She made the same mistake as the Danish liberal, Johann Struensee. She urged Ludwig to give the press its freedom. The newspapers immediately began to print the juicy details of her scandalous affair with the King. Rumour had it that he enjoyed spanking her naked bottom – or, at least, that's how cartoonists depicted the happy couple at the time.

The Jesuits pumped up the scandal by declaring that Lola was the Whore of Babylon from the Book of Revelations. In government she was temperamental, often throwing things at cabinet members when they disagreed with her. This gave the newspapers great copy. As she became increasingly unpopular among the staid citizens of Bavaria, she employed a band of young liberals to protect her. It was said that she used them as a male harem. Even her housekeeper spoke out about her frequent orgies. After two years of Lola, Bavaria was in uproar.

In 1848, there were uprisings in Berlin, Vienna, Paris, Rome, Naples, Milan, Prague and Budapest. When students barricaded the streets of Munich, Ludwig saw the writing on the wall. He banished Lola but it was not enough to save him. He was forced to abdicate in favour of his son, Maximilian II.

Lola had made off with half of the crown jewels. Back in England, she married a wealthy young guards officer, called George Heald, who was 12 years younger than her. His family were outraged. They investigated her past and the whole of the scandal came out. Undeterred, the couple went to Spain, where she quickly ran through his fortune.

She returned to London to cash in on her notoriety with the play, *Lola Montez in Bavaria*. After that, she went to America where she married a newspaperman in California. By the time she was 40, she was poverty stricken. She moved into a hostel run by the Methodists and died of syphilis at the age of 43.

AFTER the relatively scandal-free reign of Maximilian II, Ludwig I's grandson, Ludwig II, came to the throne. He fancied himself an even greater patron of the arts than his grandfather and began a scandalous association with Wagner.

At the time Wagner had met the love of his life, Cosima Liszt, the composer's daughter. She was embroiled in a messy divorce and had just had a second child for him. As usual, Wagner was penniless and, for the second time in his life, he was threatened with the debtors' prison. To escape his creditors, he fled back to Switzerland. But then he was saved by Ludwig.

On his accession, the pretty 19-year-old King summoned Wagner to Munich. The King instructed him to complete his 'Ring Cycle' and put all money worries from his mind. Wagner bowed low in gratitude. King Ludwig sank to his knees, clutched the composer and swore an oath of eternal fidelity.

Ludwig plied Wagner with expensive gifts – diamond rings, sumptuous textiles, precious ornaments, expensive furniture and, of course, paintings and busts of himself. Wagner responded with poetry, sycophantic to the point where he was in danger of committing a federal offence. In their letters, they called each other 'Beloved', 'Embodiment of my Happiness', 'Supreme Goodness', 'Source of Light in my Life', 'My One and All', 'Saviour of my Happiness' and 'Dearly Beloved Adored One'.

Naturally, Wagner hid the nature of his relationship with Cosima. Ostensibly, she was his secretary. As such, she handled their correspondence, which was passionate to the point that she grew jealous.

In Munich, Wagner's interminable private audiences with Ludwig set tongues wagging, not least because Wagner was a Protestant and a noted revolutionary. Wagner's high-camp mode of dressing in silk and furs, and his addiction to perfume were a gift to satirists. The King preferred thigh boots, tight breeches and army uniforms.

Ambitious courtiers circled. One faction tempted Wagner with a young woman called Agnes Street to use his influence with the King on their behalf. Meanwhile, with all Wagner's talk of Siegfried, Brünhilde and the joys of Valhalla, the chronically unstable King began to lose his grip on reality.

When King Ludwig discovered the true nature of Wagner's relationship with Cosima, he accused the composer of 'adultery' and 'betrayal'. Wagner grew so unpopular that he was forced to leave Bavaria. The King consoled himself by building magnificent castles. The first was the theatrically neo-gothic Neuschewanstein, decorated with scenes from Wagner's operas. In 1869, Ludwig built the even more extravagant Linderhof, which featured a huge artificial grotto illuminated with coloured electric lights, which would be the envy of any theme park ride today. He finally went over the top with Schloss Herrenchiemsee, which he intended as an elaborate copy of Versailles.

A proud Bavarian, Ludwig looked down on his mother's Prussian background. Once King, he refused to see her and referred to her only as 'my predecessor's wife'. He never got around to having a wife himself, although he was engaged to Elizabeth of Bavaria. The engagement was broken off and it is generally assumed that Ludwig was gay. For the last 17 years of his life, he was closely attached to his stablemaster.

After 22 years on the throne, Ludwig's extravagant building plans had left Bavaria practically bankrupt. In 1886, he was declared insane, although the historian Ghislain de Diesbach said that he was merely 'an eccentric and misanthrope who despised the human condition while still remaining desperately attached to it'. Forced to abdicate, he drowned himself in Lake Starnberg.

## 19 ❖ Serbian Shenanigans

The history of Serbia is peppered with scandal, which revolved around the struggle between two competing factions – the Karageorgists and the Obrenovicists. These were the followers of two of the leaders who freed the country from Turkish rule.

Serbia had fallen under Turkish domination after the disastrous Serb defeat at the Battle of Kosovo in 1389, and it remained part of the Ottoman Empire for the next five centuries. Then a rebel leader named Karageorge, or Black George, started an uprising against the Turks. Although initially successful, the uprising failed in 1813. A second Serb leader Milos Obrenovic began uprisings in 1815–17. With the Russo-Turkish War of 1828–29, Serbia became an autonomous principality under Turkish suzerainty and Russian protection. Obrenovic became Prince of Serbia, while Karageorge was killed. His severed head was put in a basket and presented to Prince Milos.

While Milos and his descendants held on to the throne, the descendants of Karageorge ran a murderous opposition. This came to a head when Prince Michael of Serbia, an Obrenovicist, was assassinated by Karageorgists in 1868. His murder was supposed to trigger a spontaneous uprising that would sweep the Karageorgists to power. However, the assassins dallied at the scene of the crime and were arrested. Although they had mutilated the body, Prince Michael's face was still intact. His corpse was propped up in a carriage and driven through the streets of Belgrade. Other Karageorgists assumed that their plot had failed and made no move. This gave the Obrenovicists enough time to call a parliament and swear in a successor before the Karageorgists had a chance to seize the throne.

The problem was the successor they chose, who, although popular, had little claim to the throne. Prince Michael did not have any children or close relatives. When searching for an heir he had come across a distant relative named Milan Obrenovic. The boy's father had died of alcoholism and, when Prince Michael's representatives caught up with her, his mother was shacked up with a Romanian nobleman, while her son lived in the stables with a bunch of gypsies.

The young Milan had been plucked from the horse dung, washed and sent to Belgrade, where Prince Michael had taken a liking to him. He had sent the boy to Paris to learn table manners and how to read and write. Milan was a quick learner. Although a gypsy at heart, he soon caught on to the ways of royalty. Princes, he realized, should gamble, womanize and spend freely.

When, on the death of Prince Michael, Milan came to the throne, the people's Prince announced ambitious plans to turn the collection of wooden shacks that was then Belgrade into a modern, stone-built capital. But by this time he was addicted to the aristocratic life style. He spent most of his time gambling in the casinos of Vienna, Paris and Budapest. Soon Serbia's treasury was empty.

The people of Serbia began to grumble about their gypsy prince and the prospect of a Karageorgist putsch threatened once more. The Obrenovicist government quickly realized that they must do what all royal families do when they are unpopular – have a royal wedding.

Unfortunately, no real blue-blooded princess was going to marry the gypsy ruler of a bankrupt principality. However, they found someone who appeared to be the perfect candidate. Her name was Natalie Keshko. She was 16, slim and breathtakingly beautiful – and her father, a wealthy Russian soldier, owned most of Moldavia. Milan was smitten.

So were the people of Serbia. When she arrived in Belgrade, the crowds took her horses from the carriage and pulled it themselves. Prince Milan bounced back in the popularity stakes.

At the time, Serbia was being pulled between Russia and Austria. Being a Slavic race, the Serbs identified themselves with the Russians, but the strength of the Austro-Hungarian Empire meant that Western influences could not be resisted.

Princess Natalie was a Russian. That was a point in her favour. But she loved haute couture dresses imported from Vienna and Paris. Milan, too, looked to the West, where he had been educated and could indulge his opulent life style. The couple even got married in Vienna, at the invitation of Emperor Franz Joseph. Prince Milan could not have afforded to stage an occasion nearly lavish enough in Belgrade.

Although this caused some resentment, crowds turned out to cheer when the Prince and Princess had their marriage blessed in Belgrade Cathedral. But the occasion was marred by a thunderstorm, which many believed to be an omen.

With his popularity once more on the wane, Prince Milan decided that what he needed was a war. So in 1876, he attacked Turkey. The Russians came in on his side, bringing victory in 1878. The Serbs were ecstatic about this Pan-Slavic alliance, but Prince Milan was less than pleased. Within a year, he had signed a secret treaty with Austria.

The Prince's popularity reached dizzying new heights when Princess Natalie presented him with an heir, Alexander. Milan pronounced himself King and Natalie became Queen. But the marriage was already in trouble.

On the surface, everything looked idyllic. Underneath, tensions were boiling. Although Queen Natalie was a rare beauty, sexually she was a cold fish. Worse, she refused to surrender her dowry. The wealth that she had brought with her to the marriage was tied up in land and she refused to sell it.

King Milan began to fool around with the ladies of the court. Queen Natalie went into jealous rages. He beat her and did everything he could to upset her. The marriage reached the point where they were living separate lives. Natalie lavished all her time and attention on her son. Milan spent his time in Vienna spending lavishly on show-girls. He proudly presented one actress with a picture of himself in a frame made of gold and set with diamonds. She sent it back with a note expressing how deep her gratitude would have been if the diamonds had been real. This naturally spurred Milan to lavish more jewels on her. It was only later that he discovered she had had a replica frame made with fake diamonds, which she had returned to him, keeping the real jewel-encrusted one.

This taught Milan a lesson. Back in Belgrade he took as his mistress a large, full-breasted Serb woman, several years his senior. Her name was Artemisia Christich and she was the wife of his private secretary. She bore Milan a son, Obren, and her husband divorced her. Milan's popularity waned still further. No one could understand how he could prefer this thickset motherly figure to his beautiful young wife.

As if driven by a political deathwish, Milan was determined to marry Artemisia. Even though he had not entertained his wife in the bedroom for several years, she had not taken a lover, so he had no grounds for divorce. Hell-bent on marrying his full-figured mistress, Milan devised a cunning plan. He announced that now that Alexander was 11, the Crown Prince should be sent abroad to see more of the world. The doting Natalie immediately insisted that she went with him. As soon as they were out of the country, Milan sent her a letter forbidding her to return to Serbia. It also told her that he was having their marriage dissolved and demanded that she return the Crown Prince immediately.

The Queen kicked up rough. When Alexander was dragged from her arms and forcibly returned to Serbia, she spread the rumour that Milan intended to murder him in order to leave Obren, his son by Artemisia, heir to the throne. Milan further scandalized the country by forcing the Orthodox Church to grant him a divorce. Artemisia was so unpopular that she could not show her face in public and there were several attempts on Milan's life.

It was then that Milan realized that, although he liked the life style of a king, he was not cut out for the politics involved in the position. So he installed a modern liberal constitution and abdicated in favour of his son. However, he did not use his new-found freedom to married his beloved Artemisia. Instead, he took the generous pension he had awarded himself before he stepped down, and hightailed it back to the show-girls of Vienna.

Twelve-year-old Alexander was left to the tender mercies of one Jovan Ristich, ex-Prime Minister of Serbia, who had been appointed Regent. With Milan now out of the way, Natalie wrote to Ristich asking permission to return to Serbia to be with her son. He refused out of hand. Obviously, Alexander's mother being in the country would lessen Ristich's influence over the child.

But Natalie returned anyway, to be greeted by cheering crowds. The palace gates were locked but she made a show of going there every day and standing outside, telling those who would listen that she was wondering if Alexander was looking out at her.

The people's sympathy was on the side of the mother who was forbidden to see her child. Soon, Ristich was the most unpopular man in the country. Desperate to find some face-saving way out of the situation, he telegrammed Milan, asking his permission for Natalie to see their son. Milan reluctantly agreed.

As Ristich had feared, Natalie used the opportunity to start to turn Alexander against him, and she used a series of newspaper interviews to further tarnish his image. Ristich asked her to leave the country. When she would not, he had a banishment order approved by Parliament and he forced Alexander to read it to her. When she still refused to go, he sent the police to her house at night to arrest her. This provoked a riot. However, when the rioters had dispersed, the Queen was left on her own and grabbed by a bunch of soldiers, who bundled her unceremoniously out of the country. Parliament passed another bill, banning her from returning. For good measure, Milan was given another million francs if he promised to stay out of Serbia, too.

Alexander remained alone and isolated, under the thumb of Ristich, until he was 16. Then one evening, he invited Ristich, his cabinet and the military top brass over for dinner. After they had eaten, Alexander gave a speech. In it, he said that he felt that he was now old enough to rule by himself and was no longer in need of a regent. However, he invited Ristich and his government to stay in the palace as his guests. When they tried to leave, they found themselves surrounded by armed guards.

The next morning Serbia awoke to the news that a radical new government was in control. Although Alexander was an Obrenovic, he shared power with the Karageorgists. Alexander saw this as a way of uniting the country against the old guard in Ristich's government. For the Karageorgists, it took them one step closer to their ambition. They were happy to bide their time. When Alexander put a foot wrong, they would be perfectly placed to exploit it.

And put a foot wrong Alexander surely would. He had inherited all the political nous of his father. His first act was to go to Biarritz to see his mother. There he met Natalie's middle-aged lady-in-waiting, Draga Mashin, and fell instantly in love. Her gentle manner and her ample bosom offered all the maternal love that Alexander had missed during his adolescence.

At first, Draga dismissed Alexander's infatuation as puppy love. But he was determined. Alexander went on to Paris where his father introduced him to the delights of the casino, the brothel and show-girls. All the time, Alexander was hatching a plan.

Back in Belgrade, Alexander declared his parents' divorce null and void. This suited Milan, who still hoped to get his hands on some of Natalie's fortune. It also allowed Natalie to return to Belgrade as the revered Queen Mother. And with her she brought Alexander's beloved Draga Mashin.

This arrangement immediately brought with it political consequences. Natalie now saw herself as Queen of the Serbs. This brought her into conflict with the constitutional government and it began to make her unpopular. In the end, Alexander was forced to send her and Draga back to Biarritz. Annoyed at having his plan thwarted, he tore up the liberal constitution his father had bequeathed the country and took power as an absolute monarch.

However, he made frequent trips to Biarritz to see Draga, who had now become his lover. One day, a love letter addressed to Draga fell into Natalie's hands. She was shocked and outraged and sacked Draga on the spot, without references. Penniless, Draga had no choice but to return to Belgrade, where she set up home with Alexander.

Milan also returned to Serbia and began to dabble in politics. While the vast majority of Serbs still saw the Russians and other Slavs as their natural allies, Milan still pushed for an alliance with the West, and urged his son to marry an Austrian or German princess. But there was only one woman that Alexander wanted to marry – Draga. Politically unpopular as the young princesses Milan paraded before the King were, at least they were nubile and attractive. No one could understand why Alexander was so stuck on his middle-aged *hausfrau*. People suspected witchcraft.

The Prime Minister, Dr Georgevich, was worried that, with Draga, Alexander was going to make the same mistakes his father had with Artemisia. He joined forces with Milan and urged the King to marry a foreign princess. Alexander appeared to acquiesce but, before any official betrothal and all the exhausting business of organizing a royal wedding, he suggested that his father and Prime Minister take a holiday.

While they were out of the country, Alexander announced that he was going to marry Draga. When he heard the scandalous news, Dr Georgevich resigned. Milan, of all people, wrote condemning his son's irresponsibility and refused to return to Belgrade. He died penniless in exile the following year.

In Serbia, the royal match was extremely unpopular. The newspapers dragged Draga's name through the mud. The government persuaded her to leave the country, but Alexander prevented it.

However, Alexander did have one powerful ally, or so he thought – Tsar Nicholas II of Russia. The Tsar suspected that Alexander, like his father, harboured leanings towards the West and was happy to see him destroy himself. He offered to be best man.

Alexander laid on a lavish wedding at Belgrade Cathedral. Tsar Nicholas sent his apologies. He could not be there in person for reasons of state. The Russian ambassador stood in as his proxy. Few Serbs turned out either.

Soon after, Draga announced that she was pregnant. Alexander hoped that although a royal wedding had not stirred the hearts of the Serbian people, an heir to the throne might do the trick. But he had reckoned without his mother, who was sending postcards to everyone she knew in Serbia, saying that Draga had had an operation that had left her infertile. Another rumour circulated that Draga's sister was pregnant and that Alexander intended to foist her child on Serbia as his heir.

Tsar Nicholas, as best man and by convention godfather to the first-born, was naturally concerned. He sent two doctors who announced that Draga was not, and never had been, pregnant. There were riots in the street.

In an attempt to restore order, Alexander imposed martial law. Draga's relatives were appointed to key posts in government and the army, and – folly of follies – he announced that Draga's brother, Nikodiye, was heir. This was the final straw. The people turned to the Karageorgists for a solution.

The Karageorgists' leader was Colonel Alexander Mashin. Draga had been married before and Mashin had been her brother-in-law. He suspected that she had poisoned her drunk and loathsome first husband, his brother. So he harboured a personal grudge.

Then something very bizarre happened. Alexander received a letter from W.T. Stead, Editor of London's *Pall Mall Gazette* and political mentor to Edward VII's lover, Daisy Brooke. He had recently held a demonstration of clairvoyance in a fashionable London restaurant. At it, Mrs Burchell, a medium from Bradford had announced that the King and Queen of Serbia were going to be murdered in their bedroom. Alexander ignored the warning.

Realizing that even with Draga's relatives in command, the army could not be relied upon, Alexander turned to his old friend, Tsar Nicholas, for assistance. The latter sent troops but it was no help. On the night of 16 June 1903, the King's bodyguards were drugged. Colonel Mashin marched a regiment of infantry to the palace. The soldiers cheered as it made its way through the streets and the police turned a blind eye.

As the soldiers smashed their way into the palace, Alexander and Draga concealed themselves in a secret chamber. For two hours, Mashin's troops turned the palace upside down and failed to find them.

The King's equerry, Laza, was captured and tortured, but he would not reveal where his master was. Mashin finally managed to persuade him that his intention was only to force the King to abdicate. He would come to no harm, Mashin gave his word of honour. Laza opened the secret panel in their bedroom, revealing the King and Queen. One of the other conspirators shot Alexander. Mashin himself shot Draga. Her naked and mutilated body was thrown out of the window to a cheering crowd below. Alexander, too, was flung out, but he revived at the last moment and clung on to the window frame. His fingers were hacked off and he fell to his death. Throughout all this, the Tsar's troops did not stir from their compound in the Russian embassy.

Mashin then rounded up the rest of Draga's family and butchered them. The massacre of loyalists became so bloodthirsty that the Austrian ambassador warned Mashin if they did not stop, the Emperor would send in the Imperial army. Three days after the coup, Peter Karageorge, pretender to the throne, returned from exile in Geneva and was crowned King.

KING Carol of Romania did things the other way around from Milan Obrenovic. His flagrant affair with Magda Lupescu forced him to forfeit his throne in 1925. Five years later, he returned, deposed his own son and installed Magda in a luxurious villa near his palace.

However, in 1940, Romania's newly installed pro-Nazi government kicked him and Magda out. Demonstrators fired on their train as they fled the country.

## 20 ❖ Mystery at Mayerling

In 1889, the Austro-Hungarian Empire was rocked to its core by scandal. The heir to the Imperial throne shot himself over the love of a commoner. At least, that is the official story. As such, it is scandalous enough.

Archduke Rudolf of Habsburg was the scion of the Habsburg family, which had controlled much of central Europe for over 600 years. True, the Empire was past its best. But, although in the late 19th century the constituent countries were agitating for their freedom, it was still ruled with a rod of iron by Emperor Franz Joseph.

Like most heirs to the throne, Rudolf liked to fool around. He kept a detailed inventory of his amorous conquests, rigidly segregating commoners from his aristocratic lovers. A sensitive lad, he also got caught up in revolutionary politics and wrote a number of influential articles demanding change.

His father brought him to heel and put him in the army, and he was married off to the delightful but brainless Princess Stephanie of Belgium. Rudolf was an intelligent man and she bored him. In frustration, he became a morphine addict and in 1888 an army inspector recommended his dismissal. This left him suicidal.

With a friend, a Hungarian patriot, he plunged himself into a harebrained plot to depose his father and seize the throne. It failed.

It was then that he met Maria Vetsera, a beautiful Greek girl. A teenage virgin she developed a crush on Rudolf and threw herself at him. He caught her, but her love and the gift of her maidenhead did not distract him from thoughts of death. The failure of his half-hearted bid for power left him with no other honourable way out, he said, but death.

He set out for his hunting lodge at Mayerling, where he and Maria wrote farewell letters together in his bedroom. Then he shot Maria with his revolver. They may have made love before he killed her. She was naked when they found her. Rudolf himself hesitated. At six the following morning, he went downstairs and asked his valet to prepare breakfast. Back in his room, he fortified himself with a glass of brandy and shot himself in the head.

Initially, it was said that Rudolf had died of a heart attack, but then the story of the suicide pact between the two star-crossed lovers came out. However there are certain inconsistencies in it. For example, if Rudolf was so in love with Maria, why did he visit a prostitute the night before he left Vienna for Mayerling? And, if his death was indeed suicide, how did Rudolf come to be buried in consecrated ground?

In 1983, the last of the Habsburg monarchs, former Empress Zita claimed that a long telegram from Franz Joseph to the Pope, explaining why Rudolf could be buried in hallowed soil, was missing from the Austrian state archives. She said it had been allowed because Rudolf was actually assassinated because of his left-wing sympathies.

He was replaced by a much sounder candidate – his cousin Archduke Franz Ferdinand, whose assassination in Sarajevo in 1914 sparked World War I.

On the other hand, the nuns who use part of the old hunting lodge as a cloister pray for the three dead at Mayerling. Maria, some think, was pregnant. The story of the suicide pact at Mayerling could well have hushed up an even bigger scandal.

# 21 ❖ Farouk, King of Playboys

The Shah of Iran was fabled for his taste in Parisian prostitutes, whom he would have flown out to Tehran for his delectation. But the most scandalous of all the Middle Eastern monarchs was King Farouk of Egypt.

Ascending the throne in 1936, at the age of 16, he was kept in power by the British. But during World War II he made little secret of the fact that he hoped that the Germans would kick the British out. At the same time, he profited shamelessly from the War. When the British finally withdrew their support, Farouk was ousted by Gamal Abdel Nasser and Anwar Sadat in a coup. After that he travelled the world, indulging his gluttony, his love of gambling and his passion for women. He became so notorious for his sybaritic way of life that it was said that if there were seven deadly sins, King Farouk would have found an eighth.

Even when he was King, Farouk could exert little power. He had to content himself with petty edicts to indulge his whims. He once issued a decree banning Egyptians from owning red cars. Then he had his royal cars – which numbered over 100 – sprayed red so that he could career through the streets without fear of being stopped.

The first real source of royal scandal in his reign was his mother, Queen Nazli. When Farouk came to power, Queen Nazli began a famous affair with his tutor, the celebrated soldier, explorer and scholar, Ahmed Mohammad Hasanein. Then she took up with a young diplomat, Riad Ghali, who was not even a Muslim but a Coptic Christian. Queen Nazli then marred him off to her own daughter, Farouk's younger sister. The three of them moved to Beverley Hills, where mother and daughter converted from Islam to Catholicism. This was too much for the then innocent young Farouk, who banned them from returning to Egypt and confiscated their property.

King Farouk did not remain an innocent for long though. A disastrous marriage to a beautiful 17-year-old named Safinez Zulficar put an end to that. Although, upon their marriage he changed her name to Farida – which means 'the only one' – she soon began to take lovers. This hurt Farouk and when Fatima Toussoun, the wife of his cousin, Prince Hassan Toussoun, threw herself at him, he could not resist the fair-skinned Circassian. They met for moonlit trysts in a palace on the banks of the Nile and he told her that if she gave him a baby he would marry her.

By the age of 23, Farouk was already suffering from bouts of impotence and is believed to have had underdeveloped genitals. But he set about creating for himself the image of a virile and insatiable lover. He invoked the *droit du roi* over the wives and daughters of his subjects and claimed to have bedded over 5,000 women in his lifetime.

To aid him in this, he became a connoisseur of aphrodisiacs. He used love potions devised in the times of the pharaohs. He also came up with his own recipe, which mixed amphetamines with hashish, caffeine tablets, honey and powdered rhino horn. In addition, he consumed vast quantities of oysters and eggs, along with pigeons and mangoes, which he believed were cures for impotence. Every morning, just to be on the safe side, he would have a vigorous rubdown by a chambermaid in his bathroom, which was decorated with mosaics showing naked slaves.

Farouk went about bedding different types of women, the way other men collected stamps. If a woman refused her, he would have her kidnapped and imprisoned in the harem in one of his five palaces. If the woman was married, and it seemed that her husband might kick up a fuss, he resorted to blackmail to get her into bed instead.

His aide, Antonio Pulli, would be sent out to comb high-class brothels for the light-skinned women Farouk preferred. European show-girls would be given diamond bracelets for their favours.

Farouk had a scandalous wartime affair with a beautiful Jewish girl, named Irene Guinle. Despite his pro-Nazi sympathies and the disapproval of his Muslim subjects, he never let race, religion or politics stand in the way of his pleasures. In fact, her Jewishness was a point in her favour in Farouk's eyes. His father, Fuad, had had a Jewish mistress for 20 years. Not only had she arranged his marriage to one of the richest women in Egypt, through her Jewish contacts, she had wisely invested his resulting wealth, and she had used her influence with the British to put Fuad on the throne, even though he was not strictly the next in line.

Irene had no time for Farouk though. She despised anyone with pro-German sympathies and she did not like sex much. She had been put off it by her first husband, English public school-educated Louis Najjar, who had turned up on their wedding night with an attaché case containing a pair of high-heeled shoes and a cane. She had fled from their Cairo honeymoon hotel in horror. He had found her cowering behind a pyramid and had dragged her back to their room. What he wanted was for her to beat him until he bled, then scrape the high heels down the cuts. This had to be done three times a day. Everyone does it this way, he told her. She stood it for four years before getting a divorce.

She met King Farouk in 1941 at a charity ball in aid of the war effort. At the time, the Germans were poised on the Libyan border and seemed unstoppable. Farouk was immediately attracted to her light skin and athletic figure. She avoided him, but he pursued her. When he suggested a moonlight dip, she fled. But she was stopped at the door by the British Ambassador, Sir Miles Lampson. He explained that it would be very much in Britain's interest to have a committed anti-Nazi close to the King.

She went swimming with the King. The next day, he called her and asked her out on a date. She said that she did not go out with men with beards. This was a deliberate ploy. Farouk's beard allied him to the Muslim Brotherhood, who wanted to kick the British out of Egypt. He shaved it off. She soon realized that Farouk was like a child and she could twist him around her little finger.

Even though Fatima Toussoun had just given birth to a baby girl,

Farouk began to be seen out publicly with Irene, although he refused to attend pro-British events with her. Although Farida was wheeled out for state occasions, Irene was Queen of Egypt in all but name. In the street, people would shout 'Long live Irene', and Farouk began to put pressure on her to convert to Islam.

Irene's mother kicked her out and she went to live with Farouk in the Abdine Palace. Although Farida and his official harem lived there, Irene was installed in Farouk's royal apartment.

At the height of the German threat, there were pro-German demonstrations in the street, and Farouk seized the initiative by sacking his pro-British Prime Minister. But with inside knowledge of Farouk's movements, Lampson surrounded the Abdine Palace with tanks, shot the locks off the palace gates and led troops up the stairs into Farouk's study. He presented the king with articles of abdication. He could either sign them or endorse Lampson's new choice of pro-British Prime Minister. Farouk chose the latter.

The affair between Farouk and Irene lasted two years, ending in 1943 when the German threat to Egypt had receded. Irene left him after she had caught him in bed with the Englishwoman, Barbara Skelton. Farouk begged Irene to stay, saying that he would marry her and make her officially the Queen of Egypt. When she refused, he threatened to declare war on all Jews. Then he said that if she left he would give the rest of his life over to prostitutes and gambling – which is pretty much what he did.

Barbara Skelton continued seeing Farouk. She was a cipher clerk in the British Embassy and, when she began accompanying him to balls in haute couture gowns that he had plainly bought her, embassy staff became worried that she might be passing secrets to him and she was posted home. She went on to become a novelist and wrote a thinly fictionalized account of her time in the Abdine Palace. She described rooftop champagne parties, where the entertainment would be provided by nude belly dancers who had had their pubes shaved. Farouk had a thing about belly dancers and he worked his way through the top stars of the country. According to Skelton, the King would take the prettiest women off to his bedroom. Skelton's protagonist enjoyed being beaten by the King with the cord from a dressing gown, although Skelton admitted in her diaries that she preferred a splayed cane.

After 11 years of marriage, Farida had produced three daughters, but still no son. She was beginning to get narked that her husband's love life was outdistancing her own. And when, one morning, a famous French opera star was seen leaving Farouk's bedroom, Farida asked for a divorce. He gave her one.

Farouk's next scandalous liaison was with Princess Patricia 'Honeychile' Wilder Hohenlohe. Born in the American state of Georgia, she had become a star of *The Bob Hope Show* and bedded Clark Gable and Tyrone Power, both of whom she threw over for her riding instructor. She even boasted a brief liaison with John F. Kennedy in a dank air-raid shelter in London, early in World War II.

Her ex-husband was the Austrian Prince Alexander Hohenlohe. When they divorced she kept her title, along with a considerable part of his wealth. When she turned up in Egypt in 1949, she had in tow a new husband, a polo-player from Argentina. He was persuaded to go big game hunting while she tried to swap her title of Princess for Queen.

However, while Honeychile was pursuing her ambitions in the bedroom of the Abdine Palace, Farouk had already found his new queen in a jeweller's shop. She was there with her – soon to be ex- – fiancé choosing an engagement ring. Her name was Narriman Sadek. She was 16, small, plump and a commoner. He smothered her with flattery and expensive gifts. Her boyfriend did not stand a chance and she dumped him.

In scandalous style, Farouk set out on a three-month movable stag party, which lurched across Europe. Prostitutes from all over the Continent flocked to join his ever-swelling entourage. In Biarritz, Farouk hooked up with Barbara Skelton once again.

The royal wedding was something out of the Arabian nights. There followed a four-month honeymoon in Europe. Narriman, a poor peasant girl, was plied with gourmet food, couture gowns, expensive jewellery and priceless art. They stayed at the finest hotels. The royal entourage numbered 60 and were ferried around in a fleet of Rolls Royces. When they went out on the royal yacht, Farouk dressed the entire party in identical white flannels, blue blazers and yachting caps.

Back in Cairo, Farouk was no more faithful to Narriman than he had been to his first wife. But he moved his extramarital activities out of the Abdine Palace. He turned the top floor of the Mossat Hospital into a bachelor pad, staffed by attractive nurses.

However, Narriman provided the son he craved and she followed him into exile in 1952. He left behind a vast collection of pornography, which included clocks and watches whose moving parts depicted sexual acts. These, along with his stamp collection, fetched more than a million dollars.

Freed from the burdens of state, Farouk established himself in Rome where the paparazzi followed every escapade in his attempt to become the world's ultimate playboy. The first scandal was the whirlwind seduction of the big-breasted 16-year-old Miss Irma Capri. He bombarded her school with flowers and jewellery, while she followed his activities with actresses and Swedish blondes in night-clubs in the gossip columns.

At the time, Farouk was seeing 18-year-old Swede, Brigitta Stenberg, a girlfriend he had borrowed from his good friend, Lucky Luciano, the mobster who had been deported back to Italy by the Americans in 1946. Despite this affair being splashed all over the newspapers, Farouk assured Irma that she would be his new queen.

She gained heart from the very public break-up of his marriage. Narriman announced that she was going to fly back to Cairo with Farouk's 14-month-old son to obtain an Islamic divorce. Farouk blamed the new regime. Although he had been deposed, the monarchy had not been abolished and it was certainly in the new regime's interest to get their hands on the heir to the throne. Farouk accused them of deploying 'that most powerful of all weapons, the mother-in-law' who, he told the press, was 'the most terrible woman in the world'.

Irma's mother's objections to the match began to wane and, despite Irma's father's continued opposition, she arranged for Irma to be sent to a convent in Rome for the summer. Farouk picked her up at the station and whisked her back to his villa at Grottaferrata. There, an entire wing had been prepared for her. The bathroom had even been remodelled to resemble one in a Rita Hayworth movie that Irma had casually mentioned seeing.

Irma was then extensively prepared for her debut on the Via Veneto, home of Rome's *la dolce vita*. They would leave the villa at nine in the evening and return at dawn. Farouk and Irma – and her dangerously low-cut gowns – became the king and queen of the night-club scene. The Italian press soon dubbed her 'Irma, Capace de Totalo' – 'Irma, Capable of Anything'.

With Irma now his very public mistress, Brigitta Stenberg decided to go back to Sweden. As a going-away present, she fixed Farouk up with the current Miss Universe, Armi Kuusia of Finland. Brigitta used her experiences with Luciano and Farouk as a basis for a new career as a novelist.

Farouk took Irma on an 18-month tour of Europe, introducing her to stars, socialites and royalty. When she expressed a desire to become an opera singer, he paid for singing lessons and arranged her triumphant debut in Naples. So that she would be rested for her performances, he stopped taking her out. Not that he stopped going out himself, of course. Gore Vidal remembered seeing the overweight ex-king in the Via Veneto, sucking on the nipple of a prostitute when a thief on a motor scooter snatched her purse. Farouk laughed, but went on sucking. He gave her enough money to compensate her for what she had lost.

From the newspapers and magazines, Irma knew that he was seeing other women – whom Gore Vidal dubbed 'chubby chasers'. But Farouk refused to discuss them. Irma herself was not allowed the same privilege. When she went to the beach at Anzio without telling him, she found half the Italian police force looking for her.

Farouk died in 1965 at the age of 45, after a midnight supper with his latest amour, voluptuous blonde Annamaria Gatti. He had eaten a dozen raw oysters laced with Tabasco, a lobster thermidor, a roast baby lamb with roast potatoes, a creamy chestnut Monte Bianco, two oranges, two large bottles of mineral water and a Coca-Cola. He was just lighting a Havana cigar – another trademark – when he collapsed over the table clutching his throat. Everyone thought he was joking. When they realized he wasn't, it was too late.

Annamaria Gatti disappeared soon after and the rumour circulated that Farouk had been poisoned. The death certificate cited a cerebral haemorrhage. Farouk was found to be carrying a Biretta. He could no longer afford bodyguards. The Rolls had been sold. Outside the restaurant was a Fiat 2300 with diplomatic plates. In his pockets were two US thousand-dollar bills, a wad of 10,000-lira notes and a gold pill box containing his blood-pressure tablets.

As mistress of 13 years' standing, Irma took her place beside Farouk's coffin, alongside his first wife Farida and their daughters. Irma went on to play the oversexed opera singer in Franco Zeffirelli's 1988 movie, *Young Toscanini*, playing opposite Elizabeth Taylor.

# 22 ❖ The Bribery of Prince Bernhard

Traditionally, royal scandals involve sex because monarchs usually have more than enough money. If they do not, people are always eager to lend it to them in the hope of preferential treatment. But in 1975, Prince Bernhard showed that the Dutch had a thoroughly modern royal family by getting himself involved in scandal concerning bribery.

For the Dutch, Prince Bernhard was a national hero. During World War II, he had escaped with his wife – then Princess, now Queen Juliana – to England where he had joined the RAF. After a distinguished war record, he returned home to accept the German surrender in Holland as commander-in-chief of the Free Dutch Forces.

When Queen Juliana took the throne, Prince Bernhard subsidized the

£150,000 he got from the state with numerous company directorships. In 1953, he publicly complained that the money he was making was failing to support his flamboyant life style.

In 1959, NATO was in the market for a new fighter plane. The stakes were enormous since, once the fighter was chosen, each member of the alliance would have to equip their airforce with the new plane.

Prince Bernhard was promoting the US company Northrop's Tiger fighter. But the Dutch parliament ruled that it was too expensive. The Germans had opted for the Lockheed Starfighter, and it was thought that if The Netherlands picked it, too, it might tip the balance.

Lockheed's Californian headquarters got a message from their chief European salesman, Fred Meuser. He was a close friend of the Dutch Royal Family and he suggested that if they gave Prince Bernhard one of their Jetstar executive jets, it would be a public relations coup for the company.

Lockheed was considering the possible downside of so public a gift, when Meuser suggested that depositing the cash equivalent of a Jetstar – a mere £500,000 – in Prince Bernhard's numbered Swiss bank account might do just as well. And it would be more discreet. Lockheed agreed, earmarking the £500,000 as 'commission'.

By this time, the Dutch deal was academic. The US Department of Defense had plumped for the Starfighter and had promised to give the Dutch a complete Starfighter squadron, paid for out of their overseas budget. Nevertheless, good to their word, Lockheed paid up.

Leaving his Queen at home in Holland, Prince Bernhard began putting this money to good use, having fun in Paris and Rome. But by 1967, his coffers were running a little low. Fortunately, Lockheed had a new naval reconnaissance plane, the Orion, they wanted to sell to the Dutch government. They offered Prince Bernhard £250,000 if he could get a decision in their favour. Unfortunately, when the Prince made enquiries in The Netherlands, he discovered that the Dutch government had already chosen the French Atlantique patrol plane over Lockheed's rival. However, Lockheed gave the Prince £50,000 just for trying.

When The Netherlands were looking for another naval patrol plane in 1973, Prince Bernhard smelt another opportunity. This time he wrote to Lockheed, offering his services. But when the company's bosses read his letter in detail, they concluded he was being just a little too greedy. His deal would have cost them £2 million in commission. They turned the Prince down, but this ruffled his feathers – so they offered him a new deal worth £500,000 if he could place an order for four Lockheed planes with the Dutch government.

Unexpectedly, the Dutch government cut their budget, but the letters remained on file. Unfortunately for the Prince, the Lockheed company ran into trouble in 1975 and turned to the American government for help. As part of the bail-out deal, the Federal government insisted on going through the company's books and found that Lockheed had forked out over £11 million in kickbacks and bribes. Prince Bernhard's 'commissions' and his correspondence naturally made headline news. On top of the US Senate investigation, Prince Bernhard faced a judicial inquiry in Holland. This rocked the Dutch Royal Family. Bernhard was forced to resign all his public posts, but it was generally accepted that Queen Juliana knew nothing of her errant husband's business deals and she withstood the scandal. However, on 30 April 1980, she stood down in favour of her daughter, Beatrice.

Even this move was not entirely scandal-free. Beatrice's marriage in 1966 to German diplomat, Claus George William Otto Frederik Geert von Amsberg, had caused a furore when it was revealed that he had been a member of the Hitler Youth before joining the German army.

Their son and heir, Crown Prince Willem Alexander Claus George Ferdinand of Orange, seems determined to keep up the family tradition. In 1985, he took part in a skating race. Although he is heir to £50 million, he accepted sponsorship from *Playboy* magazine, whose advertisement he carried on his trousers.

The future head of the Dutch Protestant Church, also once turned up to a fancy dress party dressed as a mother superior, and was photographed praying to the Great God Heineken. A close friend of the heir to the Heineken fortune, he announced to the press that he had moved into a $2 million mansion in The Hague, so that he could be near O'Casey's, his favourite Irish bar. In 1988, he drove his car into the Leiden canal. His girlfriends have included a TV presenter, an underwear model and the heiress to a Dutch gin fortune.

## 23 ❖ Fall from Grace

Along with the marriage of Charles and Diana, there has been another fairy-tale wedding this century. It was the marriage of the beautiful Hollywood movie star, Grace Kelly, to Prince Rainier of Monaco. In former times, the idea of a reigning monarch marrying an actress would have been a scandal. But in this case, the Hollywood publicity machine had worked overtime to manufacture a virginal image for Grace. It was the antithesis of the truth.

True, Alfred Hitchcock had dubbed Grace Kelly 'The Snow Princess' during the filming of *Dial M for Murder*. But he did so ironically, because of her extraordinary promiscuity on the set. Screenwriter Bryan Mawr-recalled a few years later: 'That Grace! She fucked everyone. Why she even fucked little Freddie [Frederick Knott] the writer.'

In the movie business, it was well known that Grace Kelly had slept her way to the top. The famous Hollywood columnist, Hedda Hopper, called her a 'nymphomaniac'. Also, she was not quite the high-society gal that the studios made her out to be either. Her father, self-made millionaire Jack Kelly, was the son of an Irish immigrant and a former bricklayer, who qualified for the Social Register. But he took mistresses from among the wives of Philadelphia's socialites and groomed his daughter to marry a blue-blood. Eager to please daddy, Grace cultivated a refined English accent and came on like a debutante.

She was barely 15 when men started proposing to her. Jack Kelly took it as a mark of esteem that herds of eligible young men would flock to the house. There were so many of them, he could scarcely remember their names.

'You can take her out all you want,' he said. 'But don't think you are going to marry her.'

Only one of them meant anything to her. He was Harper Davis, the son of a Buick salesman. Her father only discovered that the relationship was serious when Davis graduated from High School in 1944 and enlisted in the Navy. He forced her to break it off.

Years later, when she got engaged to Prince Rainier of Monaco, he asked her if she had ever been in love before. She said: 'Yes, I was in love with Harper Davis. He died.'

When Davis returned from wartime service in 1946, he was struck down by multiple sclerosis. By 1951, he was totally paralysed. Grace would spend hours at his bedside, although he could not move or speak. He died in 1953. When she flew back from Hollywood for his funeral, the studio made great play of the 'Philadelphia socialite' returning for the funeral of her childhood sweetheart.

Grace enrolled in the American Academy of Drama Arts in New York in October 1947. But before she left Philadelphia, she was determined to lose her virginity – but not to her own true love.

'It happened very quickly,' she explained later. 'I went round to a friend's house to pick her up, and I found that she wasn't there. It was raining outside, and her husband told me she would be gone for the rest of the day. I stayed talking to him, and somehow we fell into bed together, without understanding why.'

She did not repeat the experience with the man in question, though she stayed on friendly terms with the couple.

Grace's first sexual encounter was not as accidental as she made it seem. She explained later that she had not wanted to move to New York without knowing what sex was all about, but none of the boys she knew could be trusted to keep a secret. When a friend commiserated, saying that it was a pity that her first sexual encounter had not been suffused with love and romance, she replied: 'It wasn't that bad.'

At drama school, she dated the best-looking guy in the class, Mark Miller. But he had plenty of rivals.

'There were these guys who would call for her,' said Miller. 'I would be thinking that I'm the only love in her life, and some stud would arrive at school. So I'd ask her, "Who's that guy?" and she'd say, "Just some guy I know. He's crazy about me." She would laugh about it and brush it off, like she was just sort of doing the guy a favour. I never gave it too much thought. I was very naive, I suppose.'

She also had a month-long fling with Hollywood leading man, Alexandre D'Arcy, once hailed as the 'new Valentino'.

'She didn't dress as the sort of girl that would jump into bed with you,' D'Arcy said. But he tried it on anyway. In a taxi, he touched her on the knee. 'She just jumped into my arms. I could not believe it. She was the very opposite of the homely type of girl she seemed.'

She went back to his apartment on 53rd Street and made love to him without a second thought.

In her second year, one of the drama teachers at the Academy, Don Richardson, took her to his attic apartment on 33rd Street.

'I got the fire going and went out to make some coffee,' he recalled.

When he came back, he found she had taken all her clothes off and was waiting for him in bed.

'We had no introduction to this,' he said. 'There was no flirtation. I could not believe it. Here was this fantastically beautiful creature lying next to me... That night was just sheer ecstasy.'

They had to be discreet. At the Academy, Grace and Richardson pretended not to know each other. Grace also continued seeing Mark Miller, although she kept that from Richardson. But most weekends, Grace would sneak downtown and make love to Richardson.

The affair was the talk of the Academy. But somehow, Mark Miller remained in blissful ignorance. Then he only broke it off when he found out

**Hollywood royalty – film star Grace Kelly and husband Prince Rainier**

she was seeing some stud from Philadelphia.

To make money, Grace would take on assignments modelling lingerie. At lunchtime, she would steal away to Richardson's appartment, and they would make love. Afterwards, she would put her clothes back on and run back to model. She said that these lunchtime sessions were important for her modelling career. They put lights in her eyes. Richardson also marvelled at how she would jump out of bed on Sunday mornings, run off to Mass, run back and jump back into bed with him, naked, with her little gold crucifix around her neck.

Sleeping with Richardson helped Grace at the Academy. He made sure she got good parts in the Academy's productions and coached her. He knew she would never make it on the stage. But when he took a photograph of her he realized that she had what it took to make a movie actress and he took her to the William Morris Agency.

Grace took Richardson home for the weekend to introduce him to her family. But they took against him. He was not a Catholic. He was married, although separated from his wife and currently in the throes of a messy divorce. And he was Jewish. Grace's mother went through his bags and found a packet of condoms. Richardson was thrown out of the house and Grace was lectured on immorality.

She was only allowed to return to the Academy for her graduation. But she seized the opportunity to move in with Richardson. Grace's father tried to buy Richardson off with a Jaguar. Her brother phoned, threatening to break every bone in his body. Richardson refused to be intimidated, but the affair cooled when he discovered Grace was seeing other men.

One of them was the Shah of Iran, who spent a week with her when he was visiting New York. He plied her with gold and jewels. When her mother read about this in the newspapers, she insisted Grace return the jewellery. Grace also received jewellery from Aly Khan.

Richardson recalled her putting on a fashion show for him. She appeared in gown after gown. He could not imagine where she had got them from. Then she appeared, naked, wearing nothing but a gold and emerald bracelet. Richardson had known several girls who had been out with Aly Khan.

'When he first had a date, he would give them a cigarette case with one emerald on it,' he said. 'When he fucked them, he'd give them the bracelet. I was broken hearted. I put my clothes on, and said that I was leaving.'

On his way out, he dropped the bracelet in the fish tank. He left her, naked, fishing around the tank for her bracelet.

She had an affair with Claudius Philippe, banqueting manager of the Waldorf-Astoria who was on first-name terms with everyone from Gypsy Rose Lee to the Duke and Duchess of Windsor. She also set her cap at Manie Sachs, the head of Columbia records, who was a close friend of her father.

While touring with the Elitch Gardens stock company in the summer of 1951, she began an affair with actor Gene Lyons. Lyons was another divorcé and 10 years older than her. Then, on 28 August 1951, she was asked to report to Hollywood to appear in the film that would make her name, *High Noon*.

Her co-star was Gary Cooper. He was a well-known womanizer and, although he was nearly 50, he still lived up to the nickname Clara Bow had given him in the 1920s – 'Studs'.

The movie began with Gary and Grace in a wedding scene. All Cooper had to do was say 'I do', take Grace in his arms and kiss her. The scene was shot over and over again. Cooper kissed her at least 50 times. Grace made no secret of the fact that she preferred older men and seduced him.

Grace's affair with her co-star in *High Noon* was the first of many. Gore Vidal, then a scriptwriter in Hollywood, said: 'Grace almost always laid her leading man. She was famous for that in town.'

She also slept with screenwriter Bob Slatzer.

Cooper made a point of not being seen out with Grace. Nevertheless the affair made the gossip columns and Mrs Kelly was soon on her way to Hollywood to chaperone her wayward daughter.

Grace flew back to New York and Gene Lyons, but they were soon parted. She signed a seven-year contract with MGM and headed to Africa to film *Mogambo* with Ava Gardner and Clark Gable. From the moment she landed at Nairobi airport, she began flirting with Gable. He was unimpressed, but once they were out on the set and he found that Grace was the only available white woman for hundreds of miles he succumbed. He was 28 years her senior.

When they arrived in London to shoot the interiors in Boreham Wood, the press asked him about the affair. He denied any involvement.

'I hear you two made Africa hotter than it is,' said Hedda Hopper.

When Mrs Kelly turned up in London, Gable had had enough. He had a guard mounted at the top of the stairs at the Connaught to keep Grace out and he did not return her phone calls. A few weeks later, he was seen doing the town in Paris with model Suzanne Dadolle, with whom he had started an affair before he went to Africa.

Back in New York, Grace consoled herself with Gene Lyons, while seeing Don Richardson on the side. Her affair with Lyons ended when she started an intense affair with leading French heart-throb, Jean-Pierre Aumont, during the shooting of *The Way of the Eagle* for TV. Afterwards, he returned to France and she went back to Hollywood, where she and Gable talked of marriage. Gable considered the age difference insurmountable. In the end, she had to agree.

'His false teeth turn me off,' she told a reporter.

During the filming of *Dial M for Murder*, both Tony Dawson, who played the murderer in the movie, and Frederick Knott, who wrote the original play, fell for her. So did her 49-year-old leading man, Ray Milland.

Milland had been happily married for 30 years. Although he had had the odd peccadillo, he had steered clear of actresses, which had kept him out of the gossip columns.

His long-suffering wife, Mal, kept her eyes judiciously shut. But she could not turn a blind eye to his affair with Grace, especially when scandal sheet, *Hollywood Confidential*, got hold of the story.

When Milland was spotted getting on a plane with Grace, Milland and his wife separated and Grace moved in with him. However, when Milland's wife agreed to a divorce – their property was in her name – he thought better of it.

Hitchcock was also in love with Grace in his way, and she was happy to gratify his voyeuristic yearnings. She lived a mile down Laurel Canyon from him. He had a powerful telescope and she would purposely leave the curtains open when she got undressed, slowly, at night.

Throughout this period, Grace had also been seeing Bing Crosby. He was married, but his wife of 22 years, Dixie, was an alcoholic and was incapacitated with cancer. Crosby pretty much came and went as he pleased. He lived next door to Alan Ladd, and would use the Ladds' pool house for his trysts with Grace. This upset Ladd as he and his wife were close friends of Dixie's. Ladd suggested they go to a motel, but Crosby was a well-known skinflint. Besides, going to a motel risked a scandal.

Grace was cast in *The Bridges at Toko-Ri* with William Holden, who was just 11 years her senior and her youngest co-star yet. Although he was married with children, Holden was on the rebound from Audrey Hepburn at the time and he and Grace had a fling.

In New York, she met up with Jean-Pierre Aumont again, who introduced her to fashion designer, Oleg Cassini. An accomplished seducer, Cassini set to work. Aumont and Cassini had long been rivals in love, first over Cassini's wife, then over actress Gene Tierney. Cassini bombarded her with flowers, but Grace was heading back to California where she renewed her romantic attachment with Crosby.

Crosby's wife had died and the newspapers were soon proclaiming the affair between the 25-year-old actress and the 50-year-old crooner 'Hollywood's newest romance'. He proposed. She turned him down. But he carried a torch for her for the rest of his life.

Grace invited Cassini out to the Coast. But when he arrived in LA she had little time for him, as she had resumed her affair with Holden. *Confidential* magazine got wind of the affair when reporters spotted his white Cadillac convertible parked outside her apartment one morning. The studio claimed that he was just picking her up for an early call. Holden claimed that the convertible was Mrs Holden's.

'Does anyone think I'm so dumb as to park my wife's car outside another woman's apartment all night?' he told Hedda Hopper.

While Holden's lawyers were demanding a retraction from *Confidential*, Grace's father and brother went to *Confidential*'s office and threatened to beat up the editor. The scandal sheet changed its tack. In the next issue it said: 'Hollywood wives stop biting your nails... this new Hollywood heat wave wasn't grabbing for a guy who already had a ball and chain.' It went on to say that Grace had forsworn married men and implied that she was only bedding single men from now on.

Even though Grace was occupied elsewhere, Cassini did not waste his time in LA. He was seen at Ciro's with Anita Ekberg, Pier Angeli and other beauties. He made sure his adventures made the gossip columns so that, even when Grace was out on location, he could pique her jealousy.

It worked. When she went to France to film *To Catch a Thief* with Cary

Grant, she sent him a postcard saying: 'Those who love me shall follow me.'

He did and they became lovers. But again, her family thought he was a poor choice as a husband. Her mother thought there were too many women in his background. Her father dismissed him as a 'wop', although he was actually a Russian Jew by descent. Hollywood looked down on him, too. Hedda Hopper wrote: 'With all the attractive men around town, I do not understand what Grace Kelly sees in Oleg Cassini. It must be his moustache.'

Cassini did not improve the situation by cabling Hopper saying: 'I'll shave off mine if you shave off yours.'

In the face of this opposition, Grace was determined to marry Cassini. But during the filming of *Tribute to a Bad Man*, there were rumours of an affair with her co-star, Spencer Tracy. She was seen out with Bing Crosby and Frank Sinatra, who was a well-known stud and freshly divorced from Ava Gardner. This was all grist to Hedda Hopper's mill. Grace also began a discreet affair with David Niven.

Years later, Prince Rainier asked Niven which of his Hollywood conquests had been best in bed. Niven replied without thinking: 'Grace.' Then, seeing the shocked expression on the Prince's face, he tried to recover the situation by saying unconvincingly: 'Er, Gracie... Gracie Fields.'

Sensing the affair was coming to a close, Cassini poured out his heart to Joe Kennedy, the future President's father. Kennedy offered to intercede with Grace for Cassini, then used the opportunity to pursue Grace himself.

At the 1955 Cannes Film Festival, Grace bumped into Jean-Pierre Aumont again and they rekindled their affair. Then she received an invitation to visit Prince Rainier in Monaco. She accepted, but then tried to wheedle out of it when she found she had a hairdresser's appointment that day.

Aumont stepped in, explaining that she could not turn down an invitation from the reigning monarch because she had an appointment at the hairdresser's. At the very least it would be a diplomatic embarrassment for America.

So Grace drove the 50 miles to Monaco. She found that Prince Rainier was a good deal more attractive than she had expected. He showed her around his palace and gardens. It was not love at first sight, but Rainier was very taken with Grace. He was in the market for a princess. As thing stood, if he died without producing an heir, the principality of Monaco would be swallowed up by France.

Although charming, the Prince plainly did not make much of an impression on Grace. Two days later, she was photographed kissing and cuddling Aumont in Cannes. One picture showed Grace nibbling Aumont's fingers. *Time* magazine's caption read: 'Grace Kelly, commonly billed as the icy goddess, melted perceptibly in the company of French actor Jean-Pierre Aumont... had Aumont, who came and thawed, actually conquered Grace?'

Cassini's brother Igor, who was a syndicated columnist, claimed that it was all a put-up job, an attempt by Aumont to revive his flagging career. But Aumont told the press: 'I am deeply in love with Grace Kelly' – although he admitted that he did not think that she felt that way about him.

The Kellys were horrified. Grace immediately cabled her family, denying any romance. Her mother, who knew better, cabled back: 'Shall I invite Mr Aumont to visit us in Philadelphia?'

Prince Rainier was upset. Two years before at the Cannes Film Festival, his mistress Gisele Pascal had had a fling with Gary Cooper.

Grace received a curt note from the Prince's spiritual adviser, Father Francis Tucker, thanking her for showing the Prince 'what an American Catholic girl can be and for the very deep impression this has left on him'. And that seemed to be the end of that.

Grace and Aumont left for Paris, pursued by the press. The papers printed rumours that they were going to get married. When the reporters caught up with Aumont, they asked him whether he wanted to marry Grace. He replied: 'Who wouldn't? I adore her.'

To the same question, Grace replied: 'A girl has to be asked first.'

Then she launched into a diatribe against the press.

'We live in a terrible world,' she complained. 'A man kisses your hand and it's screamed out from all the headlines. He can't even tell you he loves you without the whole world knowing about it.'

The couple managed to give the press the slip and it was reported that they had eloped. When they were found at Aumont's weekend home in Rueil-Malmaison with his family, the newspapers took this to mean they were already married.

It was not so, but she was keen. When Grace flew back to America alone, she told reporters: 'Differences in our age or nationality present no obstacles in marriage between two people who love each other.'

Once more her family were against her choice of marriage partner. A few days later, she issued a formal statement saying that she and Aumont were 'just good friends'. And she began seeing Cassini again.

Aumont conceded that, with her in Hollywood and him in France, things would not have worked out. Nevertheless, Aumont was one of the few people who got a telegram from Grace, informing him that she was going to get engaged to Prince Rainier before the formal announcement.

He married actress Pier Angeli's twin sister, Marisa Pavan, three weeks before Grace's wedding.

By 1956, Prince Rainier had another reason to get married. Three years before, Aristotle Onassis had bought the casino in Monte Carlo, but the economy of the principality was flagging and he was losing money. Gardner Cowles, publisher of *Look* magazine suggested that if Prince Rainier married a movie star it would help lure rich Americans there. Top of Onassis's wish list was Marilyn Monroe.

'Do you think that the Prince will want to marry you?' Cowles asked her.

'Give me two days alone with him and of course he'll want to marry me,' Marilyn replied.

But the Prince had plans of his own. By chance, friends of the Kellys' had been in Monaco. Unable to get tickets for the Red Cross Gala at the Sporting Club, they had called the palace. Once they mentioned the two magic words 'Grace Kelly', they were invited to the palace. Rainier told them that he was going to America and wanted to see Grace again. Delicate negotiations between Monaco and Philadelphia began. Rainier wanted to see Grace on the set of *The Swan*, which she was filming in North Carolina, but Aumont was with her there.

Instead, the Prince made arrangements to meet her in Philadelphia on Christmas Day. Father Tucker told Grace's father that the Prince wanted to marry his daughter. As always, Jack Kelly was against it.

'I don't want any broken-down prince who's head of a country that nobody ever heard of marring my daughter,' he scowled. Jack Kelly suspected that Prince Rainier was only after Grace for her money. But when Rainier proposed Grace accepted. There were some advantages to the arrangement.

'I don't want to be married to someone who feels inferior to my success or because I make more money than he does,' she explained. 'The Prince is not going to be "Mr Kelly".'

Oleg Cassini protested: 'You hardly know the man. Are you going to marry someone because he has a title and a few acres of real estate?'

'I will learn to love him,' replied Grace.

Before Grace could marry her Prince, there was a formal marriage contract to be drawn up. Monaco was going through a political and financial crisis at the time and the Prince demanded a dowry. A figure of $2 million was mentioned. Jack Kelly went through the roof, then paid up. At last, he had one over the Philadelphia blue bloods.

Grace then had to submit to a fertility test. Rainier had taken the precaution of taking his own doctor to America with him. Rainier had had to reject his previous love, the model Gisele Pascal, because she had failed the fertility test. When he had finally given her up, he told Father Tucker: 'Father, if you ever hear that my subjects think I do not love them, tell them what I have done today.'

Later, Gisele married and gave birth to a child. Rainier was devastated. The fertility tests had been falsified as part of a plot by Father Tucker who did not consider Gisele a suitable candidate for the role of princess.

Grace was terrified that the examination would reveal she was not a virgin. Far away from Hollywood gossip, Prince Rainier had apparently been taken in by Grace's chaste screen image and actually believed she was a virgin! Grace took the simple precaution of explaining to the Prince's doctors that her hymen had been broken when she was playing hockey in high school.

Scandal dogged the match from the beginning. At their first public appearance together at a charity gala at the Waldorf-Astoria in New York, a woman rushed up to Rainier and kissed him on the cheek. Grace caused a stir by ordering the Prince to wipe the woman's lipstick off his cheek. Who was that woman? Grace demanded to know. The Prince said he had no idea. The next day, the woman identified herself to the papers as Ecuadorian socialite, Graciela Levi-Castillo.

'He knows who I am,' she said.

Grace had one more movie to make. It was *High Society*, co-starring Bing Crosby and Frank Sinatra. Fearing the worst, Rainier rented a villa in Los Angeles and appeared on the set every day. He appeared puzzled by the private jokes that passed between his fiancée and her two male co-stars.

Although Jack Kelly was pleased that his daughter was marrying into royalty, it was generally considered that Grace was marrying beneath her station. The *Chicago Tribune* wrote: 'She is too well bred to marry the silent partner in a gambling parlour.'

Much of Hollywood confused Monaco with Morocco and wondered how Grace would fare among camels and sand dunes. When he discovered that Monaco was actually a tiny Mediterranean principality, the head of MGM complained that it was no bigger than the studio's back lot.

The myth of Grace's virginity was shattered by her mother, of all people. Overjoyed at the prospect of her daughter's royal marriage, Mrs Kelly talked to reporters and spilled the beans on her daughter's former love affairs. Her revelations ran as a 10-part series in newspapers across America, headlined 'My Daughter Grace Kelly – Her Life and Romances'.

To escape the scandal, Prince Rainier headed for home. But all was not lost. Although it was too late to do anything about the stories running in the American papers, the studios managed to get their hands on the articles and edit them before they went out in Europe. So as far as the citizens of Monaco were concerned, Grace Kelly was still *virgo intacta*.

Grace still had four years to run on her contract. She wanted to make *Designing Woman* with Jimmy Stewart, but the Prince put his foot down. Realizing that they could hardly sue a princess for breach of contract, MGM swapped her appearance in *Designing Woman* for exclusive rights to film the royal wedding.

Grace made the rounds of Hollywood farewell parties, 'chaperoned' by Frank Sinatra. Then, with a party of 65 guests, she sailed for Monaco on board the *Constitution*. They were met in the Bay of Hercules by the royal yacht. Aristotle Onassis arranged for a plane to drop red and white carnations in the harbour when they docked in Monte Carlo.

Then the problems started. The Kellys and Rainier's family, the Grimaldis, did not get on. Jack Kelly could not find the bathroom in the palace. Since the servants spoke no English, he could not ask them where it was. So he took a limousine to a nearby hotel to take a leak.

At the civil wedding, Grace was read the 142 titles she would now hold as Princess of Monaco. The civil service over, Grace hoped that she could share the Prince's bed that night. He said that was impossible and retired alone.

The following day, Grace married her Prince in a religious ceremony at St Nicholas's Cathedral in Monte Carlo.

'Bride is film star, groom is non-pro,' *Variety* reported.

Of her myriad former lovers, only one – David Niven – turned up. Frank Sinatra had been invited, but turned down the invitation when he discovered that Ava Gardner would be there. Press speculation about a possible reconciliation between them would have overshadowed the wedding, he said. Cary Grant also cried off. He was filming *The Pride and the Passion* in Spain.

After the reception, the couple sailed off together on the royal yacht. Grace was not a good sailor and started throwing up as soon as they got out of port. A few days later she fell pregnant.

She spent her confinement alone in the palace. Five months after she gave birth to a girl, she was pregnant again. Despite this, the marriage was soon on the rocks and she would spend long hours on transatlantic calls, pouring out her heart to her friends.

When Grace was away visiting her dying father, Rainier was seen out and about with one of her ladies-in-waiting. On her return, Grace confronted the Prince. He denied everything, but the lady-in-waiting was fired anyway.

To get her own back, Grace invited Cary Grant to stay. Pictures of them kissing at the airport appeared in the papers. Rainier promptly banned screenings of *To Catch a Thief*, which shows them in steamy love scenes together. In fact, they had not had an affair at the time. Grant was one of her few co-stars whom Grace had overlooked. That was because Cassini was fresh on the scene at the time. But in the 1970s, after he had separated from his third wife Dyan Cannon, they began an affair. It lasted, on and off, for seven years.

By the early 1970s, like many royal couples, Prince Rainier and Princess Grace had stopped sharing the same bedroom. Soon they went one step further. They stopped sharing the same country. Prince Rainier made a life for himself in Monaco. Princess Grace lived, largely, in Paris. In 1979, there were rumours that she was having an affair with Hungarian documentary film-maker, Robert Dornhelm, whom she saw a great deal of in France. He denied any romantic involvement, but he told the press that he thought having affairs would do her good.

Dornhelm knew that Grace was seeing a number of younger men, whom her friends called her 'toy boys'. One of them was Per Mattson, a 33-year-old Swedish actor who was considered for a part in a film about Raoul Wallenberg that Grace was planning with Dornhelm. They had met at a formal dinner in New York in 1982. He had been whisked up to her hotel room and had stayed there until five o'clock in the morning.

'Grace was used by some of these men,' said her old friend, actress Rita Gamm. 'For them it was not so serious, but for her it was. They did not suffer as desperately and silently as she did.'

New York restaurateur and former model, Jim McMullen, spent a week in Monaco with her. They were also seen together at New York disco, Studio 54. She picked up executive head hunter, Jeffrey Fitzgerald, on Concorde.

'I thought he would hate my lumps and bumps,' she told a friend, 'but he doesn't mind one bit.'

As the years drew on, Grace drank too much, ate too much and put on weight. Meanwhile, the torch of sexual misadventure was passed to a new generation. Both her daughters, Caroline and Stephanie, became notorious. Stephanie threatened to run off with her boyfriend, racing driver Paul Belmondo, son of the French movie star Jean-Paul Belmondo. In a moment of turmoil, Princess Grace confessed to biographer Gwen Robyns: 'How can I bring up my daughters not to have affairs when I am having affairs with married men all the time?'

On 13 September 1982, Princess Grace crashed on a hairpin bend on the Moyenne Corniche and was killed. Although the crash had taken place on French soil, Prince Rainier invoked diplomatic protocols and hampered the police investigation. This promoted all kinds of theories into why she had crashed. A lorry driver said that he had seen the car being driven erratically and that the brake lights had never shown once as the car plunged over the mountainside.

The Mafia was active in the area at the time and it is said that they cut the brake lines. Others claimed that Stephanie, who escaped unscathed from the wreckage, was actually driving. But the most likely theory was that Princess Grace had had a minor stroke while at the wheel and had lost control of the car.

At the time of Princess Grace's death, her eldest daughter Princess Caroline, a ravishing young divorcée, was the toast of the European tabloids. In 1983, she was married for a second time to Stephano Casiraghi, the son of an Italian industrialist. He died tragically in a speedboat accident in 1990, leaving her with three small children. As Prince Albert shows no sign of getting married and settling down, Caroline has changed her children's names from Casiraghi to Casiraghi-Grimaldi, with the aim of putting her son on the throne.

Princess Stephanie maintained the role of Monaco's *enfant terrible* as a wannabe movie star, rock star and fashion designer. She is noted for being the first princess of the house of Grimaldi to give birth out of wedlock.

Fifteen years after the death of Princess Grace she hit the headlines again with an even more bizarre scandal. In December 1997, *The Sunday Times* revealed that, before her death, Princess Grace had become a member of the Solar Temple. According to the newspaper article, her initiation into the cult involved nude massage and ritual sex.

In October 1994, 23 of Solar Temple's followers were found dead in a farmhouse in the village of Cheiry in Switzerland. Another four were found dead in the cult's headquarters in Canada. Now, if Princess Grace had survived to participate in this ritual murder and mass suicide, that really would have been the biggest royal scandal of all time.